BETTER COACHING

ADVANCED COACH'S MANUAL

Second Edition

National Library of Australia Cataloguing-in-Publication

Better coaching : advanced coach's manual.

2nd ed.
Includes bibliographical references and index.
ISBN 0 7360 4113 3.
1. Coaching (Athletics) 2. Physical education and
training - Handbooks, manuals, etc. I. Pyke, Frank S. II.
Australian Sports Commission.

   796.077

Library of Congress Cataloging-in-Publication Data

Better coaching : advanced coach's manual / Frank S. Pyke, editor.--2nd ed.
     p.   cm.
Includes bibliographical references and index.
ISBN 0-7360-4113-3
     1. Coaching (Athletics) 2. Physical education and training. I. Pyke, Frank S. II.
Australian Sports Commission.

   796'.07'7--dc21

                                        2001016895

ISBN: 0-7360-4113-3

This book features text examples, or breakouts, which illustrate elements of each chapter. While some of these breakouts are obviously about real people and events (for instance, where they discuss the work of well-known coaches and athletes), the majority of them are fictional examples based on one or a number of real situations.

This book was coordinated by Sport Education, Australian Sports Commission. Any inquiries regarding this manual should be directed to the Manager, Sport Education, PO Box 176, Belconnen ACT 2616.

HK Managing Editor: Coree Schutter; **Editor:** Stephanie Haygarth, Canberra; **HK Assistant Editor:** Scott Hawkins; **Indexer:** Stephanie Haygarth, Canberra; **Graphic Designer:** Stuart Cartwright; **Graphic Artist:** Francine Hamerski; **Photo Manager:** Clark Brooks; **Cover Designer:** Jack W. Davis; **Photographer (cover):** All photos courtesy of National Sports Information Centre, except photo of Cathy Freeman from Duane Hart/Sportingimages.com.au; **Illustrator:** Mic Greenberg; **Printer:** Finsbury Press

Printed in Australia   10 9 8 7 6 5 4 3

Human Kinetics
Website: www.HumanKinetics.com

United States: Human Kinetics
P.O. Box 5076
Champaign, IL 61825-5076
800-747-4457
email: humank@hkusa.com

Canada: Human Kinetics
475 Devonshire Road Unit 100
Windsor, ON N8Y 2L5
800-465-7301 (in Canada only)
email: orders@hkcanada.com

Europe: Human Kinetics
107 Bradford Road
Stanningley
Leeds LS28 6AT, United Kingdom
+44 (0) 113 255 5665
email: hk@hkeurope.com

Australia: Human Kinetics
57A Price Avenue, Lower Mitcham,
South Australia 5062
08 8277 1555
email: liaw@hkaustralia.com

New Zealand: Human Kinetics
Division of Sports Distributors NZ Ltd.
P.O. Box 300 226 Albany
North Shore City, Auckland
0064 9 448 1207
email: blairc@hknewz.com

BETTER COACHING

ADVANCED COACH'S MANUAL

Second Edition

Frank S Pyke
Editor

National Library of Australia Cataloguing-in-Publication

Better coaching : advanced coach's manual.

2nd ed.
Includes bibliographical references and index.
ISBN 0 7360 4113 3.
1. Coaching (Athletics) 2. Physical education and
training - Handbooks, manuals, etc. I. Pyke, Frank S. II.
Australian Sports Commission.

796.077

Library of Congress Cataloging-in-Publication Data

Better coaching : advanced coach's manual / Frank S. Pyke, editor.--2nd ed.
      p.   cm.
Includes bibliographical references and index.
ISBN 0-7360-4113-3
      1. Coaching (Athletics) 2. Physical education and training. I. Pyke, Frank S. II.
Australian Sports Commission.

796'.07'7--dc21

2001016895

ISBN: 0-7360-4113-3

This book features text examples, or breakouts, which illustrate elements of each chapter. While some of these breakouts are obviously about real people and events (for instance, where they discuss the work of well-known coaches and athletes), the majority of them are fictional examples based on one or a number of real situations.

This book was coordinated by Sport Education, Australian Sports Commission. Any inquiries regarding this manual should be directed to the Manager, Sport Education, PO Box 176, Belconnen ACT 2616.

HK Managing Editor: Coree Schutter; **Editor:** Stephanie Haygarth, Canberra; **HK Assistant Editor:** Scott Hawkins; **Indexer:** Stephanie Haygarth, Canberra; **Graphic Designer:** Stuart Cartwright; **Graphic Artist:** Francine Hamerski; **Photo Manager:** Clark Brooks; **Cover Designer:** Jack W. Davis; **Photographer (cover):** All photos courtesy of National Sports Information Centre, except photo of Cathy Freeman from Duane Hart/Sportingimages.com.au; **Illustrator:** Mic Greenberg; **Printer:** Finsbury Press

Printed in Australia   10 9 8 7 6 5 4 3 2

Human Kinetics
Website: www.humankinetics.com

United States: Human Kinetics
PO Box 5076
Champaign, IL 61825-5076
800 747 4457
email: humank@hkusa.com

Canada: Human Kinetics
475 Devonshire Road Unit 100
Windsor, ON N8Y 2L5
800 465 7301 (in Canada only)
email: orders@hkcanada.com

Europe: Human Kinetics
107 Bradford Road,
Stanningley
Leeds LS28 6AT, United Kingdom
+44 (0) 113 255 5665
email: hk@hkeurope.com

Australia: Human Kinetics
57A Price Avenue,
Lower Mitcham, South Australia 5062
(08) 8277 1555
email: liahka@senet.com.au

New Zealand: Human Kinetics
P.O. Box 105-231, Auckland Central
(09) 523 3462
email: hkp@ihug.co.nz

CONTENTS

ABOUT THE CONTRIBUTORS

Editorial team

Dr Frank S Pyke	editor
Ms Stephanie Haygarth	production editor
Ms Nicole den Duyn	production editor
Ms Joyce Brown	editorial consultant
Ms Sue Hooper	editorial consultant
Mr Chris Nunn	editorial consultant
Mr Gene Schembri	editorial consultant

Chapter	Author	About the author
Section A The Coach		
1. Roles and Responsibilities of the Coach	Mr Gene Schembri	Manager, Sport Education Australian Sports Commission Canberra, ACT
2. Coaching Methods	Dr Brian Douge	Director of Activities Anglican Church Grammar School Brisbane, Qld
3. The Coach as a Resource Manager	Mr Craig Davies	Program Manager Western Australian Institute of Sport Claremont, WA
4. Risk Management for Coaches	Ms Deborah Healey	Senior Associate Blake, Dawson and Waldron legal firm Sydney, NSW
Section B The Athlete		
5. Functional Anatomy	Dr Julie R Steele, FASMF	Senior Lecturer and Head of Biomechanics Research Laboratory University of Wollongong Wollongong, NSW
	Ms Deirdre McGhee	Physiotherapist, Illawarra Sports Medicine Clinic and Lecturer Department of Biomedical Science University of Wollongong Wollongong, NSW
6. Physiology and Sports Performance	Dr Alan D Roberts	Associate Professor Centre for Sports Studies University of Canberra Canberra, ACT
7. Testing the Athlete	Dr David Pyne	Sports Physiologist Australian Institute of Sport Canberra, ACT
8. Coaching Athletes as Individuals	Dr Geraldine Naughton	Associate Professor in Sport and Exercise Science Westmead Children's Hospital Westmead, NSW
Section C Preparing the Athlete		
9. Principles of Training	Dr Frank S Pyke	Executive Director Victorian Institute of Sport South Melbourne, Vic
10. Endurance Training	Dr Richard D Telford, AM	Distance Running Coach Australian Institute of Sport Canberra, ACT
11. Speed, Strength and Power Training	Dr Warren Young	Senior Lecturer Department of Human Movement and Sports Sciences University of Ballarat Ballarat, Vic

12. Flexibility Training	Mr Victor Popov	Physiotherapist, Chandler Sports and Rehabilitation Centre Chandler, Qld
13. Performance Psychology	Dr Sandy Gordon	Senior Lecturer Department of Human Movement and Exercise Science University of Western Australia Nedlands, WA
14. Acquisition of Skill	Prof Bruce Abernethy	Head of Department of Human Movement Studies University of Queensland St Lucia, Qld
15. Biomechanics of Sport	Prof Bruce C Elliott	Head of Department of Human Movement and Exercise Science University of Western Australia Nedlands, WA
16. Sports Nutrition	Ms Karen Inge	Sports Nutrition Coordinator Victorian Institute of Sport South Melbourne, Vic
17. Medical Considerations in Sport	Dr Arjun Rao	Medical Director of Mercy, Midland and South Perth Sports Medicine Clinics Perth, WA
	Australian Sports Drug Agency	The Australian Sports Drug Agency is the national body dealing with the issue of drugs in sport.

Section D Integrating the Program

18. An Integrated Approach to Planning	Mr Peter Spence	Program Manager Victorian Institute of Sport South Melbourne, Vic
	Mr Roger Flynn	Head Squash Coach Victorian Institute of Sport South Melbourne, Vic
19. Working with Teams	Ms Jill McIntosh	Head Coach Australian Netball Team Canberra, ACT
20. Adopting a Balanced Approach	Ms Deidre Anderson	Athlete and Network Services Manager United Kingdom Sports Institute London, England

ACKNOWLEDGEMENTS

Special thanks to the following people who provided assistance in the development of the manual:

Phil Ayres

Nicholas Bailey

Neil Barras

Neville Bleakley

Angie Calder

Bob Clarke

Gillian Canapini

Matt Connell

Kay Cox

John Daly

Peter Davis

Darryl Durham

Adrian Faccioni

Paul Gastin

Wayne Goldsmith

Chris Gore

Yuli Gowling

Antonia Harmer

Emery Holmik

Michael Haynes

Julian Jones

Rebecca Layton

Michael McLaughlin

Richard McCreedy

Wendy Piltz

Warwick Povey

Jenny Roberts

Martin Roberts

Warren Robilliard

Sean Scott

Graeme Shepherd

Belinda White

Cathy White

Jeff Wollstein

ABBREVIATIONS

ACE   Athlete Career Education
ACL   anterior cruciate ligament
AFL   Australian Football League
           (Australian rules)
AIS   Australian Institute of Sport
ASC   Australian Sports Commission
ALSAS   Australian Laboratory Standards
           Assistance Scheme
ASDA   Australian Sports Drug Agency
ATP   adenosine triphosphate
bpm   beats per minute (a measure of
           heart rate)
CAD   Coaching Athletes with a
           Disability scheme
CR   contract–relax stretch
CRAC   contract–relax antagonist–contract
           stretch
CRT   choice reaction time
EIA   exercise-induced asthma
EMG   electromyography
g   grams
g/kg/day   grams per kilogram per day
HBV   hepatitis B virus
HIV   human immunodeficiency virus
hGH   human growth hormone
hr   hour
IOC   International Olympic Committee
kg   kilograms
kcal   kilocalories
kJ   kilojoules
km   kilometres
L   litres
L/day   litres per day
L/hr   litres per hour
L/min   litres per minute
m   metres
MCD   minimal cerebral dysfunction
min   minutes

mL   millilitres
mL/min   millilitres per minute
mL/kg x min millilitres per kilogram per
             minute
mmol/L   millimoles per litre
ms   milliseconds
m/s   metres per second
m/s/s   metres per second per second
N   newtons
NCAS   National Coaching Accreditation
             Scheme
NESB   non-English-speaking background
NRL   National Rugby League
NSAIDs   non-steroidal anti-inflammatory
             drugs
PB   personal best
PI   peaking index
PNF   proprioceptive neuromuscular
             facilitation
RM   repetition maximum (maximum
             force that can be exerted in a
             single movement and a measure of
             strength)
s   seconds
SDA   Sports Dieticians Australia
SSC   stretch–shortening cycle (of
             muscular function)
URTI   upper respiratory tract infection
VO_2 max   maximum oxygen uptake, or the
             capacity of an athlete's body to
             transport and use oxygen,
             measured in litres per minute (L/
             min) and millilitres per kilogram
             per minute (mL/kg x min)
WADA   World Anti-doping Agency
WNBL   Women's National Basketball
             League

INTRODUCTION

Frank S Pyke

This book is about contemporary coaching technologies and practices. It differs in a number of significant ways from its predecessors, *Towards Better Coaching*, and the first edition of *Better Coaching*, which were published over the past 20 years, because sport has changed quite dramatically during this period.

At the elite level it has become more commercial and more professional, and coaches and athletes are increasingly driven by the need to win. At the participation and junior levels, there are now more choices available and competition between sporting organisations for numbers is fierce. Teaching appropriate skills in a friendly and supportive environment has become essential to maintaining participation rates.

These and other changes that have been felt by coaches in recent years are reflected in the content of this book. The need for increasing attention to legal, ethical and behavioural issues in sport, the availability of performance-enhancing and social drugs, and information technology developments all affect the work of the coach and are discussed throughout the book.

The need to integrate the delivery of a wide range of resources to the athlete is also a constant theme. This means that the coach must be a skilled communicator, not only with athletes, but also with the providers of these resources. Coaches are in the people business, where good communication and negotiation skills are essential, as is the ability to resolve the inevitable conflicts that occur in competitive environments.

Australia's best coaches now have a good working knowledge of the physiology, psychology and biomechanics of sport, and whenever possible utilise these sciences in their programs. Science is no longer a mystery, espoused only by white-coated laboratory personnel: it is now clearly also the domain of coaches.

We have learned a lot in the past 20 years. Coaches are now more adept at prescribing training for individuals and allowing athletes sufficient time for recovery. They encourage a balanced approach to sport and life and involve athletes in planning their own programs. Coaches have become the primary facilitators of programs aimed at producing change.

The best practitioners mix art with science; some would say they mix 'high touch with high tech'. While scientific technologies are useful, there is still the matter of mind and spirit. A gemstone may be cut using precise scientific instruments, but it still needs careful polishing by the artist so that it can outshine the others. Furthermore, keeping athletes happy, healthy and committed goes a long way towards ensuring success, whether they are learning basic skills or competing at the highest level. Each of the four sections of this new coaching manual reflects these evolutions.

The first section describes the role and responsibilities of modern coaches — what they do, how they do it and what is expected of them within the community.

The structure and function of the athlete is described in the second section, along with variations in physical development, performance and individual training requirements that occur with age, sex, race and culture.

The third section discusses how the athlete's performance can be improved by applying appropriate training principles and methods. This is the largest section of the book and it deals with the best approaches to enhancing fitness, technique, mental skills and decision making. The application of sound nutrition and injury and illness prevention management programs is also an important part of this section.

The book's final section provides a holistic view of the planning and implementation of individual and team sport programs, paying particular attention to the role of the coach in managing the process.

In total, this book provides a set of principles upon which to base coaching decisions and strategies representing current modern practice. However, we must understand that what is good practice today will never be good enough tomorrow. In the future, sport will therefore need open-minded and innovative coaches who are continually search-ing for a better way to advance the profession.

In conclusion, I thank the authors of each of the chapters for their contributions and for meeting the deadlines imposed. I'm also grateful to the reviewers for their valuable expert comments on the content.

Finally, I must acknowledge my colleagues on the Editorial Committee; and the editorial assistance of Stephanie Haygarth in planning and reviewing the book; as well as Gene Schembri, Nicole Den Duyn and Rebecca Layton from the Australian Sports Commission; for their support throughout the project.

THE COACH

CHAPTER 1

ROLES AND RESPONSIBILITIES OF THE COACH

Gene Schembri

(National Sports Information Centre)

INTRODUCTION

Coaches work with athletes of all ages to help them improve at their chosen sport. The coach's role is highly varied. Coaching is as much about people as it is about technique and tactics. Coaches directly influence athletes by guiding and teaching — the heart of the coaching process — and ensuring a safe learning environment. The range of teaching skills and communication techniques at their command ensures that coaches 'connect' with the athletes under their instruction. No single coaching style suits all situations or all athletes.

Coaches also have to attend to many behind-the-scenes activities, such as planning seasons, working with committees, raising funds, recruiting and training coaches and communicating with parents. They must also reflect on their own performances as coaches, obtain feedback from others and further develop their own coaching skills. The more demanding the coaching situation, the greater the need for coaches to keep a perspective on life and avoid burnout.

ON-FIELD COACHING ROLES

The athlete-focused coaching diagram on page 4 depicts the key roles of a coach — both the on-field roles and off-field or backroom coaching roles. In their on-field roles, coaches interact directly with athletes to improve their athletic abilities, and take measures to ensure that the safety and welfare of the athletes are guaranteed. Looking beyond sport, coaches also directly influence personal aspects of athletes' lives.

Improving the athlete

The foundation of good coaching is knowledge of the sport's techniques and tactics. Putting this knowledge into action requires the coach to use an effective mix of organisational skills, teaching strategies, communication skills and group management practices. To ensure that athletes' performances continually improve, the coach must apply a variety of coaching practices based on an understanding of sport science knowledge.

Frank, an under-17s coach in the Victorian Country Football League, was chatting with fellow coaches and club officials about his coaching strategy for next season. The club had acquired a very experienced head coach whose influence was affecting the coaching of all teams in the club.

Frank thought that he would concentrate on the tactical and decision-making abilities of his team. He realised that behind 'smart play' was the need for a good team dynamic and for team cohesion. The challenge for Frank was to determine what he could actually do to make a difference on match day. He decided to start by talking to his fellow coaches and football players.

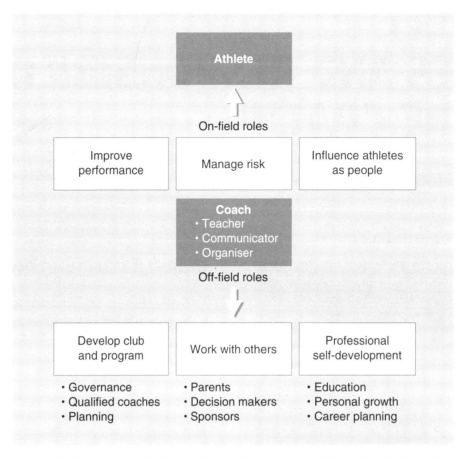

In athlete-focused coaching the coach directly influences athletes and works behind the scene to ensure that indirect influences work in favour of athletes.

Club coaches should work together to develop a united approach to coaching. If, say, the under-17s are coached in a manner consistent with the coaching at higher levels, those young players' opportunities to play at the senior level may be enhanced. A cross-fertilisation of ideas enables the strengths of coaches to be put to best use.

The coach as risk manager

The first article in a local football club's newsletter warned all coaches to be on the lookout for potholes, sprinklers and broken glass. The club's secretary had read of a case where legal action was being taken against a coach because a player had sustained serious injuries after tripping in a pothole and colliding with an opposing player. Sport, like other aspects of life, carries risks, but many can be reduced or eliminated. Risk management is an important topic for all those involved in sport.

Ensuring the safety of players by managing risk is an important part of coaching. Here is a short checklist of things coaches can do to minimise the exposure of their athletes to harm and to avoid being the subject of legal action.

(National Sports Information Centre)

Coaches must ensure the wellbeing of athletes in their care.

- Keep up to date with the sport being coached, particularly with the latest techniques and coaching methods. Holding a current coach accreditation is one way to do this.

- Sporting organisations with sound risk management practices ask their coaches to agree to abide by a code of conduct. A good code of conduct is a useful tool for making it clear that coaches intend to treat athletes with dignity and respect, as well as to look after their welfare and safety (see below for more information on this).

- An essential part of any coach's preparedness for the task is obtaining appropriate insurance. When a coach is insured by a global association or club cover, he or she should check to make sure it covers all likely situations.

- Because one of coaches' important responsibilities is ensuring a safe training and competition environment for all athletes, they must be sure that the playing areas and equipment are suitable for the activity being coached. Protective equipment, such as goggles and helmets, should be used whenever required. Environmental factors, such as fluid replacement on hot days, should not be overlooked.

- Effective coaching, including sound group management and appropriate teaching methods, will help to minimise injuries that happen when athletes become bored and behave unsuitably — including skylarking.

Peter has a long history of coaching girls in a popular team sport, and has coached all levels, from beginners to the national team. He is a typical 'dedicated coach', and has always made himself available to fit in with the schedules of the athletes with whom he works. Athletes would often say things such as, 'He is really interested in us, not just as athletes but as people', or 'Peter is a real friend and would do anything to help us'.

At the end-of-tournament function, officials noticed that Peter was sitting with just one of his athletes, 16-year-old Amanda, and that there was a lot of merrymaking that involved touching. The sport's community, including Peter's team, was shocked to read in the newspapers two months later that Peter had been arrested and was facing three rape charges, three sexual assault charges and one charge of assault. Peter denied all charges and said that he had only had a consensual relationship with Amanda.

This breakout may challenge some readers, who might ask, 'What is this doing in a book about coaching?', but it graphically illustrates an issue that is causing increasing concern in many areas of society, including sport.

The coach occupies a very significant place in an athlete's life, often being friend, guide, confidant, role model and, in some cases, surrogate parent. It is often an unequal relationship in terms of who has the most authority and power, particularly where children and adolescents are involved. Coaches owe a duty of care to the athletes they work with and should understand that, in assuming the role of coach, they also assume special responsibilities. They also contribute to the broader community: sport can help people get on with each other. When coaches don't do what is expected of them — or of any member of society — they diminish the goodwill that otherwise exists between them and the community.

Codes of conduct have been developed and implemented to supplement other measures that ensure the safety and wellbeing of the athlete (see the appendix). Athletes need special protection, not just from physical harm, but also from psychological harm. Coaches may influence athletes far beyond the field or gym, and so it's important that they consider all aspects of the lives of the athletes under their care.

Below is a list of guidelines to help coaches deal with ethical issues in coaching.

Ethical guidelines for coaches

- Sign or agree to abide by a code of ethics.
- Check that the organisation asking you to comply with a code of ethics has procedures in place that will guarantee your rights in the event of an allegation of inappropriate behaviour.
- Avoid situations where you are alone with athletes, particularly in rooms or in a car.
- Touching must be appropriate to the activity being coached. Check your club/ association's policy.
- Never make assumptions about drugs, medications and foodstuffs. Check them before allowing athletes to use them.
- Remember, coaching is not like other non-sport social experiences. Coaches owe a duty of care to the athletes with whom they work that makes the coach–athlete relationship special. This may mean that what is acceptable behaviour in the wider community is not acceptable when it occurs between coach and athlete.

- Just because a coach's behaviour doesn't break the law, coaches shouldn't assume this as a defence.

- Don't do anything you wouldn't want your friends to read about in the newspaper or that you would want to prevent happening to someone in your family!

The coach and the whole athlete

The coach is often a very significant person in an athlete's life. Athletes like Lalit, in the Australian Institute of Sport gymnastics squad, see much more of their coaches than they do of their parents. Whether coaches work in institutes of sport or in a club, they have a role in guiding and balancing the demands that sport makes of athletes with the other demands placed on them, such as home life, social needs, education and, in some cases, employment.

Getting to know the needs of an athlete is important. Coaches should ask themselves why the athletes in their programs come along to training and what other forces in their lives they are attempting to balance? An understanding of these needs will give coaches a sound foundation to working with athletes.

Coaches should ask athletes:

- what are their short and long-term goals?

- what are the best things about training and competition?

- what are the worst things about training and competition?

- do the training schedules make provision for the non-sport components of athletes' lives: for example, do coaches encourage athletes to prepare a weekly planner showing both sport and non-sport commitments?

Coaches should ask themselves:

- assuming that they monitor the weekly sport and non-sport commitments of their athletes, how do they resolve clashes?

- do they feel equipped to deal with an athlete who is having a relationship problem, and when does this cease to be an area in which they should be involved?

- when relevant, what do the athlete's parents want from her or his participation in the program?

Parent nights, athlete and parent surveys, both formal and informal conversations with athletes, and providing a parents' feedback box are some of the things coaches can do to address the questions raised above.

Some of these needs will be special and obvious. The wonderful achievements of athletes such as Australian wheelchair athlete Louise Sauvage remind us that coaches work with the complete diversity of our population. Whether they coach senior athletes, athletes with a disability, able-bodied athletes, those in regional areas or athletes from diverse backgrounds, the principle is the same. Each athlete has individual needs, and coaching techniques and methods must be modified accordingly. To apply this principle, coaches must understand the developmental needs of the athlete, attempt to understand the needs of the individual, modify the training program to fit the needs, and use effective coaching methods that recognise diversity.

Athletes with disabilities are among the range of people with whom coaches work.

(National Sports Information Centre)

A disproportionate number of senior talented athletes start their careers in 'the bush' and often do well in their early years despite having little access to regular quality coaching or being unable to train with others of a similar standard. These young athletes often have to balance playing a number of sports with school work, school sport and social commitments.

For young athletes, playing a variety of sports can develop a good physical and motor skills background that will pay dividends in later life. However, playing multiple sports can mean that valuable time is taken up by duplication: for example, playing the same sport in both school and club. If school and club coaches take the time to work out a program that eliminates some of the overlap in training and competition, the athlete's progress will be better guided. If coaches make contact with the regional or state sporting association, they may also learn about additional talent development opportunities for the athletes they coach.

Athletes and 'social' drugs

The increasing professionalism of sport is placing greater demands on coaches to be accountable for the behaviour of athletes. Coaches should make athletes aware that the abuse of any substance is likely to injure their health and reduce their performance, and that drug abuse is simply incompatible with high-performance sport. Increasingly, incidents of athletes misusing alcohol and other social drugs have resulted in a number of negative outcomes including:

- damage to athletes' and coaches' reputations and credibility, possibly jeopardising future scholarships, selections, funding, sponsorships and endorsements
- disciplinary action that may result in fines, suspension from the team or the sport, or legal action
- questions about the coach's ability to manage athletes and a perceived lack of discipline, values and consideration for athletes' welfare by the coach, and
- a decline in public, political and parental support, which could have implications for junior development.

Steve coaches the first grade football team in which Dave is a young star. After a big win, the players decide to celebrate. Steve encourages them to have a meal first, but most are already in party mode. Steve isn't going with the players and asks Tim, the team captain, to look after them.

After dancing and having half a dozen beers, Dave is feeling pretty light-headed. His mate Justin offers him a tablet, saying 'this'll make you feel good' and Dave swallows it. While dancing again he begins to feel extremely hot and disoriented, and keeps falling over. Tim pulls him off the dance floor and makes him drink some cold water. Feeling pretty sick, Dave tells his team-mates that he is going to drive home, but Tim persuades him to take a cab instead.

The next morning Dave is feeling awful. He should train in the late afternoon but doesn't think he can. He rings Steve to tell him that he can't make it. Steve has received similar phone calls from several other players, and is becoming concerned about the effects of post-game celebrations on the athletes.

Strategies for coaches

To prevent athletes misusing social drugs, coaches should:

- ensure that athletes are aware of the facts on alcohol and recreational drug misuse
- set guidelines and ensure a total commitment by all to these guidelines
- establish alternative methods of celebrating, or control celebrations with strategies such as meeting all post-match commitments before celebrating, organising a meal with the celebrations, or involving parents, and
- be available to discuss issues with athletes and know where to get help.

Practical suggestions about alcohol consumption that coaches can give athletes include:

- try a low-alcohol alternative
- eat before drinking alcohol
- quench your thirst on water or soft drinks
- have an alcohol-free drink as a spacer, and
- plan ahead, choosing a designated driver or booking a taxi.

For information on the effects of social drugs and on athletes and performance-enhancing drugs, see chapter 17, Medical Considerations in Sport.

OFF-FIELD ROLES

The on-field roles take up most of a coach's time, but coaches have to do many other things to complement day-to-day coaching.

Coaches at all levels will readily identify the numerous off-field tasks they have to deal with. Many coaches would prefer that someone else dealt with many of these tasks, which they see as distractions from the 'real business' of coaching. Some of these tasks include: recruiting athletes; fundraising; dealing with parents and administrators; providing or arranging for transport; working with/managing other coaches; providing or arranging for uniforms to be made; dealing with athlete health matters; organising equipment and venues; coordinating the off-field support team; communications, such as a newsletter; and other planning.

The wide range of potential tasks means that prioritising is very important. Some tips on prioritising include:

- identify the on-field and off-field roles and make a list

- tick the must-dos and decide whether any of these can be delegated or shared

- establish a routine to deal with off-field tasks and block out times to complete similar tasks, such as phone calls

- share or delegate other 'nice-to-do' tasks and, if some still remain unresolved, delete them from the to-do list, and

- review the situation every month or two.

Helping to build a quality program

Clubs are like any other organisation that is striving to do things better; those that are well run have a better chance of providing quality sport experiences for their members. While helping to build a stronger club or organisation is not what we think of as 'coaching', coaches often work behind the scenes to ensure indirect influences work in favour of athletes.

Sport has to compete with a range of other influences in the lives of athletes. Within sport there is strong competition for the same players. Parents are now more discerning, not only about the type of sport their children will play, but how it fits in with their increasingly busy lives. Coaches should consider whether their club is meeting the needs of its 'customers' or whether participants are 'voting with their feet'.

Efforts by sports associations, supported by government agencies, aimed at improving the quality of clubs, including their 'customer service', will be increasingly important in the competition for members and community support. Coaches have a role in this process.

Communication skills off the field

It is important that coaches use a variety of communication strategies, as a flexible approach to communicating will enable them to work with a wide variety of athletes, each with their own special needs. Such coaching skills are also valuable in other areas of sport, and life in general.

Mrs Henderson has been a regular at the parents orientation of the Hills Softball Club. The second speaker, Mark, a coach, was explaining the draw and other calendar highlights when Mrs Henderson stood up and berated the committee and coaches for their planning of last year's calendar. Her youngest son was disciplined twice last season for using foul language.

Mark politely thanked Mrs Henderson for her interest, pointed out that he would take questions and comments at the end of his presentation, and indicated that she would be welcome to submit ideas for the club's social and fundraising calendar. He turned to make eye contact with other parents, thanked those who had already helped with this year's calendar, and finished his short presentation.

Mark had learned these communication strategies at an updating seminar on how to deal with difficult people, and the incident reminded him that working with others off the field was an important part of a coach's role.

People involved with sport often bring with them a lot of enthusiasm and passion. It is not unusual for some of this energy to flow over into committee proceedings, coach–parent interactions and a range of other occasions. People skills, such as those of negotiating, resolving or defusing difficult situations, putting a case or winning an argument, and empathetic listening and reflecting, may be used to good effect both on the field and off the field.

Dealing with the media

Dealing with the media, like public speaking, is a frightening event for many. Students in the Australian Sports Commission's (ASC) graduate diploma of coaching, in which media training is a compulsory module, show that people can quickly develop good media skills. If coaches find that they are in need of help in this area, they should contact the ASC and other organisations who can provide such useful resources. More experienced colleagues can also assist newcomers who may have to deal with the media.

Dealing with officials

Referees, umpires and judges are an important group and are essential for the effective conduct of sport. They play a critical role in ensuring the game is played fairly and safely. Good officiating can enhance the flow of a game and increase its spectator value. Yet there are often misunderstandings between officials, players and coaches.

Some sporting organisations have implemented programs to improve communication and understanding between officials, players and coaches. In some cases these measures are designed to give the athletes a competitive advantage through better understanding of the rules and, in the case of officials from other countries, better understanding of different officiating styles and nuances.

Protests are allowed at Australian gymnastics championships but not at the Olympic Games. In an attempt to prepare gymnastics judges for the task of judging at the Olympic Games, the federation's national coordinator, Jill Wright, implemented a process that allowed formal protests over scores to be managed in a way that encouraged interaction and communication between judges and coaches. This became an education process for both gymnasts and judges, as the gymnasts learned what the judges look for, and the judges gained an insight into the gymnasts' performance preparation.

This is a good example of how effective off-field communications can have positive effects on players, coaches and a third party, in this case the officials.

(National Sports Information Centre)

Communication with officials is essential.

Planning

Effective planning underpins a coach's on-field and off-field roles. The coach of the Australian Olympic rowing eight must plan strategies that will guarantee appropriate attention is given to each part of the program. The organisation of each event in the life of the rower is essentially the responsibility of the coach, but coaches should delegate tasks whenever they can, to conserve their resources. A coach of an Olympic rowing eight would, for instance, be required to carry out the duties listed on page 10.

The elements in this list do not only relate to elite sport. All coaches at all levels of competition and for all ages of athlete in most sports must attend to most of the issues raised on page 10. The coach of the state schools regional under-15 softball team must consider many of these elements if he or she is required to coach a Brisbane-based team in a state competition to be held in Townsville.

Professional self-development

Sport is continually changing: rules change, techniques change, equipment is refined and coaching methods, including the application of the sport sciences, evolve. Coaches must keep abreast of these changes and adapt their coaching accordingly.

Self-reflection

Coaches should ask themselves whether the things they do and say as a coach make a difference, and whether their coaching behaviours are effective and improve the athlete's performance. It is important that coaches take control of their own learning. Self-reflection, using videos of their coaching and the support of a critical friend, will help them modify their coaching behaviours. A critical friend may act as a sounding board, offer a word of advice, ask a question, seek clarity or use other techniques that help the coach become more effective.

New knowledge and skills

Formal and informal opportunities are available for coaches seeking to update their knowledge and skills. Formal techniques include accreditation programs, tertiary study and professional development courses. These are complemented by informal ways of learning, such as updating workshops, seminars, personal study, discussion with other coaches and fact-finding visits to other programs. Top-level coaches often use a network of other coaches, including those from other sports, to compare notes with and supply new ideas.

Tasks for the coach of an Olympic rowing eight

Travel

condition athletes for travel

plan a pre-Olympic visit

confirm transport security for training and racing equipment

arrange funding and support for travel to and from pre-Olympic events and the Olympic program, and

check the quality of living conditions.

Climate and racing conditions

manufacture training conditions that mirror those probable at the Olympic venue and in the Olympic season, and

arrange competitions that offer the same mental stimuli that will be present at the Olympics.

Social activities

provide opportunities for leisure, and

establish conditions so that athletes will be able to enjoy social activity while maintaining a full commitment to the crew.

Coaching rules

prepare the cox to act as coach while racing

prepare the crew to respond to the cox during the race, and

provide rowers with updated information about the opposition.

Financial pressures

know the financial status of each rower

mobilise funding agencies to support the total campaign — crew and equipment

confirm personal finances to guarantee a personal commitment to the campaign, and

prepare the crew and the coach for life after the Olympics — win or lose.

Injuries

arrange backup in case any rower is injured

predict the impact of an injury to a member of opposing crews, and

schedule routine assessments to ensure that rowers are not attempting to mask injuries that would significantly affect the Olympic chances of the crew.

Level of competition

develop coping strategies with crew members to help them to be positive about competition for a seat in the crew, psychological strategies that might be used by the opposition, varying race strategies that will raise or lower the ratings required at different phases of the race, and coping with being an underdog or a favourite.

Player longevity

make decisions about the configuration of the training squad to guarantee that a long-serving quality rower does not prevent a young rower with greater potential from experiencing appropriate development

adjust programs for ageing rowers, and

prepare older rowers for retirement from Olympic rowing.

Mentoring

A mentor is someone, usually more experienced, who works on a one-to-one basis with a less experienced person (the mentee). A third person may sometimes assist in the matching of mentor and mentee. Mentoring may also involve an informal process where the mentor or mentee is attracted by a mutual interest or friendship. At the heart of effective mentoring is an effective and friendly relationship between the two parties.

Coaches who choose a mentor may benefit in a variety of ways. They can acquire new skills and knowledge, receive feedback from a critical friend, receive support and have access to a sounding board in difficult times, and learn how to deal with situations of a 'political' or sensitive nature from a more experienced adviser.

The 'critical friend', referred to under self-reflection on page 9, takes on part of the mentor's role.

Innovations

The best coaches are innovators. They continually question accepted practices and are not afraid to try different things. There are no recipes to teach creativity and foster innovation. A critical and questioning approach is important.

The table below gives an insight into some of the questions a coach–innovator might ask.

Avoiding burnout

Coaches are well known for working long hard hours. In their desire to optimise the performances of athletes, coaches will often do things that, in the longer term, can mean they become burnt out.

The following checklist invites coaches to reflect on their coaching behaviours and whether they are taking steps to avoid burnout.

- Have you built exercise into your daily schedule?
- What do you do to relax? Well-coached athletes have effective recovery and relaxation programs — do you need to ask your athletes for advice?
- Is time with friends and family important to you? Do you follow through with actual commitments to others?
- When you're on the road do you 'steal' those rare and precious moments to do something for yourself?
- Coaches are often not good at delegating. How good are you at letting go? Good delegation habits may save you hours each week.
- If you had to leave your position tomorrow, how well equipped would your assistants be to carry on without you?
- Are your athletes independent and self-managing?
- Do you practise what you preach when it comes to healthy living habits — nutrition, sleep, relaxation and recovery?

THE COACH: FACILITATOR, GUIDE, FRIEND OR DIRECTOR?

One of the biggest shifts in coaching methods over the last two decades has been the realisation that athletes learn over a period of time how to coach themselves. Athletes who are able to think independently and take responsibility for aspects of their training will be better equipped to deal with any situations that arise.

Questions a coach–innovator might ask

Area	Question
Technique	How much should I use technique training versus playing the game or practising the skill?
Tactics	Is practising set-plays the best way to develop thinking players?
Physical preparation	Is the physical preparation work enhancing the performance outcome? Should less, more or different work be done?
Coaching methods	How much of the coach's advice actually makes any difference? Should there be less talking or more talking? What are effective methods for changing behaviours?

(National Sports Information Centre)

Some athletes can take responsibility for aspects of their own training.

Shaun Creighton, who lives in Canberra, is an Australian international distance runner. His coach, Pat Clohessy, lives 1000 km away in Brisbane. At 32, Shaun knows how to structure his yearly training plan and translate this into daily programs of training, recovery, physiotherapy, work, study and relaxation. Shaun looks to Pat for reinforcement before and after specific training sessions and overall strategy. In this example the coach is a resource person and guide. Shaun's hands-on coaching days are in the past, but he still values highly the guidance and support of his coach.

The degree of hands-on coaching or direct intervention by the coach will depend on the circumstance. The factors involved include: the stage of development and age of the athlete or team members, whether the coach works in a team or individual sport and what its coaching traditions are, the teaching styles preferred by the coach, and the athlete's previous coaching history.

Malcolm has been working his way up the ranks as a rugby league coach. He is working with the under-15s this season, the oldest group he has coached. Malcolm's style is authoritarian. He believes the coach knows best, that he has to do the talking and that good players come out of the 'train hard, play hard school'. He is an intuitive coach rather than a scientific one. Despite his authoritarian style, Malcolm is charismatic, articulate and often humorous, though he uses sarcasm in his humour.

The season is not going well for Malcolm. Some of the players have been talking to other coaches in the club, complaining that Malcolm treats them like little kids, doesn't listen to them, uses irrelevant drills and is fostering a style of play they think is out of date. A recurring criticism is that Malcolm doesn't recognise the knowledge and skills of the team and that he never asks for the players' views.

If Malcolm sought the advice of a colleague, this might result in more of a questioning approach to his coaching. Highlighting player strengths by using players to provide some 'coaching' advice is another approach. Malcolm could employ other strategies: working one-to-one with players, spending time with athletes on goal setting or adopting a style that de-emphasises the personal attributes of the athlete and concentrates more on the athletic performance behaviours. Finally, there is a fine line between using sarcasm as a way of creating some fun and hurting people. Malcolm might try using humour that is less personal.

CONCLUSION

The model of the coaching process described above shows that coaches are always striving to balance their work with athletes with a range of other tasks. Working directly with athletes is what coaches enjoy most. Improving technique, nurturing 'thinking' players and influencing athletes for the better in their daily lives is at the core of a coach's role. In the coach's toolbox we find the skills of teacher, communicator, motivator, organiser and manager. If the coach is effective in the application of these skills, then the athlete's learning will be positive.

What of the other roles? Clubs must recruit athletes, who will need uniforms, equipment and a venue. Athletes will have to travel to training and competition. Coaches will have to deal with parents, administrators, off-field athlete support personnel and other coaches. All of these off-field roles are important, but take the coach away from coaching. Effective time management, including the ability to share and delegate, are essential if the coach is to balance the competing roles.

Working with athletes in a way that nurtures their independence, autonomy and critical thinking is what many contemporary coaches hope to achieve. This means less prescription, less direction and less of a dictatorial approach, so that athletes develop self-management and self-control skills. The art of good coaching is finding a balance between the extremes of empowerment and prescription: this balance will vary from team to team and within a team, and will change as the coach–team relationship evolves.

Finally, coaches have needs as people too. Taking time to learn, self-reflect, work with helpful colleagues, relax and achieve their potential is just as important for coaches as it is for athletes.

COACHING TIPS

- Continually seek opportunities to learn — coach education can come in many forms, including attending training courses, watching other coaches, reading and using the internet.

- Develop communication skills and adjust them to the individual needs of each athlete.

- Communicate plans and progress to athletes, parents and management staff.

- Establish high personal standards in line with the Coach's Code of Ethics (see appendix).

- Aim to develop independent, self-sufficient and responsible athletes.

FURTHER READING

Australian Coaching Council (1996) *Coaching Better: Becoming a More Effective Coach* (video and study pack). Canberra: Australian Sports Commission.

Australian Coaching Council (1996) *Video Self-Analysis: A Lens on Coaching* (video and study pack). Canberra: Australian Sports Commission.

Australian Sports Commission (1998) Harassment-free Sport series (several publications on guidelines for coaches, athletes, administrators and sport and recreation organisations). Canberra: Australian Sports Commission.

Cross, N, and J Lyle (1999) *The Coaching Process: Principles and Practice for Sport*. Melbourne: Butterworth Heinemann.

Douge, B (1997) Coaching skills: strategies for coaching athletes in the turbulent years of early childhood. *Sports Coach* 20(1): 18–20.

Douge, B (1997) Coaching skills: keeping adolescents on task. *Sports Coach* 20(4): 13–14.

Douge, B (1999) Coaching skills: coaching adolescents to develop mutual respect. *Sports Coach* 21(4): 6–7.

Douge, B (1999) Coaching skills: optimal team performance in adolescent sport. *Sports Coach* 22(1): 9–10.

Hessert, K (1998) *Coach's Communication Playbook*. Charlotte, NC: Sports Media Challenge.

Kidman, L, and S Hanrahan (1997) *The Coaching Process: A Practical Guide to Improving Your Effectiveness*. Palmerston North, New Zealand: the Dunmore Press.

Martens, R (1997) *Successful Coaching*. Champaign, IL: Human Kinetics.

Salmela, J H (1996) *Great Job Coach: Getting the Edge from Proven Winners*. Ottawa, Ontario: Potentium, the Coaching Network.

Schembri, G (1998) Code of ethics for coaches. *The Sport Educator* 10(1): 3–7.

CHAPTER 2
COACHING METHODS

Brian Douge

(Courtesy Queensland Newspapers)

INTRODUCTION

This chapter is about coaching methods. It focuses on how a coach might use different methods in different situations, what styles of coaching achieve the best results, how to use a variety of communication skills and the ways coaches can improve their coaching.

Different methods in different situations

Coaching methods will vary according to the sporting context. A coach employed by a corporation to win a championship may have to consider the requirements of the team owner when selecting coaching methods. A coach who is invited by athletes to be their coach may need to adopt coaching methods that respond to the athletes' specific requests. It is important that coaches are able to recognise how their methods should be modified to respond effectively to change.

Styles of coaching

Coaches must use a range of coaching styles to help athletes learn. Some athletes require in-depth instruction and explanation, while others learn best by practice. One contemporary coaching style involves teaching athletes how to coach themselves. This allows the coach to become a resource used by the athlete to support his or her self-development program.

Charlie Earp is a highly acclaimed golf coach. He helped Greg Norman achieve his ranking as number one in the world. However, during the peak of his career, Greg would only contact Charlie occasionally to ask him for advice, coaching himself in the meantime. By teaching Greg Norman to coach himself, Charlie Earp could make himself available to coach many more players.

To use a coaching style effectively, coaches must have a range of teaching skills, and must be able to:

- give direct instructions
- ask facilitative questions
- decrease the amount of organising and disciplining they do
- increase athletes' responsibility for performance
- develop a rapport with each athlete
- provide good models
- define athlete accountabilities and associated consequences, and
- improve athletes' decision-making and problem-solving skills.

Communication skills

Dealing with differences in the needs of athletes and teams is a major part of coaches' work, for which they need a variety of communication skills to effectively deliver information. Some of these communication skills include:

- presenting information in written, oral, live, symbolic and audiovisual formats
- listening skills
- conflict resolution skills, and
- the ability to negotiate and provide accurate feedback.

Self-improvement

Coaches of professional teams now usually select their assistant coaches. They do this because they can choose assistants who support their coaching style, with whom they have a good understanding and rapport, and who can give them considered feedback about their coaching. Effective coaches exploit these opportunities and use their assistant coaches to help them critically examine their own work (see Self-reflection on page 24).

In summary, effective coaches have the ability to manage change in, for instance, who they're coaching and what the athlete's needs are, which level of competition is relevant, and which resources are available. They can use effective tools, such as different coaching styles and teaching strategies, to adapt to change. They know how to achieve specific goals, such as athlete development and performance results, and they achieve autonomous, professional self-development through systematic study and trial and error practice.

SPORT CONTEXT

Managing the sporting context can be one of the most challenging aspects of coaching. Think about what it would be like to be appointed coach of a state tennis team in which each of your athletes has a private coach. Some of these private coaches could also be the parents of the athletes. Imagine having one of your players going to his or her private coach for advice between matches during a teams competition. It could be that this coach's advice contradicts your own. If this occurs while a match is in progress, for example between singles and doubles rubbers, then it could severely compromise your ability to enhance the athlete's performance. This is one example of how the sports setting can affect the work of a coach.

Jill has recently been appointed to the position of head coach of the state swimming team. She is concerned about travelling for a week with a group of young men and women aged between 14 and 25. Geoff, her own coach, who has experience as assistant coach of the national team, suggests the following strategies to help:

- plan the week to ensure that all athletes are occupied at all times
- use curfews where appropriate
- set up teams within the team, such as a breaststroke team and a freestyle team and appoint leaders of each of these teams, and

- conduct a meeting with team leaders and the older and more experienced swimmers to discuss the importance of keeping the focus on swimming for the week. Use the meeting to develop team rules for the appropriate use of free time.

Jill took Geoff's advice and was pleased to find that the swimmers responded well to responsibility. Most pleasing was that Ian, captain of the breaststroke team and a known disruptive influence at previous championships, behaved in an exemplary manner, contributing significantly to team spirit.

Planning is typically associated with schedules, training routines and organisation. However, effective coaches can also plan to use particular coaching strategies to cater for changes within a particular setting.

Aaron is an experienced rugby union coach who knows that his players will make mistakes during matches. Two of his players make the same mistake — attempting to pass the ball in high-risk situations. The older player does it because it is a bad habit, while the young player lacks the confidence to keep possession in rucks and mauls.

Aaron knows that the older player, John, will resent being criticised in front of his team-mates and, similarly, that this would not help the confidence of the younger player, Simon. During the week Aaron organises training drills that require John to run hard to break the defensive line and require Simon to take the ball into ruck and maul situations. He then asks the team captain and one of the assistant coaches to offer words of encouragement to the two players when they retain the ball in tight situations.

On game day Aaron speaks privately with John before the game and gives him the responsibility of running hard with the ball to try to break the opposition defensive line. He also asks one of his assistants to quietly praise Simon during the game for his efforts in taking the ball into rucks and mauls.

The ability to plan in this way can often depend on previous coaching experience. Beginner coaches should not hesitate to consult with more experienced coaches if they have a difficult situation to manage.

COACHING STYLES

There are three conditions that signal effective coaching. Athletes should:

- have the ideal time for learning
- have adequate opportunities to learn, and

- be practising the task that best helps them learn.

There have been some highly successful training techniques that almost guarantee to provide these three conditions. The golfers' driving range; tennis, baseball and cricket ball machines; net practice in cricket; repetitive cyclical drills in all sports, such as the 'drive, boast, drop' drill in squash; and self-instructional modules, such as training regimes for triathletes, are all examples of effective training techniques. Each of these examples is a practice regime that guarantees the athlete will have uninterrupted skill attempts and can control the type of skill being practised and the duration of the practice. They eliminate the time wasted having to wait for a turn, retrieve balls, work on skills that are of more benefit to other members of the team, and perform other distracting skills because the training regime has too many variables.

However, training techniques that effectively manage the time and opportunities to learn alone will not guarantee optimal learning. A golfer may hit a hundred balls at a driving range in 45 minutes, but if she has poor technique or is unable to analyse the cause and effect components of each stroke, then valuable practice time may be wasted.

The following are styles of coaching that can improve the amount of effective learning during practice.

Direct instruction

Direct instruction is one way of helping athletes to make the most of their time and involvement in practice. Quality direct instruction includes:

- setting high but realistic expectations
- being an active coach who gives accurate feedback and quality instructions
- closely supervising athlete performance
- making the athlete accountable
- setting meaningful tasks resulting in high success rates, and
- clear presentations, enthusiasm and warmth.

There are some very prominent examples of coaches who exude the direct instruction style: coaches in netball, basketball, football, and corner coaches in boxing. Some might say that many of these coaches don't seem warm towards athletes, but most of the other characteristics of direct instruction are dominant features of the coaching style of these sports.

(Courtesy Queensland Newspapers)

A water polo coach setting the standards

Facilitative questioning

Facilitative questioning is a style of coaching that aims to increase the decision-making and problem-solving skills of the athlete. After all, in most sports, the coach is not allowed to instruct during the game and, if they are, they must do it from a sideline, often a long way from the action. Athletes who have been coached to solve problems and make decisions by themselves can make changes to their game during contests, and can also analyse cause-and-effect relationships when working on their techniques and game plans. This is often called developing 'game sense'.

Facilitative questioning does not necessarily mean that the coach asks the athlete questions, although that may be the case; it may be that the coach sets tasks that require the athlete to make decisions and solve problems.

Indira, a basketball coach, asks the team how they would transfer the ball from one end of the court to the other without the opposition intercepting, while another coach, Jill, organises a drill in which the players must transfer the ball from one end of the court to the other. During the drill, Jill introduces opposition of between one and five players, who are allowed to use a variety of strategies to steal the ball. Jill gives specific direction to the defensive players and not the offensive players, and doesn't tell the offensive players what the defenders are doing or how to keep possession of the ball. As a result, the offensive players have to develop their own passing solutions for particular defensive strategies.

Increasing athlete responsibility

Players who develop a sense of responsibility for their own performance and that of their team, as well the ability to manage themselves, will make the coach's job much easier. This is essential in cricket because the captain of the team not only sets an example as a player, but also organises the team during the match, decides where the players field, who bowls and for how long, and even the order of batting. In many open cricket teams the captain is often the coach.

Coaches of junior teams sometimes feel pressure because they believe that they must control and manage everything. While quality control and management are measures of a good coach, athletes who can control and manage themselves are signs of a better coach. The subtle difference is best explained by looking at how a player thinks. At net practice, is the bowler waiting for his coach to tell him to bowl or is he looking for opportunities to bowl when there is a vacant net? Does the young soccer player move freely across the field in cover defence, or does she hesitate because she is not sure how the coach might react if she leaves her designated playing position?

Young players who arrive at training and move quickly to assist with equipment organisation, begin individual warm ups and practice, and encourage each other to be on task, are well coached. Older athletes who organise their own complementary social life, nutritional eating habits, efficient recovery programs and effective individual training modules, are also well coached.

To develop an athlete's commitment to taking responsibility for her or his own involvement coaches should:

- highlight and praise those players who support others, especially for showing initiative
- avoid judging athletes and assume they are making the effort
- become the ideal model — the athletes should see the coach bowl in a vacant net at cricket practice or assist with packing up training equipment
- make clear what is required of the athletes at the beginning of the program
- criticise the action, not the player
- devote time to explaining the reasons for the various routines that result in effective management and performance
- ensure players know that a mistake does not affect the coach's respect for them as individuals
- accept that some athletes will help, support and show initiative more often than others do. Self-management is a skill that must be learned and the coach is responsible for ensuring that the less-skilled athletes learn and improve.

(Courtesy Queensland Newspapers)

Lawn bowlers as they analyse the game situation before advising team-mates of the best strategy.

- divide the team into smaller teams — defenders, midfielders and attackers — and appoint leaders who guide their subteam in their specific role in the overall team strategy, and

- ask for players' opinions and allow them to have input into the game plan and training program.

Some sports have naturally developed a self-management ethos, for example, it is expected that gymnasts will complete warm-up and training routines without supervision. They are also often expected to use a set of performance criteria for a particular apparatus to design their own programs.

Developing a rapport with athletes

Prominent coaches often appear to have a strong and positive relationship with athletes.

Media footage often shows John Newcombe, coach of the Australian Davis Cup team, engrossed in the serious business of guiding his players on match day, then later arm-in-arm singing with his players at a social function.

Winning teams and athletes seem to have an automatic rapport with their coach. Perhaps this is because, even if the athletes question the coaching techniques, one of the key criteria for developing rapport is trust. When they are winning, athletes tend to become believers and coaches can do no wrong. However, sometimes the signs of strong rapport are only superficial. Success can sometimes overcome some of the difficulties that might exist between a coach and an athlete.

Independent of the win/loss ratio, there are other indicators that rapport exists between player and coach, including:

- players respond quickly and appropriately to the coach's requests and treat the coach with respect

- the coach understands the athletes well and can therefore set achievable tasks and goals that the players consistently attain

- the coach applies rules fairly and treats each athlete with respect by getting to know them and acknowledging their efforts

- the coach is enthusiastic about listening to the athlete and if necessary makes concessions, and

- athletes are uninhibited in offering suggestions or comments.

A coach debriefs his basketball team and asks for the players' thoughts. A spontaneous discussion ensues with comments that focus on areas that need improvement and aspects of the game that should be retained and consolidated. During these discussions players are aware of the protocol for making a comment: they must avoid criticising team-mates in front of the team, but are encouraged to comment on successes and to feel comfortable talking about their own deficiencies (though this is often more appropriate in a private conversation with the coach or respected team leader).

These indicators and strategies can only result from a well-planned coaching program that strategically develops an appropriate rapport with each athlete.

Ideally, coaches will vary the level of association with players according to the situation. For example, the coach of a professional team may need to maintain some distance from the players because there will come a time when she has to tell players that they are no longer required in the team. De-listing a player from the team is extremely difficult to manage if a friendship has developed between the coach and the affected player. Alternatively, the coach of a low-level amateur team may be required to establish strong friendships to keep players involved and working hard.

Modelling

One of the most powerful coaching tools is modelling. Unfortunately coaches do not always have at their disposal someone who can demonstrate or model good skills. On these occasions coaches often resort to creating images that athletes can use to alter their performance.

To explain to beginner swimmers the leg action for breaststroke, coach Andrew asked the athletes to get their feet wet, then sit on the dry concrete pool deck with their legs straight, toes pointing to the coach (sitting in front of them) and only heels and bottom touching the ground. Andrew then said, 'Keep your feet next to each other and move your heels along the ground toward your bottom. You have just drawn (wet mark on concrete) the body of a butterfly. Now see if you can use your heels to draw the wings without moving your bottom.' The swimmers soon discovered that, in drawing the wings of a butterfly, their legs produce a conventional breaststroke kicking action.

Some coaches do not have a kit of clever analogies to create effective images, and others choose to use real live athletes to model ideal play, either in person or on video. Coaches who use modelling as the major focus of their instruction can achieve significant gains in a short time. The key components of the modelling style of coaching are:

- using models that the athletes see as successful

- referring to models of self-management, good behaviour, attitude and sportsmanship, as well as skill and game play

- using other team members who exhibit correct performance as models (however, coaches should do this sensitively to ensure that they don't compromise the integrity of any player. They should avoid making judgements about individuals and instead direct the attention of the players to the specific quality of the movement.)

- rewarding athletes who demonstrate desirable behaviours — 'I really appreciated the sincerity of the three cheers that the opposition gave us at the end of the game', and

- selecting models to ensure that they complement the program and that the model is capable of performing at the required level.

After some expert players play an exhibition match for his table tennis team, coach Ian observes that the team members enthusiastically apply the techniques demonstrated by the experts.

Defining athlete behaviours and associated consequences

Consider the following examples:

The javelin coach offers athletes a chocolate bar (edible reinforcer) if they can throw the javelin past a designated marker three times out of five throws. The marker might be at 85% of their personal best.

Only players who attend all of the required training sessions will be selected in the team, unless absent for an exceptional reason.

Coaching strategies that connect an action to a consequence seem to be favoured by coaches who focus on the competitive elements of coaching and the need for athletes to work together. This coaching style can be extremely productive if the athletes understand and support the connection between their actions and the consequences, and they often enjoy the challenge of avoiding or pursuing the consequences.

Coaches who use such behaviour management programs should avoid relying on them, and vary the approach, phasing programs in and out. They should also always use them as meaningful activity, rather than to have fun at someone's expense. Once they form good training habits, athletes will do what they should because they want to do it, rather than to avoid or pursue a consequence.

Important principles to observe when using this coaching style include:

- accurately defining the required behaviour and ensuring that athletes accept the impending consequence

- remembering to give a reward if it is promised

- avoiding situations where the same athletes experience negative consequences most of the time

- avoiding spur-of-the-moment punishment or promises of rewards — plan to use behaviour consequences when it becomes obvious that other strategies are not working and something else is needed, and

- devising consequences that will contribute to the training or practice of skills, for example, if the athletes practise correctly, the coach will reduce the training time.

COMMUNICATION

Coaches of athletes with disabilities know only too well the advantages of being able to use a variety of media to communicate performance criteria and feedback. Hearing-impaired athletes rely heavily on visual information and the visually impaired need coaches to use a mix of verbal and tactile communication. Most people have a preference for specific types of communication or combinations of communication. Effective coaches expose athletes to the full range of communication media and use the methods that seem to work best.

Written communication

Most sports have produced excellent written instructional materials for learners. Some sports activities, such as gymnastics, diving, martial arts, synchronised swimming, rhythmic gymnastics and dance sport, have highly

(Courtesy Queensland Newspapers)

A gymnastics coach supports an athlete to provide feedback about body position.

sophisticated technique criteria and base their standards on such written guidelines.

Coaches can use written material in a variety of ways. They can give players manuals to help them understand technique, or written conditioning and skill drill programs that players can follow when their coach is not available. When selecting or preparing written material for athletes, coaches must ensure that the information is easy to understand and digest and, to do this, should:

- use diagrams to assist with visualisation
- break the material up into lessons of no more than one or two pages
- use language that everyone understands
- explain new terms
- highlight the key points
- provide a brief summary, and
- always research the current literature before preparing materials, as the material they need may already exist.

Oral communication

The human voice is used for a vast range of purposes, such as instructing, giving feedback, admonishing, praising, lecturing, questioning, prompting and urging. As well as adapting the techniques mentioned above for

effective written communication, good oral communicators should use:

- appropriate voice projection
- a tone of voice that changes to complement the purpose of the message
- questions that try to confirm understanding and/or engage the athlete's problem-solving skills, and
- precise diction.

These techniques make the material more interesting, highlight the essential elements and reduce boredom. It is also important for coaches to check that the way they present spoken instructions is suitable for all the athletes in their care.

Robyn, an experienced player, has just joined the mixed touch team coached by Angelo. When Angelo read through Robyn's medical information form, he noticed that she had a vision impairment that had never been obvious to him. During the next training session he tried to ensure that, when he was addressing the group, he stood directly in front of Robyn so that she could see him and what he was doing. But Robyn often moved to the side when he did this, and Angelo started to worry that he was making her feel uncomfortable.

After the training session Angelo spoke to Robyn and explained that he was uncertain about the best way to ensure that she could see the relevant demonstrations. Robyn explained that she had very good peripheral vision, but that her central vision was blurry so she had trouble identifying details such as faces or numbers on player's shirts. She told Angelo that, if she stood slightly to the side when she was watching a demonstration, she could see better. Robyn asked him to give her a copy of his training program before the sessions, so she knew what was going to happen and could find the best spot from which to watch demonstrations.

Angelo felt a lot more comfortable after having talked to Robyn about what was best for her, and now speaks with her regularly about how she is finding the sessions.

Practical experience

Robert, a cycling coach, decides that the best way to communicate to a cyclist about the gamesmanship that occurs in road racing is to enter the cyclist in as many road races as possible. Robert knows that the athlete learns well from experience, but does not respond well to other forms of communication. Robert plans to debrief the athlete about his performance after each race and ask such questions as, 'What could you have done to avoid being boxed in at the finish?'

Cyclists work hard to ensure that they have an opening through which to ride to the finish line.

Athletes can learn more effectively from experience if the coach structures particular experiences into the overall coaching plan and therefore communicates specific ideas to the athlete while they are performing. In the previous example, the coach chose practical experience to teach the cyclist about being 'boxed in'.

Symbolic communication

Coaches will often find it necessary to show an athlete how to visualise and feel a movement, particularly if it is a new one or if a major flaw in technique is being corrected.

A discus coach wants to explain which way the hand turns on release of the discus, and says to the athlete, 'Imagine that you are quickly and tightly twisting a lid onto a jam jar'.

Examples of symbolism exist for all sports. Developing a collection of images that help athletes visualise and feel the movement can often significantly reduce the time taken to learn a movement.

Audiovisual communication

Videotapes enable coaches and athletes to focus on key aspects of performances, because critical moments can be examined in detail at any speed, and with or without sound. Coaches use video to analyse athlete skills and game play, as well as to analyse the skill and game play of the opposition.

Video is an excellent communication tool because perceptions can be confirmed and compared. A coach may be having difficulty convincing an athlete that there is a flaw in his technique. By watching a tape of his performance, the athlete can confirm that he and the coach are talking about the same aspect of technique, and also see that he does have a technique problem. Educating athletes to analyse their own videotapes greatly enhances their decision-making and problem-solving skills and accelerates the learning process.

Listening skills

Coaches should regard it as a privilege if athletes feel comfortable talking with them. They will listen more effectively if they genuinely want to help athletes develop and perform. Coaches who want to be good listeners should remember that:

- Listening is not only an auditory experience. Being sensitive to body language, performance data and group dynamics are also skills that help coaches to accurately understand and interpret what they are told.

Ray notices that a player, Carlos, is not as energetic as usual. If he knows Carlos well, Ray may realise that the problem is either Carlos's disappointment at being left out of the team, tiredness from a heavy training schedule or social complications. If Ray does not know Carlos well, but does know that, if asked, Carlos is likely to say, 'I'm fine. Don't worry', then he should ask other athletes or coaches about the cause of the problem.

- It is important to make time to listen to athletes, but coaches should be quick to curb the tendency of some athletes to use coaches as an emotional crutch, or to play political games with the team.

- Coaches should choose a relaxed and quiet environment for conversations when possible, and respect the athlete's need for privacy. Often during the quarter and three-quarter time breaks in Australian rules football matches, good coaches can be seen moving away from the player group to talk with an individual player.

- Coaches should acknowledge the sentiment being expressed by the athlete. They should use eye contact, head movements (nods), facial expressions and supportive statements to indicate that they have heard and understood what is being said.

- Coaches should avoid judging the athlete. If the coach disagrees with the athlete then, rather than show disappointment, they should wait until the athlete has finished what he or she has to say and then express the alternative point of view. They must always support opinion with reasons.

Conflict resolution

Sport stimulates the emotions of participants. When people are highly emotional, their personality traits are sometimes exaggerated and interpersonal relationships can become more difficult to manage. Effective coaches establish expectations and policies for players in such situations before the season begins.

Lynn, a water polo coach, chooses to employ a half-court press and requires her players to swim hard from attack to defence each time the opposition gains possession of the ball. (The half-court press is when the opposition is defended from halfway down the pool rather than for the entire length of the pool.) Lynn knows that one player does not have the fitness or inclination to do this. Rather than allow team-mates to become frustrated with the player who isn't making the effort, Lynn explains her policy and sets up the team's offence so that the less fit player doesn't have to swim so far. She also talks to the team about using each other's strengths and compensating for weaknesses. The less fit player agrees to improve his fitness and support the coaching strategy.

The ability to predict areas of potential conflict and plan to prevent problems arising comes with experience. Some conflicts will not be resolved, in which case all concerned should strive to move on and not dwell on the past. There are many worthwhile conflict resolution strategies.

- Coaches of young athletes have the responsibility of establishing supportive behaviours in each player. It is great to see young gymnasts making encouraging comments such as 'Bad luck!' or 'Great try!' when a team-mate makes an error. Such comments will help the one who made the error remain positive and continue to feel part of the team. Regarding a mistake as an opportunity to support will assist in defusing possible tensions that could develop between players.

- Admit some fault and attempt to consider the conflict from the other person's perspective.

- Ask questions rather than continually restating the same argument.

- Make concessions and compromise to establish a point of agreement.

- Avoid resorting to personal attacks such as, 'You're lazy!' and 'You don't listen!'.

Feedback

'Bowling Warnie!' is a phrase that became synonymous with Australian cricket. Ian Healey, long-serving wicket-keeper for the Australian team, used it to let spin bowler Shane Warne know that the ball he'd bowled had done what was required. The understanding between the two players meant that these two words could provide feedback about a range of aspects of each ball.

Effective feedback helps the athlete learn. It can be a comment from the coach, a sensation from the equipment and/or body or an evaluation of the outcome. Several options are available to a coach to gather useful information about an athlete's performances:

- Heart rate monitors can be attached to cyclists to gather data about physiological responses during rides.

- Sensors can be attached to bike pedals to gather information about how consistently force is applied during each cycle of the pedals.

- Videotapes of an athlete's performance of a skill can be compared to video examples of ideal technique.

- Using a swing frame (a frame in the shape of the preferred arc of the swing of the golfer), a coach can show a golfer where her swing path may need realignment.

- Sprint coaches can use timing lights to provide athletes with information about their speed during various sections of a sprint.

Whatever method is used to provide useful information, the coach should:

- use questioning techniques to help athletes construct their own feedback (questioning helps athletes identify for themselves what is and isn't correct)

Jenny asks a player to hit several serves to the left and several to the right before asking, 'What was different when you hit to the right compared to the left? What felt different?'

- refrain from repeating comments and assume that the athlete is intelligent and is working on responding to the coach's observation

- give only one or two pieces of information at any time so they can be absorbed more effectively

- help the athlete understand that the technique corrections resulting from feedback may, in the short term, result in a poorer outcome

- give more feedback about what is correct than about what is incorrect in a performance, and

- avoid giving corrective or negative feedback in the presence of team-mates (if necessary that fault can be mentioned to all players, but an individual should not be associated with the problem).

SELF-REFLECTION

Young athletes may be highly successful on the scoreboard but may not be aware that they have a technique fault that could prevent them from progressing to a higher level. If such players have exceptional ability, they could be winning championships even though their coaches have not identified the fault.

Coaches have to know if they are effective or ineffective, independent of the ability of the players. How does a lawn bowls coach know that he uses effective coaching techniques? Unless coaches can arrange for someone to observe and analyse them on a regular basis, just as a coach would analyse an athlete, there is really only one method they can use to confirm the effectiveness of their coaching — self-reflection.

Self-reflection is a process where individuals compare their current practice against an ideal set of practices, using a systematic procedure to make comparisons between real and ideal.

Mentoring

Effective coaches have often had the good fortune to be coached, as athletes, by a good coach. In later life they have probably imitated many of the coaching methods adopted by their own coaches without even being aware of it.

The mentor in self-reflection is someone whom a coach respects and selects to assist with the self-reflection process. The mentor acts as an 'auditor' of the coach's interpretation of his or her own coaching practice, hearing the coach's analysis of the coaching performance and confirming the accuracy of the coach's comments. The mentor asks questions about the methods used and guides the coach toward a deeper understanding of her or his work.

Video analysis

Video analysis assists the self-reflection process because videotape provides permanent images that can help with in-depth analysis and evaluation. It can also help to identify areas in need of improvement and can be used to plan for such improvement.

(National Sports Information Centre)

Video is an effective tool for self-reflection.

Video self-analysis is a six-step process:

- recording — videotape a coaching session
- reflecting — review the tape to find a suitable segment, then analyse the segment against an ideal model
- consulting — invite a mentor to 'audit' the analysis
- planning — design a plan to improve
- implementing — carry out the plan, and
- follow-up recording — videotape a follow-up coaching session and check that the plan has worked.

Behaviour modification

A coach uses a vast range of strategies to bring about changes in an athlete's behaviour and sometimes this can be very difficult, especially if the behaviour that is to be corrected has become an ingrained habit. Unfortunately, it is sometimes just as difficult to modify coaching behaviour as it is to modify athlete behaviour. If an inappropriate coaching behaviour becomes a habit then a major commitment is required to change the behaviour.

A common flaw in a coach's delivery of information is the use of extraneous language — 'um', 'ah' or 'you know'. For some coaches, eliminating the use of such distracting language can be very difficult. Coaches who are attempting to modify their own behaviour should try these strategies:

- identify the behaviour to be modified
- establish the characteristics of the new behaviour
- look at models of the new behaviour
- assess how important the change is — how will it affect the coach's effectiveness?
- obtain feedback about the behaviour, and
- reassess the effects of the change on all coaching tasks.

Committed coaches certainly need ongoing self-development programs. Once coaches decide to make that commitment, they must then find the time to improve their coaching, as well as work to make a living, unless the coaching role also provides an income. Fortunately today's aspiring coaches have access to an abundance of resources that can be used to support a self-directed program, including:

- websites about coaching that are informative and comprehensive
- a system of progressive study offered through the Australian Sports Commission, and
- coaching positions at all levels that are readily available in clubs and schools and can provide coaches with vital experience.

CONCLUSION

Every coaching session is an opportunity to trial different coaching methods. Using those we have discussed in this chapter, in conjunction with the self-reflection process, coaches have all the ingredients at their disposal to prepare athletes in the most effective and efficient ways possible. If they also manage their own self-paced training program effectively and efficiently, coaches can be assured of achieving the best results on and off the field.

COACHING TIPS

- Vary coaching methods for different athletes and situations.
- Adjust your coaching style to meet changing circumstances.
- Learn from both mistakes and successes.
- Think creatively to find a better way.
- Remember the three 'eyes' — personal-eyes, individual-eyes and empath-eyes.
- Show the athlete how much you care, not just how much you know.

FURTHER READING

Australian Coaching Council (1996) *Video Self-Analysis: A Lens on Coaching* (video and study pack). Canberra: Australian Sports Commission.

Kidman, L, and S Hanrahan (1997) *The Coaching Process: A Practical Guide to Improving Your Effectiveness*. Palmerston North, New Zealand: the Dunmore Press.

Martens, R (1997) *Successful Coaching*. Champaign, IL: Human Kinetics.

Siedentop, D (1991) *Developing Teaching Skills in Physical Education*. Mountain View, CA: Mayfield.

CHAPTER 3
THE COACH AS A RESOURCE MANAGER

Craig Davies

(National Sports Information Centre)

INTRODUCTION

Coaches are often selected for positions because of their technical abilities and knowledge of the sport. This happens whether they are full-time head coaches of national teams or volunteer coaches of local club teams. However, the achievements of the athletes and the success of a coaching program depend on far more than coaches' technical skills and their ability to impart their knowledge to the athletes.

Coaches of the current era must sometimes be able to develop and manage a wide range of support personnel and other resources to help them obtain the best performances from athletes. However, all coaches should remember that, whatever they do, the wellbeing of the athletes is always the first priority. This chapter looks at the supporting resources that are available to coaches at any level, and coaches can use them to help athletes achieve their full potential.

Planning is crucial to deciding what support personnel and resources are required. At the beginning of a season or planning phase, coaches therefore usually conduct a needs analysis of the program and identify the re-

sources they require. To do this they might ask the following questions:

- What are the strengths and weaknesses of the athletes (physical, skill-based, tactical, mental)?
- What is the injury and health status of the athletes?
- What support services could assist the athletes?
- What expertise exists within the club, sport or program that could assist the athletes?
- What expertise do I need to seek out to assist the athletes?

The way resources are used will depend on the ages and standards of the athletes, the type of sport they play, the resources available and the phase of the training program. A national coach would probably use all of the resources outlined in this chapter, but a club coach may only select a few essential ones. However, many coaches, particularly those in rural or isolated communities, may have very limited access to such assistance and resources. In such cases, coaches must prioritise their needs carefully, and focus on effectively obtaining and using the few resources available.

For example, coaches should ensure that 'the basics' are covered, including:

- technical and tactical skills development
- injury prevention and management
- access to safe facilities and equipment, and
- individualisation of training programs to suit the needs of each athlete.

If a coach can achieve these things, this sets a good foundation for the development of the program.

Sonia, a level 2 lacrosse coach, was starting to prepare for the forthcoming season and was reading through some of her training program notes from the previous season. She noticed that the team had scored poorly in the beep test for endurance, and had showed signs of fatigue at training and during the second half of matches. Sonia realised that, if the team was to have any chance of reaching the finals, she had to improve their fitness.

Sonia consulted a sports physiologist for advice, who designed a fitness program for Sonia to implement. The conditioning expert offered to run a few fitness sessions during the pre-season period. Routines to maintain fitness throughout the season were also recommended to Sonia. The team's fitness results were markedly improved, giving them a better chance of making the finals at the end of the season.

THE COACH AS A RESOURCE MANAGER

The task of the coach of any team is to develop the resources available to the team or individual athlete, including a team of support personnel or service providers whose input can be integrated into the program. The members of this team, and some of the other resources coaches can use, are shown in the diagram below.

Developing a network

Coach education programs go some of the way to giving coaches a wide range of skills, but no matter how much coaches read or study, they cannot be expert in all domains. Many of the chapters in this manual will provide background information on subjects such as sports science, sports medicine and so on, but they cannot make readers experts in those fields. Coaches must turn to experts in sports science and associated professions for help in developing the specialised parts of their programs.

Coaches should be resourceful and develop a network of people who can assist them as required. The cheapest and easiest way to develop a network is to advertise within the sport. A coach may find that there is a parent or club administrator with special expertise relevant to the program. An alternative is to ask around to find out about the sports science and sports medicine professionals in the local area.

Coaches can also contact the nearest institute, academy or university that specialises in sport science or human movement studies and make an appointment to see the specialists there. They should discuss the important needs of their sport with these experts: for example, flexibility, injury prevention, technique improvement, sensible eating, relaxa-

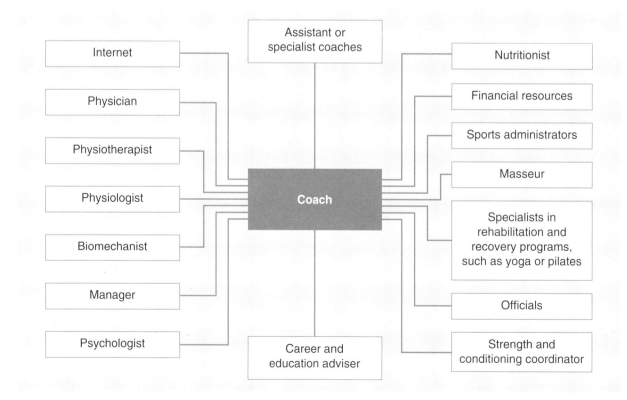

Network of coaches' resources

tion and goal setting. Sometimes these experts are willing to be involved in a coaching program in some capacity. For example, the local hospital dietician may be willing to talk to parents and athletes about sensible nutrition before the competitive season. Coaches also shouldn't forget about those around them in their club or association.

Antony, an Australian rules football coach, moved to remote far north Queensland and was appointed coach of the predominantly Indigenous local under-19 team. Antony's initial training sessions went reasonably well, but he noticed that the Indigenous players, in particular, were reluctant to make eye contact with him while he was giving instructions. He also tried to use a 'questioning' style with the players when discussing tactical issues, but this didn't work well either.

Antony discussed these problems with Steve, an Indigenous senior coach at his club. Steve was happy to help Antony and explained to him that, in some Indigenous communities, eye contact is generally avoided. He also told Antony that, in some Indigenous cultures, it is considered rude to ask a question if you already know the answer, which explained why Antony's questions were not being well received!

Antony was able to use this advice to adapt his communication style in future sessions, which were much more successful. He also got to know Steve and others at the club and learned more about the local culture.

(National Sports Information Centre)

Coaches of indigenous athletes may find it useful to learn more about indigenous cultures.

There are many ways that experts can help! With a few phone calls, a personal visit and a positive attitude towards incorporating the knowledge of the services and resources that are available to the training program, coaches can create their own Institute of Sport.

Managing the team of providers

Because coaches must sometimes manage a large and complex group of people who contribute to the development of the athletes, they must also learn good management and administrative skills. They must know how to best manage their own time and that of others when it is a scarce and valuable resource, and how to deal with people to obtain the best from them and for them.

Administrative skills are also vital to coaches, as they are often responsible for a range of administrative tasks, including:

- registering the team/athletes for competitions
- planning the program
- booking training venues
- record-keeping (athlete details, personal bests, statistics from training and competition)
- budgeting and financial management
- purchase and care of equipment
- making travel arrangements
- ensuring that their own accreditation is up to date
- ensuring that all insurance paperwork is complete, and
- arranging storage of files and training programs.

The self-reflection process (see chapter 2, Coaching Methods) will help coaches assess their skills in these areas to some extent, and those who need to improve should consider these avenues of assistance:

- the Australian Sports Commission produces a range of relevant resources
- some state and regional departments of sport and recreation run courses on management skills in sport
- many local and regional colleges and tertiary institutions run basic-level people-management courses, and
- other more experienced coaches or administrators can often help by sharing strategies they use to manage their time and people.

Assistant or specialist coaches

Additional coaching resources are important for any coach, but unfortunately assistance is not always readily available. Coaches may need to seek out interested ex-players or parents as assistants. Assistant coaches can add value to a program by providing technical assistance, support (both on and off the training field), another 'set of eyes', ideas and a different perspective.

Generally an assistant coach will work with the head coach throughout the season, whereas a specialist coach may conduct regular or one-off sessions during the year. A specialist coach who has expertise in a particular area can help the athletes while also benefiting the professional development of the participating coaching staff.

When working with assistant coaches, it is important for coaches to ensure that all coaches on the team have common goals for the program, and share a clearly defined approach to issues such as team selection and court time for players. Head coaches and assistant coaches should discuss these issues and agree on their approach.

It's vital that the head coach and assistant or specialist coaches communicate well to ensure that athletes are treated consistently by the whole coaching team — mixed messages can be confusing and counterproductive. A head coach can find it useful to have regular meetings with assistant or specialist coaches. Initially, issues such as clarifying roles, the autonomy of each team member and how decisions will be made should be discussed. Future meetings may focus more on how to deal with particular athletes, or on technical or tactical issues.

The roles of assistant and specialist coaches can vary and may include:

- providing technical and tactical coaching
- giving feedback to the head coach
- acting as the head coach on certain occasions
- observing national and international competitions to provide feedback on players and opponents
- recording statistics, and
- providing specialised advice on specific skills, such as batting, goalkeeping and goal shooting.

Local, club and regional coaches can also be a useful resource, especially for coaches of state squads, who may coach athletes from regional areas who don't often train with their state coach. In this case, it is important for coaches to communicate with the local, club or regional coach who is helping the athlete train. This will ensure that coaching support for the athlete during training is comprehensive and properly coordinated, and so more effective. If the athlete doesn't have a local coach, the state coach may be able to locate a coach from a similar sport to help.

Sports scientists

Sports science support staff aim to help coaches and athletes achieve excellence in performance through a multidisciplinary approach. The sports science services that can be used by the head coach are discussed below. Coaches can seek access to these services through regional or state institutes/academies of sport, universities, TAFE colleges, local hospitals, fitness/health centres or community clubs. They can also speak to coaches from other sports in their area to see how they access such resources.

Physiologists The role of the physiologist is to assess, evaluate and enhance fitness — an athlete's ability to produce energy and force and to use them skilfully (see chapter 6, Physiology and Sports Performance, for more information). Methods of assessment include field and laboratory testing to determine the physiological status of an athlete. Relevant measures of body composition and aerobic and anaerobic ability can be closely monitored. After the athlete's test results have been analysed and evaluated, the coach is provided with recommendations for training that will help the athlete to achieve the best performances possible.

Physiologists can also help the coach in structuring and producing a periodised plan into which the requirements of the other service providers can be integrated. They can provide assistance with planning training programs, as well as designing specific training sessions to improve the fitness of athletes.

The physiologist can also evaluate the impact of external factors (for example, altitude, heat and nutritional supplements) on body function and ultimately how these factors will influence athletes' performances. To do this they must measure and monitor the response of specific physiological variables to these influences.

For further information on physiology contact the Australian Association for Exercise and Sports Science or Sports Medicine Australia.

Psychologists The role of the sport psychologist is to explain the psychology of different aspects of performance to an individual player, a team, a leadership group, the medical team or the coaching staff (see chapter 13, Performance Psychology, for more information). The psychologist's involvement with an individual or a team may cover several major areas, including:

- assisting the coaching staff to cope with player issues related to on-field performance. This may include helping with the development of pre and post-competition routines, arousal control, reactions to setbacks or errors, consistency in performance and lack of confidence.

- managing issues that are non-sport specific, but that influence an athlete's performance. This process may require the development of 'life' skills, such as communication skills (an important part of being a team member), assertiveness skills or anger management, and may extend to neutral and confidential one-on-one counselling in which a range of issues can be discussed, such as relationship problems or excessive drinking.

- helping the coaching staff to establish a team culture and build team cohesion, and working with the team as a whole or as sub-groups within the team (for example, the defenders or the team leaders), and

- helping the medical staff to manage injuries by monitoring and dealing with issues that arise in the minds of injured athletes.

It is important that the coach introduces psychological skills training as a normal part of the program, rather than as a crisis management tool. Generally, psychological intervention or counselling will occur on an individual basis, rather than being a requirement for all athletes in the squad.

There are many coaches and athletes who are capable of dealing with psychological issues and who operate effectively without further assistance, but having a well-structured program of support in this area is important.

Biomechanists Biomechanists can assess how effectively athletes perform movements and measure all aspects of their performances. However, coaches should ensure that the athletes they are training have reached the stage at which they are performing consistently before testing them biomechanically. If an athlete is not giving consistent performances then the biomechanical measurements won't hold true in the future and time, money and resources may have been wasted.

Videotapes are affordable and effective tools for analysing both individual technique and team performance in competition. Methods of assessment include slow motion and freeze-frame video analysis, which assist the coach to identify technical and tactical faults that may not be obvious to the naked eye. The biomechanist can also help in the evaluation of sporting equipment through the application of specific assessment techniques (see

Sports scientists assisting coaches and athletes.

(National Sports Information Centre)

chapter 15, Biomechanics of Sport, for more information on biomechanics).

Following an assessment and evaluation, the biomechanist provides recommendations to the coach to help the athlete achieve better performances. Club coaches can't always access biomechanical services (because factors such as the cost or the location of the resource prevents access). However, video analysis is available to most coaches and is a valuable learning tool in terms of skill and tactical development.

Nutritionists   The aim of this service is to provide athletes and coaches with nutrition education that promotes healthy eating practices centred on achieving the best athletic performance (see chapter 16, Sports Nutrition, for more information). This includes sport-specific advice for training and competition. The service can be provided through:

- personal consultation, including diet analysis and recommendations (the issues most commonly discussed are the reduction of skinfold measurements, addressing low blood iron levels and diet-related fatigue), and

- group education, in which a forum on specific nutritional topics is presented for athletes, coaches and parents (these sessions may include specific cooking sessions, nutritional advice in preparation for competition, and particularly for the off

season, to ensure that athletes do not gain excess weight during this time).

It is vital that the coach knows about problems that can prevent athletes applying the nutritional advice they are given, such as an inability to cook, family pressures and movement restrictions resulting from injury.

The best way to establish contact with a good nutritionist is to contact the Sports Dieticians Australia (SDA). This network of dieticians is committed to promoting healthy eating to enhance the performance of athletes, whatever their level of performance. The SDA can give coaches the names of nutritionists who can provide assistance for athletes, conduct group sessions and offer advice to coaches. The SDA also provides fact sheets that coaches can use to improve their knowledge of nutrition in sport.

It is important that coaches adopt an educative approach to nutrition and reinforce the message of nutritionists. The coach should also establish a link between the physiologist and the nutritionist on the team, to ensure athletes are given dietary advice that matches their bodies' needs.

Strength and conditioning coordinators   This service aims to help the athlete become as fit and strong as possible, and can include individualised strength training programs, training supervision and routine strength and

(National Sports Information Centre)

Strength and conditioning experts can provide valuable assistance in the preparation of athletes.

fitness assessments for individuals and squad members (see chapter 11, Speed, Strength and Power Training, for more information).

The importance of strength and conditioning to the athlete depends on the sport they play and, to a large extent, the deficiencies that have been identified in their performances. Information about appropriate practitioners can be gained through the Australian Strength and Conditioning Association. As a general rule it is recommended that the service providers have National Coaching Accreditation Scheme level 1 or 2 strength and conditioning accreditation.

Coaches can often obtain the advice of second or third-year sport science students, who should also have the knowledge to implement a program.

Special programs Special programs have been instigated by many coaches to provide variety in training, develop movement skills and improve mental and physical recovery between training sessions. Examples include yoga, pilates (a method of training to develop trunk stability) and meditation classes. Coaches should think broadly about the needs of athletes, and consider what can be achieved by using resources other than just those that are strictly sports related.

Accessing sports science services

It is important that all coaches base their training programs on good scientific principles. One of the difficulties facing club-level coaches is gaining access to sports science expertise. While there are some private practices, one alternative is to use tertiary institutions. Tertiary students can be a valuable resource to the coach in this area. However, you should consider the fact that students will usually have general, rather than sports-specific expertise.

There are three levels of assistance available through tertiary institutions that coaches could build into a program.

1. **Contract services** Tertiary institutions are often prepared to negotiate a contract for specific assistance. This may relate to regular testing or assessment, or one-off group work. Although this service is available, it is often not financially viable for coaches with limited resources.

2. **Research studies** A research study for an honours or masters student could also benefit a club coach, who may be able to incorporate the training program requirements into those of the study. Under these circumstances,

the coach must be aware that the research may not always produce information that is directly applicable to the development of the athletes. However, the return to the coach and athletes in terms of test results can often be very useful, if it is provided at the appropriate time.

3. **Practicum programs** Tertiary students may have to complete a certain number of hours in a practical field environment to satisfy course requirements. A postgraduate student who requires field experience may be available to assist a coach at minimal cost, particularly physiologists and psychologists.

Tertiary institutions will usually view each request on a case-by-case basis and generally limit assistance to the testing process, as distinct from programming. Information on suitable practitioners can be obtained from:

- the relevant scientific society in each state (for example, the Australian Psychological Society or the Australian Association for Exercise and Sports Science)
- the relevant department at a tertiary institution (for example, psychology or human movement), or
- state (or regional) institutes or academies of sport.

Medical staff

Medical staff are responsible for the diagnosis, treatment and rehabilitation of sport injuries. The process should be carried out in consultation with other medical providers, such as physiotherapists. Medical staff should also be familiar with the doping guidelines of the Australian Sports Drug Agency and the World Anti-doping Agency and the doping policies of specific sports.

Sports physicians Every club, team or individual should have a sports doctor. A list of sports medicine doctors can be obtained from Sports Medicine Australia. The ideal sports doctors are either:

- sports physicians who have completed postgraduate specialist training in sports medicine, or
- general practitioners who have completed a short course in sports medicine or have demonstrated significant interest and experience in the field.

Physiotherapists The role of the physiotherapist is to provide programs to prevent injuries and to treat and rehabilitate injuries as they occur. This also includes screening athletes for potential injury problems. This service is provided in close consultation with the doctor and coach regarding the athlete's condition.

It is useful if a coach can locate a physiotherapist who can work with a team or squad. The crucial aspects are communication and time. The time a physiotherapist spends with a squad is often not remunerated, but the practitioner may benefit financially if athletes also attend the physiotherapy practice privately. While it is not crucial for the doctor and the physiotherapist to work in the same practice, it is important that they communicate regularly.

It is crucial that the coach and other support staff provide immediate injury treatment and then refer an injured athlete to the team doctor. While the coach cannot force an athlete to see a particular service provider, if all team or squad members use the same medical providers it becomes easier for the coach to build a professional relationship with those health professionals.

Rehabilitation and recovery specialists

Rehabilitation and recovery programs help with mental and physical recovery from training. Recovery programs may include yoga, massage and cross-training. Massage is widely used to help athletes repeat performances and to minimise injury. Yoga can increase flexibility and improve relaxation. Water-based and other cross-training activities are used when the continuation of normal weight-bearing training would result in significant unwanted fatigue or injury.

After routine medical and physiotherapy monitoring, a coach became concerned about the reduced back flexibility and strength of one of the national women's hockey squad members. The issue was raised by the medical physician at one of the regular meetings between the squad's service providers and the national coaching staff. The national head coach was concerned that the weakness may lead to chronic lower back and hamstring problems, as the program intensified in the final preparation for the Olympic Games.

The squad's medical physician, physiotherapist and exercise physiologist worked in close consultation to review the athlete's current program. They made appropriate modifications to the flexibility, strength and recovery aspects of her program, and set regular dates for reassessments. The player's increased flexibility and strength gave her a better chance of an injury-free preparation for the Olympics.

(National Sports Information Centre)

Injuries can be prevented through specialist advice.

Other resources

Coaches can have a wide range of other resources at their disposal, including the internet, financial resources, equipment and facilities. As with people-based resources, the key is determining what is needed, assessing what is available and making use of it as effectively as possible.

The internet is a very good tool for research and for keeping in contact with athletes or other coaches quickly and cheaply. The Further reading section of this chapter lists some useful websites that are relevant to managing coaching resources. It is important to remember that those using the net must check the sources of the information they take from it, as in many cases there is little control over what appears there. They must also remember that copyright applies to internet material just as it does to other forms of publication.

Other support services

Drug education

Coaches should be familiar with the doping policy of their sport and the resources of the Australian Sports Drug Agency (ASDA) and the World Anti-Doping Agency, so that they can accurately inform athletes and the support team about banned substances and testing procedures. Seminars about drugs in sport issues are conducted by ASDA for athletes. See chapter 17, Medical Considerations in Sport, for more information on drugs in sport.

Athlete Career and Education (ACE)

The aim of the ACE program is to enhance the personal development and performance of elite athletes by providing career and education counselling services. The program does this by helping with personal development, career planning, career referral, educational guidance and transitional support strategies.

COORDINATING AND INTEGRATING THE PROGRAM

Coaches must be the coordinators and the driving force behind their training programs. They should utilise the expertise that is available to them and should not feel inadequate because they need to seek advice from experts.

Program integration begins with the head coach, who, in consultation with other members of the coaching staff, determines the competition schedule. Through consultation with all service providers, the head coach then schedules the requirements of all planned services on the periodised plan. He or she must ensure that all coaching staff are receiving regular information and communicating with all of the specialist and service providers involved in the program.

Regular coordination meetings are also a good idea. The progress of individual athletes can be discussed in detail at these meetings. The subsequent plan for each athlete can then be formulated by the head coach, based on the information that has been presented, and in close consultation with the athlete.

For example, the medical information relating to an injured player will be useful to the psychologists and physiologists. It is from this information that the head coach is able to make an informed decision about whether a player is fit to train or play. Information is then provided to strength and conditioning and nutrition staff who can adjust the program in view of the requirements of individual athletes.

The physiotherapist must work in close consultation with the medical coordinator, the coach and the sports science staff to develop injury prevention programs, as well as to manage injured athletes. It is important that athletes are involved in the planning and implementation of their programs. They should know their own strengths and weaknesses and progressively take responsibility for their own development. Athletes and coaches must work together, enlisting the assistance of others, to enhance individual and team performance.

The coach must consider every issue that may affect the athletes, ranging from family issues and work commitments to study and examination demands. Often the club coach must deal with these problems without a great deal of assistance.

WORKING WITH OFFICIALS

Coaches at all levels have to interact with officials involved in their sports (for example, umpires, referees, judges, timekeepers and scorers). While relationships between coaches and officials have not always been good, both these groups are now realising the benefits of working together. It is now becoming common for officials to attend training sessions and interact more broadly with athletes and coaches. There are many benefits for coaches and athletes in fostering positive relationships, including:

- a better understanding of each other's roles
- a more cooperative approach to conflict resolution, and
- increasing harmony between rule interpretations and coaching techniques.

Felicity, a national level gymnast, was preparing for a selection meet to determine squad members for the national gymnastics team. In previous competitions, only one or two technical errors divided the leading competitors. Felicity's previous best score for the balance beam was 9.25, but she needed a 9.45 to have any chance of making the team.

Felicity's coach, Noel, was uncertain about one aspect of Felicity's routine, which could mean up to a half point deduction. To help finalise Felicity's routine, he invited Judy, a senior judge for 20 years, to a training session. Judy observed the practice routine with Noel, indicated some technical errors and also mentioned other points that the judges would be looking for (even though Judy was not judging the forthcoming competition).

After spending time with Judy, Noel saw the benefits of working together with experienced judges to help the athletes. Felicity also felt more confident at the selection meet, as she could focus on many of the tips provided by Judy. The final score for Felicity was a 9.5 on the beam, which saw her selected ahead of the last competitor to miss out with a score of 9.4.

(National Sports Information Centre)

Officials can provide technical advice to assist performance.

ADMINISTRATIVE SUPPORT

Many club-level team coaches will have the benefit of a team manager, who can provide support in some of these areas, while coaches may have to take on much of the coordination work themselves. Often club coaches have limited administrative support. However, there are often many people within the club administrators', team managers' and the athletes' families who can assist with aspects such as uniforms, public relations, planning travel and competitions, distributing information on training and competition schedules and fundraising, such as sponsorship or grant proposals. Where possible, coaches should leave the coordination of these people to club officials.

Darryl, a level 2 basketball coach uses the expertise of many people within the Southern Junior League Development Program. Darryl selected two assistant coaches and two coaches from the age group squads with whom he wanted to work. He also conducted a skills audit of the families of the athletes in his team to find out whether they were skilled in areas that would be of use to the program, such as management, communication, information technology, medicine and sports science.

Darryl asked parents for expressions of interest in assisting with the development of the program and managed to find a team manager, a video assistant, a newsletter editor and a nurse who was interested in sports medicine and first aid. He also found specialists among the parents who would make presentations on three relevant subjects. Each player made a small financial contribution to help with the cost of these basic lectures in recovery, nutrition and sports psychology.

Some national coaches have the benefit of administrative support, a person or people responsible for the management of the program and for ensuring communication between all those involved in it. The responsibilities of such positions can include athlete welfare, allowances, coordinating the medical process, including ASDA requirements, player reports, venue bookings, travel and camp itineraries and consultation with national and state associations.

GETTING COACHING INFORMATION

Information is a critical resource for modern coaches, for learning, for teaching and for communicating ideas to others. It's vital that coaches stay up to date with the latest news and information on their subjects and sports. If they don't they risk both their effectiveness as coaches and, more importantly, the health and wellbeing of the athletes they coach.

Club coaches can obtain valuable information from national and state elite coaching programs. Coaches involved in elite programs in each sport, in conjunction with sports science coordinators, are usually more than willing to share information with club coaches. This encourages a consistent approach to coaching throughout the sport and benefits the 'up and coming' athletes aiming for the elite level. This sharing of information can happen through seminars, workshops, publications, the internet, and coaching networks and associations.

Additional information for the coach can also be located through the following sources:

- state and territory coaching centres
- the Australian Sports Commission's magazines *Sports Coach*, *Coaching Australia* and *The Sport Educator*
- government departments for sport and recreation
- institutes and academies of sport
- the National Sports Information Centre, other information centres and libraries

- tertiary institutions
- internet sites such as Sport Discus and Medline, and
- national and state sporting organisations.

CONCLUSION

Modern coaches must be able to act as program facilitators, integrating the input of a group of people and other resources so that they make a significant contribution to the development of the individual athlete or team. They know that good coaches offer better programs and will ultimately produce the best results.

COACHING TIPS

- Bring together a support team of people with different expertise to enhance athletes' performances.

- Enlist local professionals to provide medical and scientific support for athletes. For example, a local physiotherapist can teach athletes how to stretch at training, a doctor can talk with parents about drugs in sport, and a dietician can take the team on a supermarket visit and teach members how to read labels and select healthy food.

- Conduct regular support team meetings to share information and integrate the contributions of individual members.

- Develop management skills to coordinate helpers and add value to the program.

FURTHER READING

Internet

Australian Association for Exercise and Sports Science website <http://www.artesys.com.au/>.

Australian Sports Drug Agency website <www.asda.org.au>.

Pubmed (US medical publications database) website <www.ncbi.nlm.nih.gov/PubMed/>.

Sport Discus (international sports database) website <www.sirc.ca/datab.html>.

Sports Dieticians Australia website <www.ausport.gov.au/sda/>.

Sports Medicine Australia website <www.ausport.gov.au/sma/>.

World Anti-Doping Agency website <www.wada-ama.org>.

Publications

Burke, LM (1995) *The Complete Guide to Food for Sports Performance: Peak Nutrition for Your Sport*. St Leonards: Allen and Unwin.

de Castella, R, and W Clews (eds) (1996) *Smart Sport: The Ultimate Reference Manual for Sports People*. Canberra: RWM Publishing.

Fleck, SJ, and WJ Kraemer (1997) *Designing Resistance Training Programs*. Champaign, IL: Human Kinetics.

Goldsmith, W (1995) Coaching with imagination. *Sports Coach* 18(1).

Martens, R (1987) *Coaches' Guide to Sports Psychology*. Champaign, IL: Human Kinetics.

Martens, R (1997) *Successful Coaching*. Champaign, IL: Human Kinetics, chapter 14.

Sports Medicine Australia (1998) *Sports First Aid Manual*. Canberra: Sports Medicine Australia.

CHAPTER 4
RISK MANAGEMENT FOR COACHES

Deborah Healey

(National Sports Information Centre)

INTRODUCTION

Most coaches are genuinely concerned about the wellbeing of the athletes under their care and aim to prevent incidents that might affect or injure them. Physical injuries affect athletes, but issues such as contractual disputes, unfair treatment and discrimination can also affect their wellbeing and their performances.

This chapter will help coaches to identify sports risks and minimise them. Risk management involves the analysis of all situations involving coaches and athletes under their care, and the development of a risk minimisation plan that will reduce risks. The most pressing legal risks for coaches are those that concern the safety of those they are coaching.

SOME OF THE RISKS

People are today becoming more aware of their rights. They are no longer prepared to accept serious injury in circumstances where it could have been avoided, and they are seeking compensation when injury occurs. Organisations and individuals involved in sport should consider carefully the risks they face. Organisations, coaches, trainers and managers may be liable for the care and instructions that they give to athletes or for other aspects of their behaviour that cause injury, loss or damage. Risks may arise through the nature of equipment or facilities, the danger of a particular activity or through inappropriate advice or coaching methods.

Coaches must be aware of issues such as discrimination and harassment, which can result in emotional or physical injury to athletes, and deal with them in accordance with the relevant laws. The areas of discrimination and harassment are regulated by different laws at federal and state level (for more information on legislation see the Australian Sports Commission's Harassment-Free Sport series of booklets).

The law of negligence

The law does not provide compensation for every physical injury because not every injury is caused by someone else. There is no provision at law for compensation where no-one has been at fault, although some insurance policies provide compensation for any injury.

What is negligence?

Negligence is the area of law that provides a remedy to people injured as a result of the act or omission of another person. It does not matter that the person who caused the injury did not mean to hurt the injured person. To show negligence, an injured person must establish that a **duty of care** was owed to him or her by the person causing the injury. A duty of care exists when there is some relationship between the injured person and the person causing the injury, and the person causing the injury should have understood that his or her action might injure someone. This need not necessarily be the person who was actually injured.

If the coach or injured party is a volunteer, that person may still be found liable, though the potential is not the same as if he or she were employed, and this also may affect the test applied to determine whether or not the individual has been at fault. A volunteer may be responsible for an injury. A professional coach is assumed to have greater knowledge and perform to a higher standard. If a coach is paid for coaching duties, this may mean that he or she could be expected to exercise more care than otherwise.

Participants, organisers and referees have been found to owe a duty of care to other participants and spectators, and there is no doubt that coaches and other officials also owe a duty of care to participants. Facility operators are routinely found to owe a duty of care to users and to be liable for injuries suffered.

How careful does a coach have to be?

Even if coaches owe a duty of care, they are not liable for all injuries. Liability depends upon breach of the duty of care by a failure to observe a reasonable standard of behaviour. The standard of care expected will vary depending upon the circumstances, including matters such as the ages of the people involved. The injury must have been caused by the act or omission (that is, the failure to take action) of the person being sued.

In a case involving a jockey, for example, the test of negligence was whether the jockey had ridden in the manner of a reasonable jockey. The judge found that the jockey had not observed that standard, and that he was therefore liable for injuries to another jockey.

In a famous 1987 case, where a schoolboy was injured in a rugby league match and sued the Department of Education and the teacher/coaches, the court found that the coaches were not liable. The teachers employed by the department were not informed that people with 'long thin necks' should not be playing in a scrum. The department knew, but had not told the teachers. The department was liable because it should have informed the teachers, and it owed a special duty to all its students that it had failed to discharge. The standard of care that educational authorities owe to students is usually very high, and it is very difficult for educational authorities to show that they have exercised sufficient care when a student is injured.

All coaches must ensure that their behaviour and the level of care they apply to athletes is appropriate to the circumstances of their sport and of particular athletes. Facilities must be safe and appropriate. The ages and condition of the athletes are often critical in deciding this issue.

(National Sports Information Centre)

Coaches should take precautions to prevent injury.

Managing the risk of injury

Coaches can substantially reduce the risk of injury and legal action by:

- providing a safe environment (including taking the weather into account) and properly maintained equipment
- adequately planning activities and appropriate steps in the teaching of new skills, especially potentially dangerous skills
- being more careful where children are concerned
- matching young athletes not only according to age, but also height, weight, maturity and, if possible, skill levels and experience
- warning athletes of the injury risks of the sport
- knowing and keeping up to date with first aid and basic emergency procedures, and procedures for managing injuries (see chapter 17, Medical Considerations in Sport, for more information on emergencies and managing injuries)
- having a written emergency plan and ensuring that appropriate medical assistance is available when necessary
- developing clear, written rules for practice and general conduct to prevent injuries that often result from fooling around in change rooms and practice venues
- ensuring that medical decisions are made by medical personnel (refer athletes to doctors or trained medical staff rather than guess about the consequences of injury during a game or while training, and err on the side of caution)
- keeping accurate records, which can be useful aids to planning and are essential in all cases of injury These should include relevant general and medical information, progress reports and accident reports (not diagnoses).
- keeping up to date with the latest information involving their sport, likely injuries and appropriate equipment and techniques
- giving clear and specific instructions, particularly in situations that they know carry risk
- not overreaching their qualifications or ability (they should ensure that they know what they are doing and, if they do not, seek answers from experts)

- removing injured participants when they are in danger of further injury or of injuring others
- considering whether action should be taken against aggressive or dangerous participants
- maintaining their objectivity and not allowing others, be they officials, coaches, parents or athletes, to pressure them into wrong decisions
- if a preventable injury occurs, considering how it happened and what can be done to ensure that it does not happen again
- ensuring they have the medical history of the athletes, particularly children, they are coaching
- ensuring that they are fully aware of their sport's doping policy, particularly which substances are banned, and
- ensuring that they have appropriate professional indemnity insurance.

Exclusions and waivers

Contracts, tickets and signs often use words that attempt to protect against liability for injury to athletes or people coming onto premises, or undertaking a particular activity. Coaches often ask their pupils to sign such documents.

These clauses are always examined very carefully by courts in legal cases, and they may or may not be effective. To have any chance of successfully protecting someone such as a coach from legal action, these clauses must be very specific and must be carefully drafted. There are some situations in which it is impossible to exclude liability because the Trade Practices Act prohibits this being done. Coaches should think about using such a device to protect themselves, but they should obtain legal advice about the form of words.

In some situations it is possible to reduce risk by using signs on sporting premises to warn of particular danger. Although, from a legal point of view, this does indicate that the risk was known, in many situations it is well worth pointing out the risk, because it may be easily avoided. Warning signs about slippery floors around a swimming pool, the depth of a particular pool area or an instruction that running on a pool deck is prohibited are examples of these warning signs. If risks are identified, however, coaches must ensure that any instructions are enforced. A notice will not protect the coach or reduce risk if the coach or supervisors ignore the instructions. A coach, official or venue operator who ignores clearly identified risks could be in a worse position should an injury occur.

Managing the risks with exclusions and waivers

■ An appropriate exclusion clause can protect a coach from liability for injury.

■ Coaches should use only clear and appropriate warnings, disclaimers and exclusion clauses, otherwise they may actually increase the risks.

■ They should enforce any specified safety rules.

■ They should also have the rules checked by their legal advisers.

An athlete dived into shallow water at a pool, hit the bottom, and was badly injured. The pool became shallower very suddenly and deceptively and others had also been hurt in that way. The court found that, in the circumstances, a warning sign would have prevented the injury, and the failure to erect one was a breach of the duty of care owed to athletes by the pool operator. A coach who does not erect warning signs on his or her premises or give appropriate warnings to participants may also be liable for any injury that results.

A coach, Francis, was found to be negligent in a legal case resulting from Jennifer's injury in a riding accident. Francis's athlete enrolment form, and his riding club's membership form, both of which Jennifer had completed, contained clauses excluding liability for any negligence on the part of the club and its employees. The court upheld the exclusion clause and the coach was not liable to compensate Jennifer.

Dealing with children

The law recognises what we all know — that children are not able to make appropriate decisions because of their lack of experience and objectivity. The courts have actually stated that people cannot expect children to look after their own interests properly, and that people who are in charge of them must act in the children's best interests. This means that anyone coaching children must take more than the usual care to protect them.

The nature of care will vary considerably depending upon the sport. Young cricketers need supervision to ensure that they do not injure each other with the bat. In other sports, particular care must be taken to ensure that mouthguards are used. Young gymnasts often undertake complex routines that demand significant skill and concentration. Coaches of other young children may, however, be more concerned about them running onto the road during training. In each situation the coach must assess the real risks.

(National Sports Information Centre)

Coaches should take particular care when working with children.

Managing the risk when dealing with children

- Take particular care where children are concerned and expect the unexpected.

Milan, a track and field coach, let some young boys under his care play with a javelin unsupervised. One of the boys threw the javelin, intending only to frighten another, but hitting him in the leg. The boy was temporarily hospitalised, but recovered fully. Milan owed a duty of care to the boys, but he hadn't given any instructions as to the proper use of the equipment, nor had he ensured that it was used correctly, so breaching his duty of care. He also knew that it was likely that a high-spirited group of boys would misuse the javelin. Milan realised that, in future, he would have to take his responsibilities more seriously, or risk injury to young athletes and litigation against himself.

Where sports involve dangerous equipment, coaches must instruct children on its use and supervise them closely at all times. They must expect the unexpected at all times.

Discrimination

Sometimes discrimination is illegal. Most states in Australia have laws that prohibit discrimination on various grounds, such as skin colour, sex, social origin, age, medical record, disability, nationality and sexual preference in *some* areas of public activity, as does the Commonwealth. Authorities have the power to investigate, and to make orders against those guilty of inappropriate behaviour, including awards of damages to an injured person. Laws prevent discrimination occurring in some situations, but of course it should never happen at all.

After watching an interschool soccer competition, David decided that he would like to try out for the team, so he spoke to Leon, the coach. Leon had noticed that David walked with a bit of a limp, that he slurred his speech and that one of his hands was bent and appeared tight. Leon explained that soccer probably would not suit David, as it is quite a physical game and he may get hurt.

David was a little disappointed with Leon's reaction, but calmly explained that he had an acquired brain injury as a result of a car accident, which just made his muscles a little weak on one side of his body. He explained that he had no greater chance of being hurt than any other player, and that Leon was discriminating against him as a result of his disability. David asked Leon to watch him play to see if he was good enough to fit into the team. Leon, a little embarrassed, apologised to David and asked him to come along to the next training session so that he could see him play. Coaches must be watchful to prevent such discriminatory incidents occurring in their sport.

Managing the risk of discrimination

Coaches should ensure that they follow all the principles covered by the Coach's Code of Ethics (see the appendix). This will help them avoid discriminating against others and help them to prevent members of their sport or organisation acting in a discriminatory way to others.

Harassment

Harassment on specified grounds is unlawful under Australian anti-discrimination laws, but it is increasingly a real concern in sport. Coaches often have enormous influence over athletes, and if this is used recklessly or irresponsibly it can cause great harm. It is therefore essential that coaches operate at all times with professionalism and integrity.

Harassment is *unwelcome* offensive, abusive, belittling or threatening behaviour directed at a person or people, usually because they are different from the harasser. The difference may be in sex, race, disability, sexual orientation, age, power (relative to the harasser), or some other characteristic. **Sexual harassment** is *unwelcome* behaviour that has a sexual element.

Harassment upsets people. It makes participation in sport unpleasant, humiliating or intimidating for the person or group targeted by this behaviour. It should not be confused with legitimate comment and advice, including relevant negative comment or feedback from coaches on athletic performance, or on

(National Sports Information Centre)

Harassment is unacceptable within sport.

the work or sport-related behaviour of an employee or an athlete. Feedback differs from harassment in that it is intended to help the athlete improve his or her performance or behaviour.

Managing the risk of harassment

Coaches should:

- only touch athletes when absolutely necessary and understand that interpretations of touching will be influenced by cultural differences and religious implications, and by other individual circumstances

- take necessary steps to make the facilities safe and appropriate (including reporting poor lighting, graffiti, litter or broken windows, and removing any offensive pictures)

- understand what constitutes a reportable sexual harassment or sexual assault offence and familiarise themselves with their sport or club's procedures for dealing with such offences or alleged offences

- avoid unaccompanied and unobserved activities with athletes, including being alone in a room or vehicle with an athlete

- make it clear that they will not tolerate any discrimination, prejudice or harassment in their sport, and

- avoid focusing on an athlete's disability unless this is the only way to find out what adjustments the athlete requires.

Refer to the appendix, the Coach's Code of Ethics, for more advice on how coaches can avoid discrimination and harassment in sport.

Contract negotiation

A **contract** is a legally enforceable agreement between parties. A contract consists of an offer, an acceptance, and an intention that the agreement should be enforceable at law. There must be 'consideration' (the payment or value of the bargain), which moves between the parties.

The parties must be able to enter into the agreement: children and certain other people who may have trouble forming an intention to contract are treated differently by the law, and special rules apply to contracts with people under 18 years old. Unincorporated bodies also have difficulty contracting.

Contracts such as player agreements (including employment contracts), sponsorship contracts, and the rules of an association are

routinely considered by the courts. The courts may decide that employment contracts are unfair under legislation in some states. The bottom line is, however, that coaches and athletes should never sign a contract the requirements of which they are unable or unwilling to perform, or do not understand.

Managing the risks with contracts

The main issues coaches should think about when entering into a contract are:

- Do they understand their commitment and is it realistic?

- Are they able to do what they say they will do?

- Can they pay for any commitment?

- Are they giving something which is theirs to give (have they already given it away, for instance, to another sponsor)?

- Does the agreement contain evidence of the main contractual obligations of the other party, particularly those important to the coach involved?

- Are the important contractual terms clearly spelt out?

- Does the other party understand what the coach involved wants?

- Have all formalities been complied with?

Coaches should seek legal advice before terminating a contract or, in areas where there is some uncertainty about the application of a contract, before acting in a way that disadvantages the other party to the agreement.

Selection issues

Organisations should have well-documented selection policies and should ensure that these are observed when selecting representative teams. The series of appeals that occurred after the selection of teams for the Olympics demonstrated the importance of this.

It is almost impossible for a sporting organisation to detail all selection possibilities, so policies should give selectors documented discretion. To avoid difficulties later, and in the interests of fairness to athletes, selection policies should always be implemented in good faith. If organisations wish to keep selection disputes out of court, they should have athletes agree that some other sports-related forum will be the only one used to resolve selection disputes.

Natural justice

Natural justice or procedural fairness means that proceedings against a person must be dealt with fairly. The ways in which disciplinary proceedings will be run are generally set out in the rules or constitutions of sporting bodies. These must be drafted carefully to ensure that members and others are able to understand their obligations.

Tribunals are set up by organisations to interpret rules and to discipline those within the sport who are in breach of the constitution, of playing rules, or of codes of conduct. These tribunals interpret rules and are run in a similar fashion to courts. Where the rights of individuals are affected in a material way by the decision of a domestic tribunal, the courts will sometimes intervene to protect those rights.

Disciplinary proceedings

Disciplinary proceedings may exclude people from a sport, or involve a fine. In some circumstances they may deprive the person concerned of their capacity to earn a living.

Disciplinary proceedings must be conducted in accordance with the principles of natural justice but the approach that is taken will differ according to the circumstances — an organisation need not run its proceedings as formally as a court of law.

Natural justice gives those accused of breaking the rules the following basic rights:

- They should know the nature of the accusation made and the circumstances in which the breach of the rules is said to have occurred.

- They must be given an opportunity to put their case.

- The tribunal considering the matter should act in good faith.

The hearing must be conducted in accordance with the rules of the organisation. The accused must have proper notification of the time and place of the hearing. Some representations must be heard from both sides and all evidence against the accused should be 'on the table'. Any other charges that may arise out of information given at a particular hearing should be left for consideration at another time, to give the accused opportunity to provide an explanation.

Whether lawyers are allowed to participate will depend upon the rules of the tribunal. When the accused is at risk of a large loss, further consideration should be given to the issue. If the rules are silent, it is often wise to allow legal representation, as this will prevent subsequent claims in court that the process was flawed because a lawyer should have been present.

If a coach is found guilty of a charge, he or she should have the opportunity to address the tribunal on the issue of appropriate penalty.

Contrary to popular belief, the area of natural justice is largely irrelevant to player or team selection, unless the organisation provides for a process of reviewing selections in its own rules. Complaints about selections are generally contract related or rely on misleading conduct or representations by officials, not natural justice.

Managing risks at hearings

At disciplinary hearings, it is essential that:

- the accused is informed of the accusation and its details

- the accused has a proper opportunity to put his or her case, and

- the tribunal acts in good faith in determining the issue.

A sporting body convened a hearing to decide a charge against a coach, Denise, although she had already said that she could not attend because she would be working at her paid employment. At the hearing, the tribunal fined her in her absence. She refused to pay the fine on legal advice and another meeting was held at which she was disqualified until she paid the fine. A court found she had not been given a proper chance to present her case, and ordered a re-hearing.

Restraint of trade

The law of restraint of trade aims to protect people's right to work. Contracts, rules or constitutions may contain clauses that aim to limit the right of employees or members to undertake a particular activity or participate for a competitor.

The law looks at the restriction imposed, whether it is reasonable in the interests of the parties to the transaction, and in the public interest. The courts have invalidated many examples of such restraints but have enforced some, even in a non-professional context, over the last few years. The courts generally look at whether an organisation is doing *more* than is necessary to protect itself.

Managing restraint of trade risks

- Coaches and athletes should consider whether the rules go further than is reasonably necessary to protect the organisation.

- Coaches should ensure that they are fully aware of the contents of all agreements and contracts that apply to them.

In a 1998 case, three rugby league players in an amateur rugby league competition claimed that the rules of the league were a restriction of competition under the Trade Practices Act. They wanted to move to another club, but the rules required players to play for one club only during the three-year term of registration. The players' claim failed because the judge regarded the nature of the rugby league competition as a sport played for its own sake, as distinct from a trade. This case is important for those involved in sport because it suggests that a player and perhaps a coach can be restrained from moving to another club even where there is no payment involved.

Insurance

Insurance is a form of contract under which the insurer agrees to indemnify or compensate the insured for a loss suffered. Most organisations have public liability and directors' and officers' insurance cover. Coaches should have a professional indemnity policy to cover them for the expert advice that they give to those they are coaching.

Professional indemnity policies are generally drafted as 'claims made' policies, which means that the coach has to be insured at the time the claim is made, rather than at the time the incident occurs. This is an important distinction for coaches. Sports organisations generally have public liability insurance policies, which they are required to have to maintain their incorporation if they are associations. Some sports have personal accident cover for their members.

Managing insurance risks

- Coaches should read all policies to ensure they are appropriate.

- Coaches should have a professional indemnity policy, either through their sport or on their own behalf.

- Coaches should also comply with the requirements of maintaining their accreditation.

ETHICAL BEHAVIOUR

These days, coaches have to deal with a range of ethical issues, including drugs in sport, abuse of power, harassment, sportsmanship, cheating, eating disorders, respect for officials and knowing when an athlete should return to sport after an injury. These types of issues have a serious impact on athletes.

Coaches often have enormous influence over athletes and their sense of self-esteem. If used recklessly, irresponsibly or illegally, this influence could cause great harm. An athlete's experience and enjoyment of sport and life can be enhanced or destroyed by the coach–athlete relationship.

There are extra ethical considerations for coaches to consider when they are coaching children. It is essential that they develop skills in the following areas: dealing with parents, discipline issues, giving equal opportunities to all children despite ability levels, encouraging sportsmanship and having fun rather than overemphasising serious competition.

Coaches must apply ethical principles to all aspects of their working life and in all aspects of sport. The Australian Sports Commission's (ASC) Coach's Code of Ethics is a set of principles voluntarily adopted by the ASC and coaches accredited under the National Coaching Accreditation Scheme (NCAS) (see the appendix for the ASC's Coach's Code of Ethics). The code is a series of rules that describe the features the community would like to see in the ideal coach.

Observing the code is a form of risk management for coaches. Treating athletes and others in sport well will clearly bring its own rewards, but treating them badly creates all sorts of problems. At their most extreme these problems manifest themselves in damage to coaches' and athletes' health, performances and professional reputations.

Rule 1, 'Respect the rights, dignity and worth of every human being', for example, helps coaches to avoid acts of discrimination of any kind. Discrimination on the basis of sex, disability, ethnic origin, religion and other characteristics is against both state and federal laws.

Rules 9 and 10 relate to harassment and verbal abuse. New South Wales has recently enacted child protection legislation that requires the screening of people to be employed, or volunteering, to work with children. People who have been convicted of a serious sex offence must not be employed or permitted to volunteer in such situations. It is expected that legislation of this kind will become more widespread in Australia.

The most extreme forms of verbal abuse may constitute an assault at law and these provisions help coaches avoid both the immediate and the legal consequences of assault, which may be both a civil and criminal issue. Sexual harassment is also prohibited by law, and rules 8 and 10 discuss what is appropriate behaviour between coaches and athletes and what coaches' ethical responsibilities are in this area.

The ASC believes that all sporting organisations should have a code of conduct for their coaches and should ask coaches to reinforce their commitment to ethical behaviour by signing this code. They may base their code on the one used by the ASC and the NCAS or create one of their own. A process for dealing with those who fail to comply with such a code should be clearly defined and should be included in the rules of the organisation. Coaches should make themselves familiar with this procedure.

RISK MANAGEMENT PLANNING

Risk management is about identifying risk, eliminating or reducing it where possible, and insuring against the risks that cannot be eliminated. The risks in sport vary greatly depending upon the requirements of the particular discipline, the level at which the sport is being undertaken, the age of the participants and the degree of sophistication of the venue and equipment being used. By reviewing the way in which they work in light of the perceived risks, coaches can eliminate many risks before they occur.

In developing a plan, coaches should assemble risks in order from greatest risk to least risk, and address them in that order. They should set achievable goals for risk reduction (see the workbook that accompanies this manual for ideas about setting out a risk management plan). Many risks can be reduced by taking more care, giving better instructions or changing the focus of an activity or the way business is done.

Coaches should focus on those areas where participants are routinely injured, where people most often complain of unfairness or mistreatment, and those that generate most correspondence, particularly legal

(National Sports Information Centre)

Coaches should develop a plan to manage the risks in their sport

correspondence. They should systematically consider how they might amend their practices in these areas to minimise future difficulty.

Developing a risk management plan doesn't have to be an onerous task. By following the steps below, coaches can develop a simple and practical risk management plan for their coaching situation:

1. identify risks (consider risks related to environment, equipment and people)

2. develop strategies to minimise the risks identified

3. prepare a timeline for implementing the strategies

4. include a review process (an evaluation) in your plan, and

5. list those responsible for implementing each part of the plan.

Planning to manage risks

When developing an individual risk management plan, coaches should consider the following questions:

- What is the greatest risk to participants in their sport?

- If the facilities were the cause of the risk, how can they be made safer?

- Do they periodically review facilities, equipment, procedures, policies and techniques to ensure that both they and the athletes are operating in a completely safe environment?

- Are they aware of harassment or discrimination incidents in their sport and are they aware of what they must do to prevent or to deal with such a situation?

- If technique or coaching methods were causes of injury, how can they modify their behaviour or the athlete's behaviour to decrease the likelihood of future injury?

- If the cause of an injury or other problem is unknown, is there anything coaches can do to find out how it happened (they may contact their sport for help)?

- Can they set guidelines or formulate instructions for their athletes that will minimise further risks from a particular cause?

CONCLUSION

Coaches should remember that their relationship with those they coach is paramount, and that all the risk minimisation steps suggested here are intended to ensure the continuation of a fruitful and harmonious relationship. Coaches become involved in their industry to improve the results and performance of athletes. If they develop and implement good systems for managing risk, they will be free to spend more time on developing athletes, rather than dealing with injuries or legal disputation.

COACHING TIPS

- Make the first priority the care and safety of the athletes.

- Take all possible steps to reduce or manage the risks of the sport.

- Pay particular attention to the chances of risk or injury for younger or less experienced athletes.

- Always have professional indemnity insurance.

- Create a 'culture of care' in risk management planning and practices.

FURTHER READING

Australian Sports Commission (1998) *Harassment-free Sport: Guidelines for Coaches* (part of the Harassment-free Sport series). Canberra: Australian Sports Commission.

Australian Sports Commission (1998) *Harassment-free Sport: Guidelines for Sport and Recreation Organisations* (part of the Harassment-free Sport series). Canberra: Australian Sports Commission.

Healey, D (1995) Disclaimers, exclusion clauses, waivers and liability release forms in sport. In: M Fewell (ed), *Sports Law: A Practical Guide*. Sydney: LBC Information Services.

Healey, D (1996) *Sport and the Law*. Sydney: New South Wales University Press.

Martens, R (1997) *Successful Coaching*. Champaign, IL: Human Kinetics.

The ANZSLA Commentator (the quarterly journal of the Australia and New Zealand Sports Law Association) contains many useful and relevant articles on this subject.

THE ATHLETE

CHAPTER 5
FUNCTIONAL ANATOMY

Julie R Steele and Deirdre E McGhee

(National Sports Information Centre)

INTRODUCTION

Human anatomy describes the shape and structure of systems that make up the human body. Studying anatomy can seem as difficult as learning a new language, because there are many new words with which coaches must become familiar. So why bother? Developing basic anatomy knowledge is essential for all coaches because:

- to analyse and understand how the body moves efficiently, coaches must know the structures that make up the body and how these structures interact
- it helps them to better understand how sporting injuries occur, and
- by being familiar with anatomy terms, coaches can keep up to date with relevant reading, as well as being able to communicate with personnel involved in treating and rehabilitating injured athletes.

Once you become familiar with the jargon, you will notice that the words are merely descriptive terms that are really quite logical.

GENERAL ANATOMY TERMS

To describe motion, a reference position called the **anatomical position** is sometimes used, in which a person is standing upright, arms by his/her sides, and palms facing forwards. From this position, the relative location of all body parts is described using the terms listed below, most of which are organised in pairs of opposites, just like the North and South poles.

Some directional terms used in anatomy

Terms	Direction relative to the anatomical position
anterior — posterior	forward — backward
superior — inferior	upward — downward
medial — lateral	near the midline of the body — away from the midline of the body
distal — proximal	further from the trunk than another body part — closer to the trunk than another body part
superficial — deep	towards or closer to the surface of the body — away from the surface of the body
plantar — dorsal	on the sole of the foot — on the top surface of the foot
palmar — dorsal	on the palm of the hand — on the back of the hand

THE SKELETAL FRAMEWORK OF THE BODY

Bone

The 206 bones of the skeleton support the body's soft tissues, while protecting delicate structures such as the brain and heart. Bones are made of living tissues that alter their size, shape and composition in response to hormonal changes, injury, disease, and the loads they carry during exercise. They are designed to resist **tensile** forces (forces pulling outward) and **compressive** forces (inward pushing forces, usually caused by bearing weight). Differences in their make-up mean that younger bones are more pliable than older, more brittle bones.

Committed to his sport, but failing to understand what his coach had told him about the dangers of overtraining, Riley continually overloaded his leg in training. As a result, his bone tissue broke down quicker than it could be replaced and, being weaker, it was less tolerant to further loading. At first Riley had no symptoms of the pending injury. However, as he continued to overload the bone, pain and swelling developed at the injury site and his coach noticed and asked him about it. This overuse injury is called a **stress reaction** and can cause the bone to break, a **stress fracture**. Coaches should watch for the symptoms in athletes who are training hard. If it occurs, the athlete's physician and coach should ensure that the athlete rests the bone, removing any stress until a balance between bone growth and breakdown is achieved. At his coach's request, Riley rested his leg completely, and his injury recovered well.

Bones in younger athletes grow by replacing cartilage along growth plates, known as **epiphyseal plates**. Bone growth is usually complete by the late teenage years, when people normally reach their full height. Bone develops partially in response to the forces imposed on it. When intermittent, non-traumatic stress is applied to growing bones, such as the stress experienced during everyday activities like brisk walking, bone cell growth is stimulated. Regular exercise is therefore very important to the health of both young and old bones.

However, growing bones, particularly delicate epiphyseal plates, are vulnerable to injury if overloaded. If the epiphyseal plate is damaged, bone growth may be affected, possibly causing permanent damage to that bone and its associated joints. Trauma to a growth plate in a child or adolescent is therefore a serious injury and requires specialised care. Some growth plates become injured for no known reason, such as in Perthes disease, which can restrict leg length and hip joint development, most often in boys of eight to ten years.

The outer surface of a bone is called the **periosteum.** Tendons and ligaments attach to bone by penetrating this periosteum. It has a rich nerve supply and can cause considerable pain when bruised. Anyone who has ever struck their shin against a hard surface will have experienced this pain!

Bones also have a rich blood supply and so when they are broken they bleed profusely. There are two main categories of broken bones. If a bone is cracked, but maintains its normal alignment, it is called an **undisplaced fracture**. This fracture type can heal well and will not affect the associated joints. However, if the crack disrupts the normal bony alignment, so that the two pieces are at an angle to one another, this is referred to as a **displaced fracture.** Such a fracture may require surgery by a doctor to put the two ends of the bone back together. It may not always be possible to regain the correct bony alignment and the joints associated with this bone may be permanently affected.

Remember that when the body has absorbed enough force to break a bone, other tissues are usually damaged, such as muscle, tendon, ligament and skin. Fractured bones are normally placed in fibreglass or plaster of paris casts to immobilise them while they heal. All these patients need muscle and

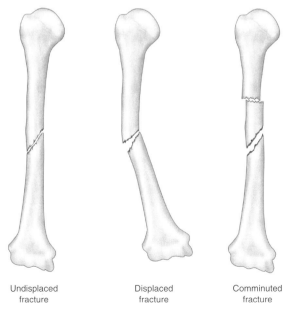

Undisplaced fracture   Displaced fracture   Comminuted fracture

The main types of bone fractures

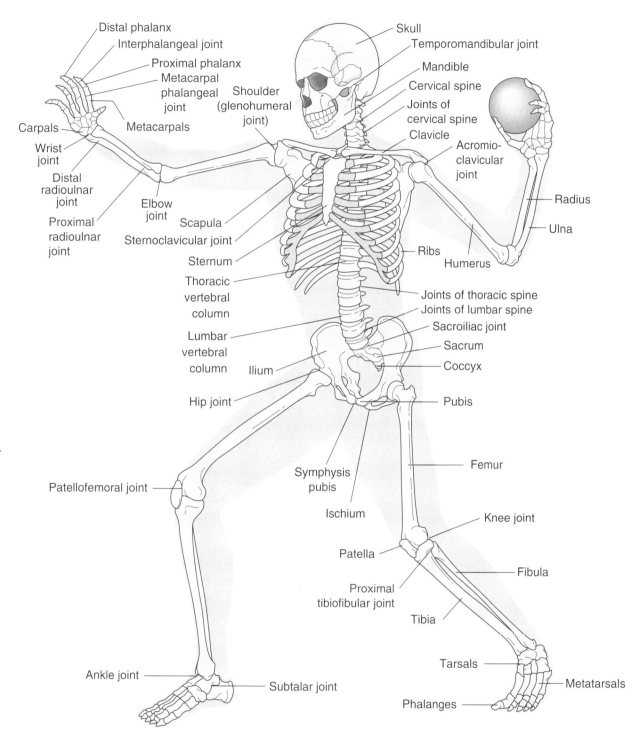

Distal phalanx
Interphalangeal joint
Proximal phalanx
Metacarpal phalangeal joint
Shoulder (glenohumeral joint)
Metacarpals
Carpals
Wrist joint
Distal radioulnar joint
Proximal radioulnar joint
Elbow joint
Scapula
Sternoclavicular joint
Sternum
Thoracic vertebral column
Lumbar vertebral column
Ilium
Hip joint

Skull
Temporomandibular joint
Mandible
Cervical spine
Joints of cervical spine
Clavicle
Acromio-clavicular joint
Radius
Ulna
Ribs
Humerus
Joints of thoracic spine
Joints of lumbar spine
Sacroiliac joint
Sacrum
Coccyx
Pubis
Femur

Patellofemoral joint

Symphysis pubis
Ischium
Patella
Proximal tibiofibular joint

Knee joint
Fibula
Tibia

Ankle joint
Subtalar joint

Tarsals
Metatarsals
Phalanges

The main bones and joints of the human body

movement rehabilitation after the cast is removed, as their muscles typically weaken and shrink when not used. Coaches can play an active role during rehabilitation by encouraging athletes to stick to their rehabilitation programs so that they quickly regain normal function.

Joints

Joints are located where two or more bones meet. They are designed to give varying degrees of mobility and stability, depending upon their structure. As a general rule, the more mobile a joint, the less stable it is. Apart from providing stability, less mobile joints also absorb shock by allowing a small degree of give when forces are applied to the bones.

There are three main types of joints: fibrous, cartilaginous and synovial joints. **Fibrous joints**, such as the joints between bones of the skull, are designed for stability and essentially allow no mobility. **Cartilaginous joints** mainly provide stability with limited mobility. Discs of the vertebral column and symphysis pubis (the anterior joint between the two pelvic bones) are examples of cartilaginous joints. **Synovial joints** (those that contain fluid to lubricate the joint), such as at the shoulder, hip and knee, are designed predominantly for mobility and so are the focus of this chapter.

Coaches must ensure that all players are physically prepared for the demands of their sport, particularly those returning from a long lay-off, or injuries could result. At 35, Mathew decided to return to basketball. He had previously played the game, but retired at 25 after failing to regain condition following anterior cruciate ligament (knee) surgery. Despite being 10 kg heavier and relatively out of condition, Mathew joined the local over-35 basketball team.

Though it was only a local competition, the team coach, Ben, realised that physical preparation was as important as the social aspects of the game, especially given the previous inactivity of players such as Mathew. Ben planned the training program for the team with this in mind. Ben was aware of Mathew's previous knee injury and made sure that the training program included some specific strengthening exercises for him.

Although varying in size, shape and mobility, all synovial joints have similar characteristics. For example, **hyaline** or **articular** cartilage, a very smooth and slippery tissue, covers the surfaces of the bones within these joints. This cartilage protects the bone surface

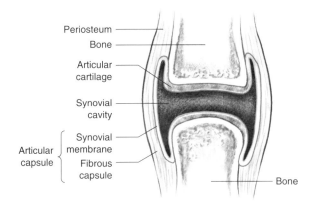

A typical synovial joint

from wear by minimising friction between the bones, and providing shock absorption by bearing and distributing loads. The bones are surrounded by a joint capsule which is lined with a **synovial membrane** that makes a very slippery fluid, known as **synovial fluid**. This synovial fluid helps to lubricate and nourish structures inside the joint.

Injury to structures inside the joint can cause the synovial membrane to become inflamed and, in response, produce excessive amounts of synovial fluid. This excess of fluid, called a **joint effusion**, will make the joint swollen and feel stiff. It is the body's way of forcing the athlete to rest the injured joint to allow healing. When structures within the joint are injured such that they bleed (called a **haemoarthrosis**), swelling will occur within minutes following injury, but an effusion may take more than 30 minutes to form.

Stable joints need a strong bony arrangement, where the bones fit together snugly. The hip, for example, is an extremely stable joint as the head of the **femur** (thigh bone) fits snugly into a deep socket within the **pelvis**. The shoulder, on the other hand, is less stable, as the head of the **humerus** (arm bone) only partially fits into the shallow hollow of the **scapula** (shoulder blade). All joints depend on other structures around them, including ligaments, discs, bursae and muscles, to help provide mobility or stability.

Ligaments

Ligaments are strong, stiff, relatively inelastic structures that connect bone to bone. They are designed to limit a joint's movement in specific directions and so assist its stability. As ligaments are relatively inelastic, there is a limit to how far they can be stretched and still return to their original length. If a ligament is repeatedly overstretched by poor technique or by trauma, it may permanently lengthen and, in turn, make the joint less stable. In such cases it is important to regain joint stability to prevent further joint damage. Depending on the degree of ligament lengthening, coaches and athletes may compensate for the joint instability by retraining muscles, taping, bracing or, in severe cases, by surgery.

George sprained his ankle playing rugby league at the beginning of the season. The swelling and bruising lasted for about two weeks. George was advised by his physiotherapist to delay his return to play until the swelling had gone. He was also encouraged by his coach to keep up the regular ankle rehabilitation exercises suggested by the physiotherapist, and to tape his ankle when he returned to play.

However, like most players, George was very eager to return to the game and started playing and training only one week after his injury. He taped his ankle for the first session and did a few exercises, but then these lost priority. During that season George sprained the same ankle another four times. After the fourth ankle sprain his coach insisted that he return to the physiotherapist, who revealed that George's ligament was now permanently lengthened, giving him an unstable ankle. George's coach now ensures that George wears his ankle guard during all training sessions and games, and that he adheres to his ankle exercise program. George still has to be very careful or he will resprain his ankle.

Articular discs

Articular discs are fibrocartilage tissue pads found within some joints. These pads improve the fit of the joining bones, enhancing the joint's stability and its ability to tolerate impact. Pads that only partially subdivide the joint cavity are called **menisci** (such as those in the knee), whereas pads that completely divide the joint into two separate cavities are called **discs** (such as those between the bones in the spinal column).

Both menisci and discs generally have a poor blood supply and therefore do not heal well. Menisci in the knee are commonly injured because of the high loads placed on the knees during sport. Injuries to the menisci are one of the causes of joint effusions. Although some meniscal tears can be repaired, most tears are treated by surgically removing the torn piece of cartilage. As this cartilage will not grow back, the injured joint will not be as stable or able to tolerate impact in the future.

Bursae

Bursae are small synovial fluid sacs found at high friction sites. They prevent two adjacent body tissues, such as tendon, bone, ligament or skin, from rubbing together, allowing free gliding of the tissues during motion. Without bursae, a tendon passing over a joint could wear and tear like a rope rubbing against a rock.

Bursae are normally so thin that they are just a fluid film between adjacent tissues. However, if they become irritated by factors such as a direct blow or repeated excessive loading, they can become inflamed and dramatically increase in size. For example, the bursa between the skin and the bony prominence of the elbow can swell to the size of an egg when inflamed. Inflammation of the bursa, called **bursitis**, can cause local pain, tenderness and swelling, restricting joint motion. Swelling of the bursa can also cause fluid to leak into the joint cavity, resulting in a joint effusion.

MUSCLES

There are three different types of muscle in the body:

- smooth muscle, which is found in the walls of internal body organs
- cardiac muscle, which is found in the heart, and
- skeletal muscle, which attaches to bones and can be voluntarily contracted to move body parts.

Without skeletal muscles, all actions, including movements as simple as standing and walking, would not be possible, so this chapter focuses on these muscles.

Muscle and tendon structure

The building blocks of skeletal muscle are long, cylindrical **muscle cells**, also called **muscle fibres**. The belly of a skeletal muscle is composed of various bundles of muscle fibres that produce force. These bundles are bound together by tough connective tissue, which is able to return to its original length, even after having been stretched by as much as 40%.

Either overstretching or overcontracting a muscle can tear its fibres, causing a **muscle strain**. When they are torn, muscles bleed a lot as they contain many blood vessels. Blood and swelling can develop scar tissue, forming lumps within the muscle. The rich blood supply ensures that muscles heal well. However, it is important to ensure that normal muscle fibre length is restored after a muscle strain. If scar tissue remains, the muscle tissue will be less pliable, weaker and prone to reinjury.

A blow to the muscle can also cause muscle fibres to bleed. This bruising of the muscle is called a **muscle contusion** or **haematoma**. Again, during treatment it is important to ensure that no scar tissue remains and that muscle length and strength are restored. If training is begun too early or the haematoma is not treated correctly, the scar can calcify, producing **myocytis ossificans**. Surgery can sometimes be necessary to remove such calcified lumps, and muscle strength and extensibility may be permanently damaged.

The connective tissue layers of a muscle may extend past the muscle belly, in cord-like structures, to form **tendons**, which attach muscles to the periosteum of bones. Tendons are designed to withstand tensile forces that pull outwardly on them with each muscle contraction. A **tendon sheath**, containing synovial fluid, surrounds tendons in areas of high friction. The Achilles tendon, which extends from the calf muscles to the heel, is one example. It has a sheath that minimises friction as the tendon slides along the surface of bones or other muscles during repetitive movements. Excessive friction from overuse or poor technique, where the tendon pulls at an abnormal angle, can cause the tendon and its sheath to become inflamed. This is called **tendonitis** and **paratendonitis**, respectively. It is important to treat both the inflammation and the biomechanical cause of the tendonitis.

Muscles are involved in many aspects of sporting performance. Whether coaches are primarily concerned with developing muscular speed, strength, flexibility or skill, they should consider the structure and function of muscles. For example, Tina, who coaches women's gymnastics, spends a great deal of time developing athletes' muscular flexibility. She has to be aware of factors such as where muscles connect, which muscles cross joints and the role of connective tissues. Armed with this information, Tina is able to develop stretching routines that are safe, develop flexibility appropriately and are specific to her sport.

Muscle actions and roles

Most muscles are attached to at least two bones and can span either:

- one joint, such as the **vastus medialis** (anterior thigh) crossing the knee
- two joints, such as the **hamstrings** (posterior thigh) crossing the hip and knee, or
- several joints, such as the **erector spinae** muscle group, which extends along the length of the spine.

To prescribe and analyse exercises appropriate for strength, flexibility or skill development, coaches should know what actions muscles produce and where they are attached, remembering that muscles crossing more than one joint can influence motion across all of these joints simultaneously. Standard terminology is used to describe movement of body segments, to prevent ambiguity. Further detailed information describing the main attachment sites of these muscles is provided in most anatomy textbooks (see Further reading).

Muscles can only pull, not push, a bone. When a muscle contracts and shortens it pulls on both of the bones to which it is attached, moving one or both of the bones towards the other. However, movement is not produced by a single muscle, but rather by a group of muscles working together, and for this reason muscles are found in functional groups opposing each other. A coordinated group of muscles creating a movement is called a **muscle synergy**. Muscles acting in synergy have different roles in producing the movement.

The main muscle that produces the movement is the **prime mover** or **agonist**, and the muscles that assist it, if more force is required, are the **synergists**. For example, the prime mover for elbow flexion is usually **brachialis**, assisted if necessary by **biceps brachii**. Although helping the prime movers, synergists often produce other unwanted actions, requiring other muscles (**neutralisers**) to cancel out these undesirable movements. Using the same example of elbow flexion, biceps brachii is a synergist to brachialis. However, biceps brachii produces elbow flexion and **supination** (turning the palm of the hand upward). **Pronator teres** can neutralise the supination, so that only the desired elbow flexion is produced.

For a movement to occur without resistance, the muscle opposite in action to the

Movement Terminology

Terms	Definition
Flexion	Decreasing the angle at a joint. Flexion of the foot at the ankle is called dorsiflexion
Extension	Increasing the angle at a joint or returning a body part to the anatomical position. Extension of the foot at the ankle is called plantar flexion
Hyperextension	Extension of a segment past the anatomical position.
Abduction	Movement away from the body's midline
Adduction	Movement towards the body's midline
Rotation	Movement about an axis, either medially (inward) or laterally (outward)
Eversion	Rotation of the foot to turn the sole outwards
Inversion	Rotation of the foot to turn the sole inwards
Circumduction	Moving a limb so that the end of the limb draws a circle
Supination	Moving the flexed forearm so that the palm of the hand is turned anterior or superior
Pronation	Moving the flexed forearm so that the palm of the hand is turned posterior or inferior
Elevation	Moving a body part upward
Depression	Moving a body part downwards

See also illustrations on pages 62-64

prime mover, the **antagonist**, must relax. As an elbow extensor, **triceps brachii** is an antagonist to brachialis. If the antagonist does not relax, but instead contracts, the muscles are said to be in **cocontraction**. Novice athletes often have difficulty coordinating an efficient muscle synergy, struggling to generate the desired amount of muscle force together with the correct type, sequence and timing of muscle contractions, and producing uncoordinated movements as a result.

Some movements, particularly those done at high speed, place distracting forces on joints that tend to pull the joints apart. Such movements require other muscles (**stabilisers**) to stabilise the threatened joint. In joints such as the shoulder, strengthening these stabilising muscles following injury is an important part of rehabilitation. Skilled athletes sometimes use cocontraction to stabilise a joint. In our example of elbow flexion, the brachioradialis would act as a stabiliser to the elbow joint. Conversely the elbow could be stabilised via cocontraction of the brachialis and triceps brachii.

NERVOUS SYSTEM

Movement of the body is controlled by the nervous system. This movement is under both conscious (when we make decisions about what to do) and unconscious control (when we don't have to think about doing it, such as standing upright). The nervous system can be divided into two parts:

- the **central nervous system (CNS)**, including the brain and spinal cord (this is the control centre which is responsible for interpreting information and making decisions about appropriate responses and movements), and
- the **peripheral nervous system**, including the nerves that connect the CNS to all the muscles, skin and glands of the body (this system acts as the communication wiring to bring information to the CNS and taking decisions from it to the rest of the body).

To produce a response, **sensory receptors** located throughout the body first detect information about what is occurring both inside

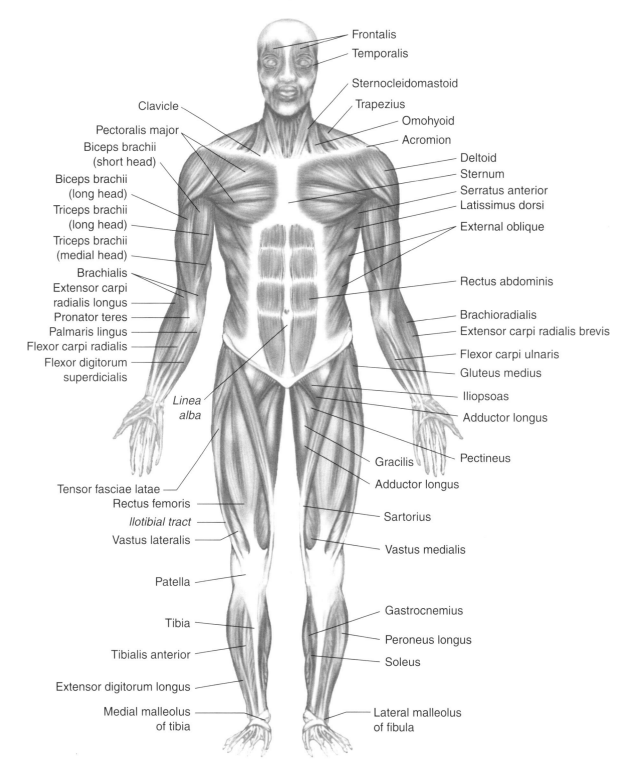

Frontalis
Temporalis
Sternocleidomastoid
Trapezius
Omohyoid
Acromion
Deltoid
Sternum
Serratus anterior
Latissimus dorsi
External oblique

Clavicle
Pectoralis major
Biceps brachii
(short head)
Biceps brachii
(long head)
Triceps brachii
(long head)
Triceps brachii
(medial head)
Brachialis
Extensor carpi
radialis longus
Pronator teres
Palmaris lingus
Flexor carpi radialis
Flexor digitorum
superdicialis

Rectus abdominis

Brachioradialis
Extensor carpi radialis brevis
Flexor carpi ulnaris
Gluteus medius
Iliopsoas
Adductor longus

*Linea
alba*

Gracilis
Pectineus
Adductor longus

Tensor fasciae latae
Rectus femoris
Ilotibial tract
Vastus lateralis

Sartorius

Vastus medialis

Patella

Gastrocnemius

Tibia

Peroneus longus

Tibialis anterior

Soleus

Extensor digitorum longus
Medial malleolus
of tibia

Lateral malleolus
of fibula

The major muscle groups in the human body

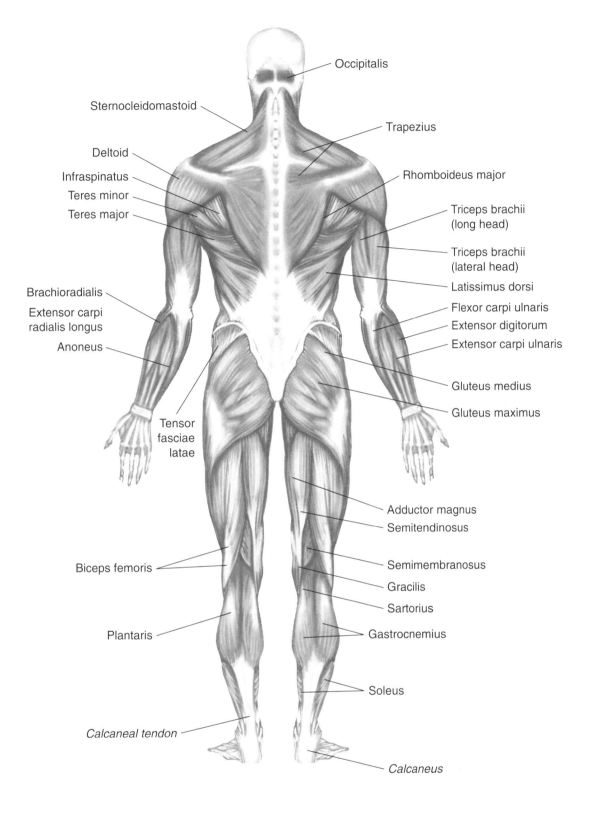

Occipitalis

Sternocleidomastoid

Trapezius

Deltoid

Rhomboideus major

Infraspinatus

Teres minor

Teres major

Triceps brachii
(long head)

Triceps brachii
(lateral head)

Latissimus dorsi

Brachioradialis

Flexor carpi ulnaris

Extensor carpi
radialis longus

Extensor digitorum

Extensor carpi ulnaris

Anoneus

Gluteus medius

Gluteus maximus

Tensor
fasciae
latae

Adductor magnus

Semitendinosus

Semimembranosus

Gracilis

Biceps femoris

Sartorius

Gastrocnemius

Plantaris

Soleus

Calcaneal tendon

Calcaneus

The main muscles involved in gross motor activities

Muscle	Main action
Abdominal muscles	
External oblique	Flex spine and/or compress abdomen, involved in activities such as abdominal curl exercises
Internal oblique	
Rectus abdominis	
Transversus abdominis	
Movers of the shoulder girdle	
Serratus anterior	Upwardly rotates and abducts scapula
Trapezius	Extends and laterally flexes head, rotates and adducts scapula
Rhomboids	Adduct and rotate scapula downward slightly
Pectoralis minor	Abducts scapula
Levator scapulae	Elevates and downwardly rotates scapula
Arm movers	
Pectoralis major	Flexes, adducts and medially rotates arm at shoulder
Deltoid	Extends, flexes and abducts arm at shoulder
Latissimus dorsi	Adducts, extends and medially rotates the arm
Teres major	Extends, adducts and internally rotates humerus
Rotator cuff group: subscapularis supraspinatus infraspinatus teres minor	As a group, the four muscles strengthen and stabilise the shoulder joint and act as chief arm rotators.
Forearm movers	
Biceps brachii	Flexes arm at shoulder, flexes forearm at elbow and supinates hand
Brachialis	Flexes forearm at elbow
Brachioradialis	Flexes forearm at elbow
Triceps brachii	Extends forearm at elbow, extends arm at shoulder
Supinator	Supinates forearm and hand
Pronator teres	Pronates forearm and hand
Movers of the hand	
Common wrist extensor	Extend and either adduct or abduct hand at wrist (extensor carpi) muscles
Common wrist flexor	Flex and either abduct or adduct hand at wrist (flexor carpi) muscles
Flexor digitorum muscles	Flex phalanges of each finger and flex hand at wrist
Extensor digitorum muscles	Extends phalanges of each finger

Movers of the vertebral column

Quadratus lumborum	Flexes vertebral column sideways
Erector spinae group	Extends various sections of the spine

Thigh movers

Gluteal (buttock) muscles: gluteus maximus gluteus medius gluteus minimus	 Extend and laterally rotate thigh at hip Both muscles abduct and internally rotate thigh at hip; active during walking to stabilise the pelvis
Iliopsoas	Flexes thigh at hip, flexes lumbar spine
Tensor fasciae latae	Flexes and abducts thigh at hip
Adductor muscles	Adduct, flex and rotate thigh at hip
Lateral rotators	Laterally rotate thigh at hip

Leg movers

Quadriceps femoris: rectus femoris vastus lateralis, vastus medialis and vastus intermedius	 Extend leg at knee and flex thigh at hip Extend leg at knee, control tracking of patella
Hamstrings: biceps femoris semitendinosus and semimembranosus	 Flex and laterally rotate leg at knee, extend thigh at hip Flex and medially rotate leg at knee, extend thigh at hip
Popliteus	Medially rotates leg on thigh

Movers of the foot

Gastrocnemius	Plantar flexes foot, flexes leg at knee
Soleus	Plantar flexes foot
Peroneus longus and peroneus brevis	Plantar flex and evert foot
Tibialis anterior	Dorsiflexes and inverts foot
Tibialis posterior	Plantar flexes and inverts foot
Extensor hallicus and digitorum longus	Extends toes and dorsiflexes foot
Flexor hallicus and digitorum longus	Flexes toes and plantar flexes foot

Use this table to work out specific muscle stretches for training. The muscle action gives you the movement produced when the muscle shortens as it contracts. The opposite movement will stretch the muscle. For example, the main action of the hamstring muscles is hip extension and knee flexion. To stretch the hamstrings, simply use the opposite movements — hip flexion and knee extension. Coaches can also use this table when developing strengthening exercises to ensure that they are using the correct action to train a muscle.

Those not shown in the illustrations on pages 58 and 59 of muscle groups are deep muscles, lying under those depicted in the illustrations.

The terminology of body movements

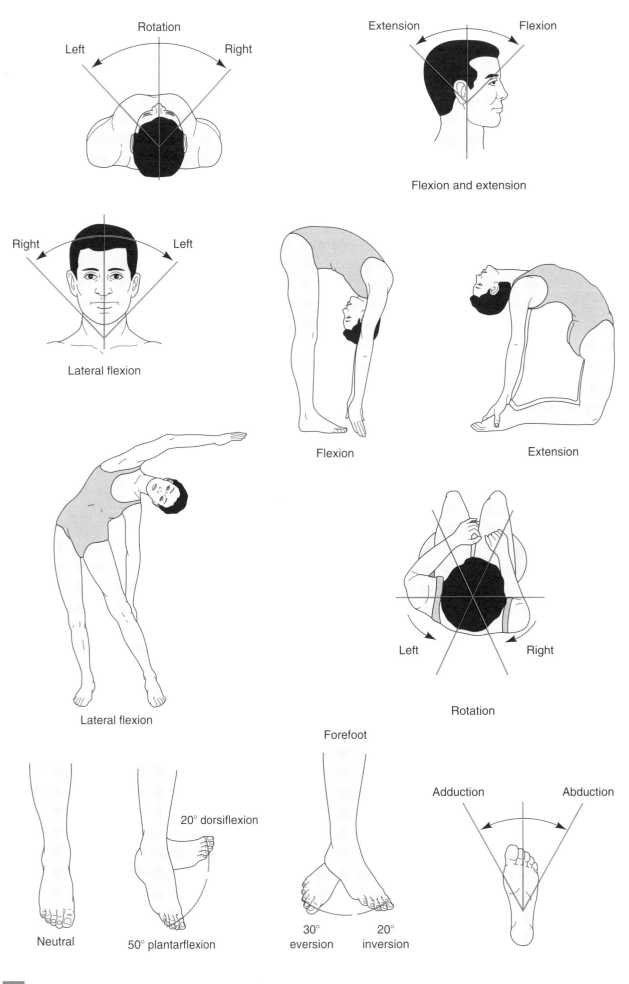

Rotation
Left   Right

Extension   Flexion

Flexion and extension

Right   Left

Lateral flexion

Flexion

Extension

Lateral flexion

Left   Right

Rotation

Forefoot

Neutral

20° dorsiflexion

50° plantarflexion

30° eversion   20° inversion

Adduction   Abduction

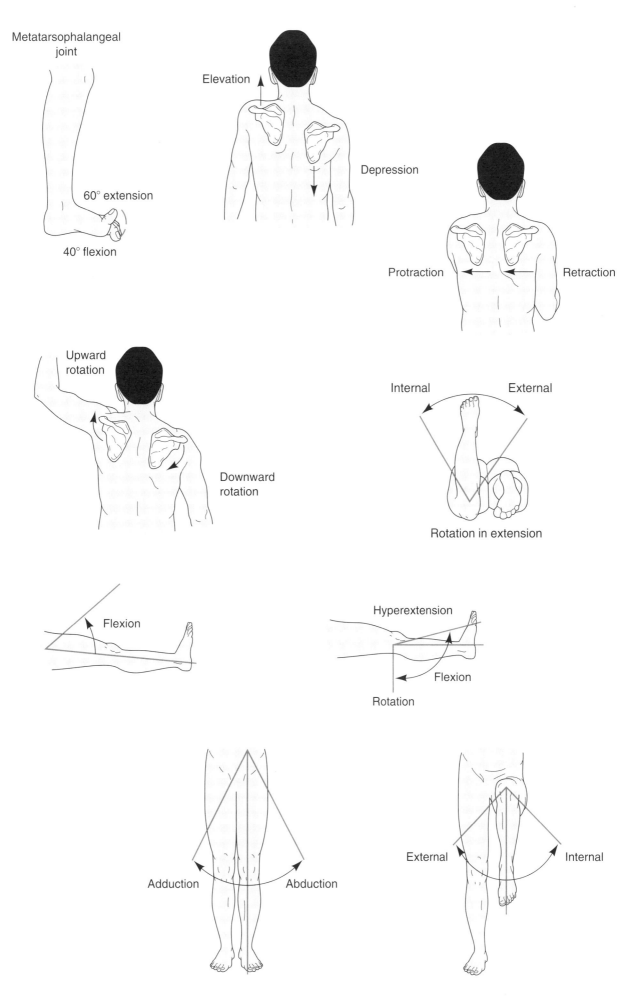

Metatarsophalangeal joint

60° extension

40° flexion

Elevation

Depression

Protraction   Retraction

Upward rotation

Downward rotation

Internal   External

Rotation in extension

Flexion

Hyperextension

Flexion

Rotation

Adduction   Abduction

External   Internal

Flexion and extension

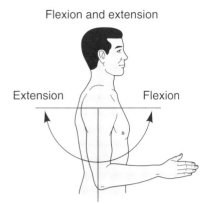

Extension   Flexion

Abduction

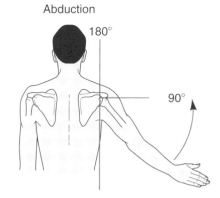

180°

90°

Elevation

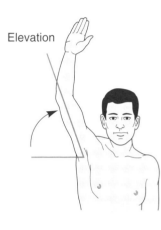

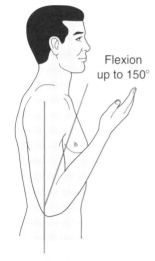

Flexion
up to 150°

180° extension

Neutral

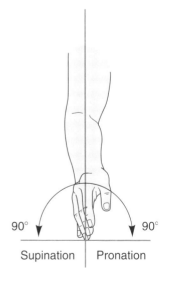

90°   90°

Supination | Pronation

and outside the body (for example, temperature, pain and smell). These receptors stimulate different sensory nerves to carry this information to the CNS. **Motor nerves** carry movement information from the CNS to muscles and glands to stimulate or inhibit movement or glandular activity. The nervous system functions to sense change, interpret these changes and respond appropriately. For example, if you stand on a sharp object, the nervous system interprets the sensation as being painful and responds by making you lift your foot away. The sensory and motor systems work together, controlling movements.

The fact that what the senses tell the nervous system will affect the movement produced has important implications for training and coaching. If an athlete performs a movement incorrectly by training, for example, with pain or when excessively fatigued, the nervous system may receive 'faulty' sensory information. If this occurs often enough, the incorrect input can change the resulting movement (muscle synergy) permanently, even when the pain has been resolved.

Practising a movement incorrectly may ultimately compromise the quality of movement, even in a skilled performer. Coaches must focus on maintaining the quality of athletes' performances and once their technique starts to deteriorate, coaches should ensure that they stop practising. To ensure complete rehabilitation of injuries, coaches must be sure that athletes have regained their pre-injury quality of movement before they start normal training schedules again.

The skin

The skin, made up of two layers known as the **epidermis** (or outer layer of skin) and the **dermis** (or inner layer), contains sensory receptors that detect and send sensory information to the nervous system to coordinate movement. For this reason using tape to strap a joint is thought not only to protect the joint because it mechanically limits its range of motion, but also by providing sensory information about joint position to the CNS via the skin. The sensation of the tape on the skin stimulates the sensory receptors that, in response, send information to the brain so that the brain can modify the movement accordingly.

However, the nervous system will become desensitised to any prolonged continual stimulus. For example, when someone puts on a woolly jumper for the first time it may feel scratchy to them, but after they have been wearing it for a while they may not notice it any more. It is therefore important to use tape intermittently, taking it off when it is not required, to limit any desensitisation.

Although the epidermis is designed to withstand friction, there is a limit to what it can tolerate. As a result of excessive friction from wearing new netball shoes during a carnival, the epidermal layers on Jessica's heel broke down, creating a **blister**. Because the skin contains so many nerves, blisters can be very painful. Through sensory feedback to the brain, pain associated with blisters can affect movement during subsequent games, possibly leading to other potential injuries. Jessica's coach therefore removed her from the court until the blister was treated appropriately. A small amount of friction applied over a long period can stimulate a thickening in the epidermal layer, called a **callus**.

THE CARDIORESPIRATORY SYSTEM

The cardiorespiratory system is composed of two major components, the **cardiovascular** and **respiratory** systems. These two systems work together to supply oxygen and nutrient-rich blood to tissues of the body so that these tissues can continue to do what they should. For example, skeletal muscles require oxygen to produce the energy required for longer duration activities. Circulating blood also removes waste products, including carbon dioxide, from these tissues. Coaches should develop a basic understanding of the cardiorespiratory system so that they are able to train the cardiovascular fitness of athletes. The better this system works to deliver oxygen to athletes' active muscles, the better and longer they will be able to exercise.

Cardiovascular system

The cardiovascular system delivers oxygen to and removes carbon dioxide from tissues all over the body. As the body's plumbing system, it is made up of a central pump, the heart, and an extensive, complex system of pipes, the blood vessels, through which blood circulates.

The heart is made of specialised cardiac muscle that beats automatically. The amount of blood that the tissues receive with each heartbeat varies according to the **cardiac output**, or amount of blood pumped by the heart. This cardiac output is determined by the

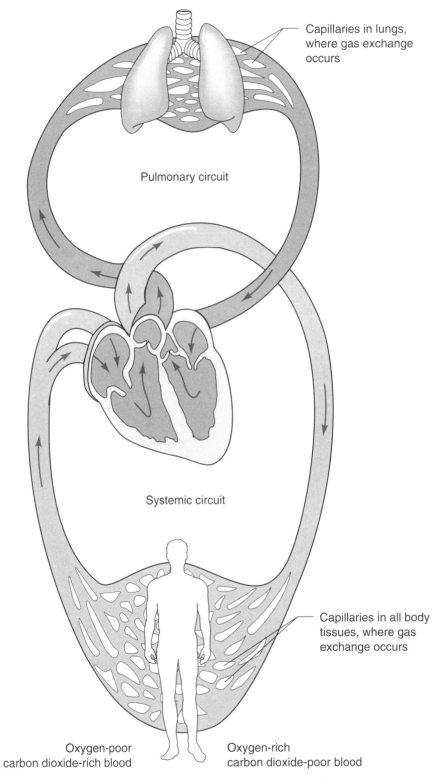

Capillaries in lungs, where gas exchange occurs

Pulmonary circuit

Systemic circuit

Capillaries in all body tissues, where gas exchange occurs

Oxygen-poor carbon dioxide-rich blood

Oxygen-rich carbon dioxide-poor blood

The cardiovascular system (after Marieb 1995)

speed at which the heart pumps and the force with which the heart muscle contracts. When people are exercising, their hearts beat faster and pump harder to deliver more blood to the working tissues. As it is a muscle, the heart can also grow stronger and more efficient with training, just like skeletal muscle. The heart beats about 100 000 times a day and pumps about 3784 L of blood through over 100 000 km of blood vessels each day.

There are three types of blood vessels in the cardiovascular system:

■ Arteries carry blood away from the heart, exiting the heart as large vessels and gradually becoming smaller. Arteries have smooth muscle in their walls that helps the heart pump blood.

■ Capillaries are microscopic vessels connecting arteries and veins, and are located near most cells in the body. They permit the exchange of nutrients, such as oxygen, and wastes, such as carbon dioxide, between blood and tissues.

■ Veins carry blood back to the heart, becoming larger in diameter as they approach the heart.

These blood vessels form two main plumbing circuits within the cardiovascular system, which extend from either side of the heart. The **pulmonary circuit** carries blood to and from the lungs where the gas exchange of oxygen and carbon dioxide occurs. The blood returning to the heart from the lungs is rich in oxygen and low in carbon dioxide. This oxygen-rich blood then travels within the **systemic circuit** to all the body tissues. Once the cells of the body use up the oxygen, the depleted blood travels back within the systemic circuit to the heart and to the lungs to repeat the cycle.

Respiratory system

The respiratory system brings oxygen into the body with each breath, transfers it to the blood in exchange for the waste product carbon dioxide, and then expels carbon dioxide from the body on the out breath. To achieve this, the respiratory system has two main parts:

■ air-filled sacs, called **alveoli**, where gases are exchanged, and

■ a system of tubes, or **airways**, to bring air from outside the body to the alveoli. These airways start at the mouth and nose and end in the lungs, branching until the smallest airways at the end of the system are only .5 mm in diameter.

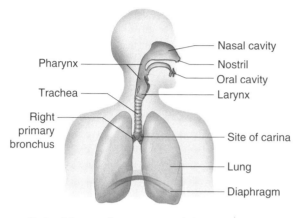

Parts of the respiratory system (after Marieb 1995)

The lungs contain about 300 million alveoli. The very thin walls of the alveoli are covered in cobweb-like capillaries. The walls of the alveoli and capillaries fuse to allow oxygen to travel from the alveoli into the blood, and carbon dioxide the other way.

CONCLUSION

Coaches are responsible for the health and wellbeing of athletes with whom they work and they are also responsible for educating themselves about the needs of athletes. Those who are familiar with basic anatomy will better understand how the body works, and how to adapt exercises and design relevant training programs for athletes. They will also better understand the nature of injuries suffered by athletes, and so how to prevent them and to help with the rehabilitation of athletes in their care. All coaches should care enough about the athletes they work with to help them in this way.

COACHING TIPS

- Learn and understand the structure of the body so as to understand the basis of techniques and skills, and the mechanisms of injury and illness.

- Use this information to help prevent and rehabilitate injuries.

- Learn anatomical terminology to enable further learning through reading, seminars and conferences.

- Use scientific terms to better communicate with members of your professional support team.

FURTHER READING

Biswas, SV, and R Iqbal (1998) *Mosby's Crash Course: Musculoskeletal System*. London: Mosby.

Hinkle, CZ (1997) *Fundamentals of Anatomy and Movement: A Workbook and Guide*. St Louis, MO: Mosby.

Jenkins, DB (1998) *Hollinshead's Functional Anatomy of the Limbs and Back*. Philadelphia, Pa: WB Saunders Company.

Marieb, EN (1995) *Human Anatomy and Physiology*. Redwood City, Ca: the Benjamin/Cummings Publishing Company.

Martini, FH, and MJ Timmons (eds) (1997) *Human Anatomy*. Upper Saddle River, NJ: Prentice-Hall International.

Wirhed, R (1997) *Athletic Ability and the Anatomy of Motion*. trans AM Hermansson. London: Mosby.

CHAPTER 6
PHYSIOLOGY AND SPORTS PERFORMANCE

Alan D Roberts

(National Sports Information Centre)

INTRODUCTION

An athlete's ability to train and compete in sport depends on maintaining a supply of energy for muscle action. Energy can be made available in rapidly released forms for the explosive activities associated with many sports, and in longer lasting forms to support the steady-paced activities in endurance sports. This chapter will explain how these various sources of energy are used, and will discuss the energy and fitness requirements of different sports.

ENERGY FOR SPORTS PERFORMANCE

Energy for activity is provided in the muscles in the form of a high-energy chemical substance, **adenosine triphosphate (ATP)**. The small amount of ATP in muscles is sufficient to support only a short burst of muscular effort, such as in a throwing event or a golf swing. If a sports performance requires repeated movements, such as in running and cycling, the ATP required must be constantly replenished from other fuel sources in the muscle.

Athletes can obtain short-term energy supplies for sprints from other substances already in the muscle, and these are called the **anaerobic energy supplies** because the body doesn't need oxygen to access them. Anaerobic energy may come from either high-energy phosphate substances in the muscle (the **phosphate energy system**), or from carbohydrate stored in the muscle as glycogen, which results in the production of lactic acid (the **lactic energy system**) when it's used to provide energy in the absence of oxygen.

A supply of oxygen is needed to provide energy for activities of longer duration, the **aerobic energy supplies**. The diagram below shows the relationships between the various energy systems.

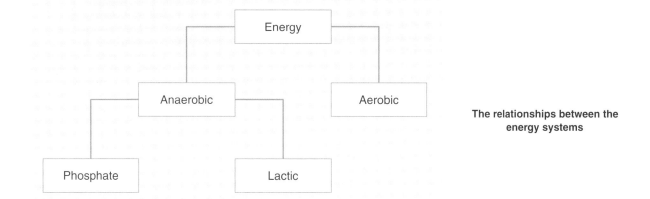

The relationships between the energy systems

A 110 m hurdler relies heavily on both phosphate and lactic energy systems.

(National Sports Information Centre)

Anaerobic energy

Phosphate energy system

The ATP already in muscle, and another high-energy substance, creatine phosphate, together provide enough energy for only a few seconds of activity. These energy sources are being used heavily during 100 m track races and the short dashes of a soccer goalkeeper. They are quickly rebuilt after an effort, to the extent that 50% of the energy supply is available again 30 seconds later, and it is completely restored within two to three minutes.

Lactic energy system

During a sustained maximum effort, additional energy is provided from glycogen stored in the active muscles. Anaerobic use of glycogen produces lactic acid, resulting in a feeling of fatigue that will eventually cause the athlete to slow down. Continuous activities that lead to exhaustion in 45 to 60 seconds accumulate the most lactic acid. This energy source is heavily used in 400 m track races and 100 m swimming events.

Once lactic acid is produced, the body can take as long as 45 to 60 minutes to remove it and, until then, the athlete will be unable to repeat a maximum effort, at training or in competition. The body can remove lactic acid more quickly if the athlete continues some light exercise rather than resting completely, but the level of effort must be below what would normally produce further lactic acid. Levels of exercise that are no more than 40–50% of maximum effort (resulting in heart rates in the range of 120–140 beats per minute) are recommended to help remove lactic acid from the system. Athletes should not be asked to make two maximum competitive efforts such as this with less than one hour between events.

(National Sports Information Centre)

Road cyclists use both the aerobic energy system (for level riding) and the lactic energy system (for establishing breakaways and hill climbs).

Aerobic energy

During longer and less intense efforts, oxygen is used to provide an aerobic supply of energy for muscle contraction. Oxygen is used to release energy from glycogen and fat stored in the muscle or in other tissues in the body, for example, glycogen in the liver. In these longer events, the better athletes can transport and use oxygen, the better they can perform.

In most endurance activities, the level of muscle glycogen available at the beginning of an exercise determines how much fuel will be available for continued performance. If athletes train hard or don't eat or drink enough carbohydrates before competition, their performance may be reduced. In events longer than one hour (for example, marathon running or team games), depleted muscle glycogen stores will eventually affect the athlete's ability to sustain a fast running pace. Athletes in these sports should consume additional carbohydrates during performance, usually in their drinking fluids.

The contributions of energy systems to sports events

The importance of each energy system to an activity depends on the intensity and duration of the exercise involved, and on the nature of the activity, that is, whether it's steady-paced or interval exercise. Very few sports performances rely on a single energy system to supply ATP for muscle contraction. Athletes in most events obtain their energy supply from a combination of the three energy systems.

Short-duration explosive events draw most of the energy needed by the body from the anaerobic (phosphate and lactic) systems. Long-term endurance events draw the energy from the aerobic system. Between these extremes there is wide variation in the contributions of the three systems to provide energy for a sports performance. However, the body does not change suddenly from one energy system to another during an event, and all three energy systems involved will be used simultaneously.

In maximum performance efforts less than one to two minutes long, the anaerobic energy systems provide most of the energy. When the performance time increases beyond one to two minutes, the aerobic energy system provides most of the energy. A 50 m swim event, for example, derives energy in different proportions from the phosphate (65%), lactic (30%) and aerobic (5%) energy systems. An 800 m track event also requires energy from the three energy systems, but in these proportions: phosphate (5%), lactic (35%) and aerobic (60%).

Estimated contributions of the energy systems to sports performance

Event, sport or playing position	% of energy derived from each system		
	Phosphate	Lactic	Aerobic
Track events			
100 m	35	55	10
800 m	5	35	60
10 000 m		8	92
marathon		4	96
Swimming events			
50 m	65	30	5
200 m	10	50	40
1500 m	5	20	75
Rowing	5	15	80
Hockey/soccer (except goalkeeper)	30	20	50
Basketball/volleyball	45	15	40

(Adapted from Finn et al 2000, McArdle et al 2000 and Pyne et al 2000)

Hockey goalkeepers use anaerobic energy for short explosive efforts.

(National Sports Information Centre)

In team games, such as soccer and hockey, the length of the game and the distance run by players mean that there's a high aerobic contribution to the energy supply. These games also contain short, intense periods of running, which require an anaerobic energy supply. Players who have to run further in the game (for example, mid-fielders in soccer and centres in netball) might use equal proportions of anaerobic and aerobic energy, as in the table on the previous page: phosphate (30%), lactic (20%) and aerobic (50%). Players in relatively set positions (for example, the goalkeeper in hockey) use more anaerobic energy for short explosive efforts and might use these proportions: phosphate (70%), lactic (15%) and aerobic (15%).

Even though marathon running and volleyball are both sports events lasting more than two hours, the energy system contributions to each of these events will be very different. The sustained running in the marathon will require aerobic energy almost exclusively. The repeated, short, explosive efforts in the volleyball game will make use of the high power of the phosphate energy system, because it can be quickly rebuilt in preparation for the next rally.

Training programs for athletes in these sports will obviously also be very different, so that training is specific to the energy demands of competition.

Event	% Phosphate	% Lactic	% Aerobic
Marathon		4	96
Volleyball	45	15	40

The exact contribution of the energy systems to the performance of any athlete will depend on many factors, including the athlete's age, sex, competition level and training status. If coaches monitor the way athletes respond to competition performances and training sessions, they can use this information to help select the best athlete for an event or position, and design the best training programs.

OXYGEN SUPPLY TO THE MUSCLES

The supply of oxygen to working muscles depends on a large number of factors, combining the respiratory, circulatory and muscular systems. These include the:

- movement of air in and out of the lungs
- transfer of oxygen from the lungs into the blood
- transport of oxygen by the blood
- effective circulation of blood to the muscles
- unloading of oxygen within the muscles, and the
- ability of the muscles to use oxygen.

Breathing (or respiration)

When athletes exercise, the volume of air passing through their lungs may increase by up to 30 times that of resting athletes. This is because the athletes breathe both more deeply and at a faster rate. The ventilation of the lungs during exercise probably doesn't limit oxygen supply in athletes with normal lung function, although preventive measures are appropriate for athletes with some respiratory conditions, such as asthma.

Circulation

Physical effort causes the heart rate to increase. The relationship between heart rate and intensity of exercise is direct and predictable in most exercise, and forms the basis of many fitness tests and ways of monitoring training intensity.

A characteristic maximum heart rate is recorded during exhausting work: for athletes aged 20, around 200 beats per minute is expected, but by the age of 50 this reduces to about 170. Well-trained athletes have a lower maximum heart rate — the heart is a more effective pump when it beats more slowly, even by as little as a few beats per minute. Maximum heart rate values also vary with the type of exercise, depending largely on the amount of muscle tissue engaged, for instance, maximum heart rates are higher in running than in cycling and swimming. This also means that typical training heart rates will be higher in running than in cycling and swimming.

The amount of blood pumped by the heart also increases with effort. An athlete's blood volume is usually between 4 and 6 L, depending on body size, sex, training status and so on. During exercise, the total volume of blood pumped by the heart can be as high as 20–25 L each minute, which means each blood cell may take only 12–15 seconds to circulate completely around the body!

Oxygen is carried in the blood largely in chemical combination with haemoglobin, which is located in the red blood cells. The circulatory system distributes blood and oxygen to the muscles during exercise. During exercise, the active muscles receive a greater proportion of blood and oxygen than they do at rest, and certain inactive tissues, such as the kidney and the gut, receive a lower proportion of the blood flow. In hot conditions, extra blood is directed to the skin during exercise to help the body reduce heat loss by sweating.

Oxygen use by the muscles

During exercise, more oxygen is extracted from the blood by the muscles. The capacity of muscle to effectively use the oxygen that is offered to it depends on certain structural and biochemical characteristics of muscle, such as muscle fibre type.

MAXIMUM OXYGEN UPTAKE, ANAEROBIC THRESHOLD, ECONOMY AND PERFORMANCE

Endurance fitness is an important part of most sporting activities. The best single measure of endurance fitness is the **maximum oxygen uptake (VO_2 max)**, which measures an athlete's capacity to transport and use oxygen. An athlete's VO_2 max can be measured in the laboratory by collecting air exhaled during exercise, or predicted in the field from tests such as the 20 m shuttle run (the beep test). Elite endurance athletes have higher VO_2 max values than all other types of sports performers. This measure varies with the type of exercise being performed, and is most directly related to the amount of muscle mass used by the athlete, so the VO_2 max of a triathlete will be higher if it's measured during running than during cycling and swimming.

The type of exercise influences both the heart rate and the VO_2 max of an athlete, depending mainly on the amount of muscle mass used in each activity. VO_2 max is shown in the table below in litres per minute (L/min) and millilitres per kilogram per minute (mL/kg x min) and heart rate is measured in beats per minute (bpm). This type of information can be used practically to determine ideal training heart rates for each triathlon sport, which will be lower in swimming than in cycling and running (adapted from Kerr et al 1996).

Maximum oxygen uptake is only one predictor of performance in endurance events. There is also a clear relationship between endurance performance and the level of oxygen uptake that can be achieved in exercise before an increase is seen in the level of lactic acid in

Type of exercise	VO_2 max (L/min)	VO_2 max (mL/kg × min)	Heart rate max (bpm)
Running	4.41	63.2	184
Cycling	4.14	59.4	178
Swimming	3.57	50.5	158

the blood (lactic acid build-up indicates fatigue is developing in muscles). The level of effort at which this occurs is called the **anaerobic threshold**. This point represents the transition between the aerobic and anaerobic energy systems, and in practical terms will be the highest speed or power output that can be sustained for an extended training session or race. There are wide variations in how hard athletes can work before they reach their anaerobic threshold and begin to accumulate lactic acid in the muscles and blood. In an untrained individual, the anaerobic threshold may be as low as 50% of VO_2 max, with this increasing to more than 85% of VO_2 max in endurance athletes.

High-level endurance athletes also don't need as much oxygen to perform at any given speed, which means they will be less fatigued by training or competing at that pace. This is a measure of **economy**, and is also shown in lower heart rates and lactic acid levels during training or competing at race pace. It also means that, at any particular level of oxygen uptake, the athlete with greater economy will be able to sustain a faster pace without fatigue, which will result in better performance.

Information on how to test for VO_2 max and anaerobic threshold can be found in chapter 7, Testing the Athlete, and information on training programs for endurance can be found in chapter 10, Endurance Training.

MUSCLE CONTRACTIONS

Muscle fibre types

Athletes have two main types of muscle fibres, and although they have been classified in different ways, they are usually called fast-twitch and slow-twitch fibres.

Fast-twitch fibres respond more quickly to stimulation, produce force faster, and reach a higher peak force than slow-twitch fibres. They also contain high levels of the chemicals needed to breakdown muscle glycogen into lactic acid, so that the muscle can continue to contract even when the oxygen supply can't meet the full energy demands of exercise.

Slow-twitch fibres are associated with greater endurance than fast-twitch fibres. Slow-twitch fibres are surrounded by more blood vessels and contain more of the chemicals needed for aerobic energy release than do fast-twitch fibres, which means that they can better extract and use oxygen. The high aerobic capacity of slow-twitch fibres gives them the potential to break down some of the lactic acid produced in fast-twitch fibres, im-

proving the endurance athlete's ability to sustain high-level performance without fatigue.

Endurance athletes have a high percentage of slow-twitch fibres in the muscles used in their events (for example, greater than 80% slow-twitch fibres), while sprint athletes possess relatively few of these fibres (for example, 30% slow-twitch fibres).

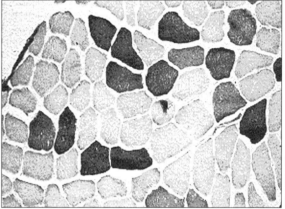
(Alan Roberts)

Microscopic view of the lower leg muscle of a distance runner, with approximately 80% slow-twitch fibres (the light fibres) and 20% fast-twitch fibres (the dark ones)

Middle distance runners and team sport athletes often possess approximately equal proportions of fast-twitch and slow-twitch muscle fibres in the leg muscles, because both middle distance track events and team sports require both speed and endurance.

Human skeletal muscle is highly responsive to training. The essential composition of muscle in terms of the percentage of slow and fast-twitch fibres is not altered by training. However, some of the chemical characteristics of muscle can be improved, for example, the capacity of the fast-twitch fibres to use oxygen to release energy can be increased by training.

Variations in muscle force

The force produced by a contracting muscle varies widely, and depends on a number of factors, including the type and number of muscle fibres that are active. Muscle also contracts more forcefully when it is stretched immediately before it contracts. Mechanical energy stored in the muscle while it is being stretched is released to increase the strength of the contraction that follows. The volleyball player who uses a two-foot take-off for spiking first uses body weight to stretch the muscles in the front of the thigh. When these muscles contract in the jump, the force produced will be greater, and the athlete will jump higher. This principle is applied in bounding exercises (plyometrics), used as training for explosive power activities.

The speed of a muscle contraction also influences how much force it generates: a muscle that contracts quickly doesn't have time to develop force: a relatively slow movement is needed to generate a forceful contraction.

MUSCULAR FITNESS

The key characteristics of muscular performance are strength, speed, power, flexibility and endurance. The strength and speed of muscle action combine to produce power, flexibility is vital to achieving a full range of movement, and endurance is the ability to perform repeated muscle contractions. Successful performers in most sports need these characteristics to some extent, but the importance of each will vary between sports. Coaches should assess the importance of strength, speed, power, flexibility and endurance to their sport to develop an effective resistance training program for their athletes.

Strength

Strength is the maximum muscular force that can be applied in a single effort. Athletes' ability to use strength in their sports performance is influenced by a number of factors.

The force a muscle can exert is proportional to its thickness, and so larger athletes with big muscles tend to be very strong. However, many smaller athletes have an advantage in terms of strength per unit of body mass. This explains why heavier athletes dominate sports requiring high absolute strength (for example, throwing events in track and field), yet smaller athletes succeed in those requiring ability to control the body (for example, gymnastics).

Athletes are usually at their strongest between 20 and 30, and thereafter strength declines slowly. However, athletes can retain substantial strength into later life, especially those who remain active, and this is important in everyday life as well as in sports performance. Differences in strength between male and female athletes are largely the result of differences in muscle mass, but female athletes can use resistance training to achieve high levels of strength without excessive muscle bulk.

Speed

Speed is the rate of movement of a limb, the body or an external object. Athletes' ability to achieve maximum acceleration and speed depends to an extent on their developing large muscular forces. They can also improve both reaction time and movement time and practice the ability to perform complex skills at speed, all of which are important in team sports.

Power

Power is the rate of doing work, and represents the efficient combination of strength and speed. In most activities there is an optimum combination of strength and speed, which will result in the greatest power. The development of power will generally involve using lighter rather than heavier weights, and faster rather than slower movements.

Flexibility

Flexibility is the range of motion at a joint or a series of joints. A full range of motion is important for effective performance in almost all sports, and it can also contribute to a sport's aesthetic appeal (for example, in gymnastics and diving). Flexibility also helps to prevent injury during sports activities.

The structure of the joint(s), and the soft tissues that surround it limit flexibility. As the bony structure of the joint cannot be altered, the key to flexibility is maintaining the range of motion permitted by these soft tissues (muscles and ligaments). To achieve optimum performance and to prevent injury, athletes should develop sufficient range of motion to accommodate all the static and dynamic positions associated with their sport.

Endurance

Muscular endurance is the ability to repeat contractions or movements without loss of performance. For example, in the 40 km cycle section of an Olympic distance triathlon, the triathlete will perform approximately 5000 repetitions of a movement combining hip and knee extension, with each leg! Muscular contraction, even at relatively light loads, results in a reduction of blood flow through the muscle, and so reduces both the availability of oxygen to produce energy aerobically, and the rate at which waste products from the resulting anaerobic energy release can be removed.

Information on testing and training procedures for muscular strength, power and endurance can be found in chapter 11, Speed, Strength and Power Training.

CONCLUSION

Each athlete has a unique physiological profile that will determine the extent of his or her success in sports performance. In the population at large, very few people possess all the qualities for top-level competition in their sport. Coaches should have a detailed understanding of the energy and the fitness needs of their sport, so that they can select sports and events for which athletes are best suited, and develop in athletes those capacities essential for optimum performance.

COACHING TIPS

- Determine the contribution of the energy systems to your sport in order to plan effective training programs.

- Ensure that training replicates the energy systems being used in competition (that is, long-distance runners should run long distances and weight-lifters should lift weights).

- Learn how to measure, manage and monitor the intensity of athletes' training using, for example, time, speed, heart rate and power output as indicators.

- Teach athletes to monitor their own responses to training by, for instance, taking their own heart rates and counting their strokes.

FURTHER READING

Costill, DL, EW Maglischo and AB Richardson (1992) *Swimming*. Oxford, UK: Blackwell Scientific Publications.

Finn, J, P Gastin, R Withers and S Green (2000) Estimation of peak power and anaerobic capacity of athletes. In: *Australian Sports Commission*, CJ Gore (ed), *Physiological Tests for Elite Athletes*. Champaign, IL: Human Kinetics, 37–49.

Gregor, RJ, and F Conconi (2000) *Road Cycling*. Oxford, UK: Blackwell Scientific Publications.

Hawley, JA (2000) *Running*. Oxford, UK: Blackwell Scientific Publications.

Hawley, JA, and L Burke (1998) *Peak Performance: Training and Nutritional Strategies for Sport*. St Leonards: Allen and Unwin.

Kerr, CG, TA Trappe and SW Trappe (1996) Maximal aerobic power during swimming, cycling and running. *Medicine and Science in Sports and Exercise* 25(5), S127 (abstract).

Komi, PV (1992) *Strength and Power in Sport*. Oxford, UK: Blackwell Scientific Publications.

McArdle, WD, FI Katch and VL Katch (2000) *Essentials of Exercise Physiology*. Baltimore, MA: Lippincott Williams and Wilkins, 124–41.

Pyne, D, G Maw and W Goldsmith (2000) Protocols for the physiological assessment of swimmers. In: *Australian Sports Commission*, CJ Gore (ed), *Physiological Tests for Elite Athletes*. Champaign, IL: Human Kinetics, 372–82.

Shepherd, R (2000) *Endurance in Sport*. Oxford, UK: Blackwell Scientific Publications.

CHAPTER 7
TESTING THE ATHLETE

David Pyne

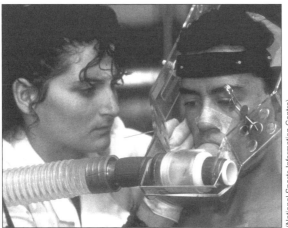

(National Sports Information Centre)

INTRODUCTION

While coaches use their experience and knowledge to prepare athletes for performance, organised testing gives them a more systematic and objective assessment of an athlete's or a team's progress towards a goal.

A well-designed and well-organised testing program provides several benefits. The primary aim of physiological or fitness testing is to assess the level of fitness of athletes and monitor changes in fitness over a prescribed period of time. A secondary aim, particularly in individual sports, such as running, cycling, rowing, swimming and triathlon, is to use the results of testing to prescribe training activities. Fitness testing can also be used in both individual and team sports to evaluate new training methods, technology and equipment.

Testing is now widely used in organised talent identification and development programs, particularly in sports where high levels of fitness are linked with successful performance. It is appropriate to test senior and older teenage athletes who aspire to higher level sport, but it's not usually appropriate for junior sporting programs, which should generally focus on skill acquisition, training and competitive aspects of sport.

In recent years there has been a gradual move away from laboratory-based testing to field-based testing, where athletes can be assessed in the same surroundings as they train and compete. Field testing can be easily and simply administered to athletes without the need for sports science personnel or sophisticated testing equipment.

BASIC PRINCIPLES OF TESTING

A coach should consider several basic principles of testing before starting a testing program. Although the tests used will vary widely between sports, any test being considered, either in the laboratory or in the field, must conform to certain basic principles. Fundamentally, testing should provide an accurate assessment of characteristics associated with success in a chosen sport or event.

To ensure that this is achieved, coaches should understand and implement the basic principles of testing:

- specificity
- validity and reliability, and
- standardisation.

Specificity

Testing must be as specific as possible to the sport requirements of the athlete being tested. There are three points that coaches should consider to ensure the specificity of their testing is maintained.

Testing should be as sports specific as possible, that is, runners should undertake running-based tests in the field or laboratory, swimmers should do swimming-based tests in the pool, and so on.

Second, testing should reflect the nature and energy requirements of the relevant sport or event. For example, coaches should conduct endurance testing for distance runners, road cyclists and triathletes, but sprint and agility testing should be used for soccer players, cricketers and netball players.

Third, testing should focus on the muscle groups predominantly used in the relevant sport. For example, a combination of lower and upper-body testing should be used for the combat sports such as wrestling and judo, and endurance sports such as speed skating and cross-country skiing.

Validity and reliability

Tests must be both valid and reliable. Validity means the degree to which a test reflects an activity of a sport or event. For example, a treadmill test would have low validity for a rower, but high validity for a soccer or hockey player. The validity of some field tests has yet to be established, and coaches must be cautious when experimenting with new tests or making modifications to an existing test protocol.

Reliability means the degree to which a test consistently reproduces a given result. For example, an exercise bike that is not properly maintained or calibrated may produce unreliable results over a series of tests. Coaches should check for local variations in testing protocols, equipment and environmental conditions, and periodically review the validity and reliability of testing procedures.

Standardisation

Many sports in Australia require all nominated national-level athletes to complete a selected series of tests. State, national and international level athletes are usually tested in laboratories accredited with the Australian Laboratory Standards Assistance Scheme. This scheme involves accreditation of testing staff, calibration and maintenance of equipment, and documentation of testing protocols, to give assurance to coaches and athletes that test results are valid, reliable and accurate.

In the field, all testing equipment should be well maintained and kept in working order, and appropriate testing protocols and procedures should be used. For example, a netball coach may conduct a 20 m sprint test on the first Tuesday of each month, in the evening training session at 5.30 pm, and always using the same 20-minute warm-up routine of running, stretching and acceleration drills.

The Australian swimming team usually comprises about 40–50 male and female swimmers selected from the open championships each year. The team then undertakes a 14–16 week preparation, depending on the scheduling of the major international swimming meet (see the testing plan on the next page). The scheduling of tests is done by the support staff in consultation with the head coach. Early season and taper tests are conducted during team camps (camps 1 and 2), while the mid-season testing is administered in each swimmer's home city. Test results are collated and analysed by team support staff and presented to the head coach, team coach and swimmer for discussion and analysis.

Medical screening involving a review of medical history, recent or current illnesses or injuries, and a blood test, is conducted at the start of the preparation and in the taper prior to competition. Body composition testing is conducted at the start, mid-season and during the taper. Endurance fitness and stroke efficiency are assessed with the 7 x 200 m and 7 x 50 m tests respectively. Twenty-five-metre speed is checked throughout the preparation with regular monitoring during the taper period prior to competition.

DEVELOPING A SPECIFIC TESTING PLAN

Testing plans are developed in a similar way to the annual or yearly training plan. Once the competition schedule and training program has been prepared, testing should be planned and integrated within the overall training plan. There are three steps to a testing program: identifying physiological requirements, testing athletes and prescribing individualised training that matches the results of testing with the physiological requirements of the event or sport. Testing is the link between the basic requirements of the sport, and the specific details of the training program prepared by the coach.

PREPARING ATHLETES FOR TESTING

Athletes should report to the laboratory or field venue in a well-prepared state. They should not engage in exhaustive exercise before testing to ensure that measurements are not influenced by the effects of residual fatigue. Athletes should have plenty to drink and should be tested two to three hours after eating a meal, to allow for adequate digestion (a well-balanced, nutritious, low-fat, high-carbohydrate meal is ideal).

Week	0	2	4	6	8	10	12	14
Meet				Open selection trials		Camp 1		Camp 2 International meet
Medical screening		•						•
Body composition		•			•			•
7 × 200 m aerobic capacity		•			•			•
7 × 50 m stroke efficiency		•			•			•
25 m speed		•			•		•	•	•

Swim team testing plan

Testing should be postponed in adverse weather, such as hot or humid conditions, persistent rain or high winds. Coaches may have to move the test to a more suitable outdoor venue or indoors, or postpone it. Athletes should complete a standardised warm-up before any strenuous physical testing. Those who have not completed a full warm-up, or have undertaken extensive or excessive exercise before being tested, may not be able to produce their best effort.

BODY COMPOSITION TESTS

Body composition testing can be useful for both developing and mature athletes. For younger athletes, basic measurements of height and body mass (weight) are used to monitor growth and maturation during the adolescent years. For older athletes, who have completed their adolescent growth spurt and have attained a mature adult physique, measurement of body composition provides useful information on the impact of training and dietary programs.

Basic testing usually involves measurement of height (cm), body mass (kg), and sum of skinfolds (mm). In Australia, the sum of skinfolds is used as an indirect indicator of body fat and involves the measurement of skinfold thickness at seven specific sites around the body (biceps, triceps, subscapular, supra-iliac, abdomen, thigh and calf).

These measurements are most useful when made on a repeated basis. A number of factors should be considered when interpret-

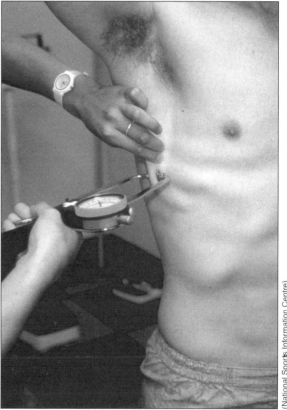

(National Sports Information Centre)

Skinfold testing

ing these data: the athlete's age, level of physical maturity, current fitness and training background, and previous body composition measurements, as well as normal biological variations in body mass and skinfolds, measurement error associated with taking skinfolds, any underlying medical conditions, and dietary practices.

ENDURANCE FITNESS TESTS

Three different measures of endurance fitness are commonly assessed in the field or laboratory: maximum oxygen uptake (VO$_2$ max), anaerobic threshold and economy (see chapter 6, Physiology and Sports Performance, for more information on these).

Laboratory tests for endurance

Maximum oxygen uptake

Maximum oxygen uptake (VO$_2$ max), which measures an athlete's capacity to absorb oxygen into the blood and utilise it, is tested by collecting an athlete's exhaled breath during a standard exercise test. Several sports-specific ergometers, including the motorised treadmill (for running, walking and running-based games, such as soccer and netball), bicycle (for cycling or mountain biking), the rowing machine and the arm–leg ergometer, can be used.

Athletes being tested do a progressive incremental exercise test until they can no longer hold the designated workload. Athletes complete several different workloads or stages of one to five minutes duration, graded from light to maximum. The subject breathes through a specialised respiratory valve, which directs all expired ventilation into a series of tubes where it is analysed for oxygen and carbon dioxide concentration. When the oxygen uptake fails to increase despite a further increase in workload, the VO$_2$ max is considered to have been reached. This point typically occurs during the last minute or two of a VO$_2$ max test where the subject becomes exhausted and cannot sustain any further increases in workload.

The VO$_2$ max is usually expressed as an absolute figure in litres of oxygen consumed per minute (L/min) in weight-supported sports such as rowing, cycling, kayaking and swimming, and as a relative figure in millilitres of oxygen consumed per kilogram of body mass per minute (mL/kg x min) for sports such as distance running, hockey and football, where the athletes have to support their own body weight.

The VO$_2$ max value for individual athletes will increase during their adolescent years and early adulthood as they attain a mature physique and train extensively. During the mid and latter phases of an athlete's sporting career, the VO$_2$ max value may approach a genetically predetermined upper limit that can be difficult to improve on. While VO$_2$ max is considered a very good indicator of endurance fitness, other related parameters, such as the anaerobic threshold and economy, should also be investigated.

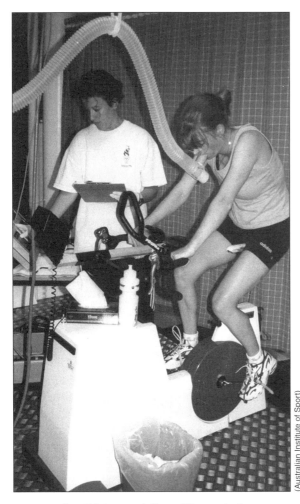

(Australian Institute of Sport)

An athlete completing a VO$_2$ max test

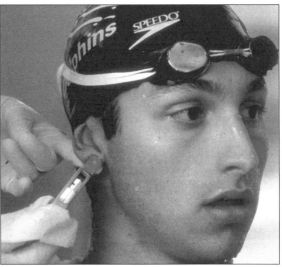

(National Sports Information Centre)

Blood lactate testing

Typical values of VO$_2$ max in athletes tested at the Australian Institute of Sport

Sport	Approx mean VO$_2$ max (L/min)	Typical range	Approx mean VO$_2$ max (mL/kg × min)	Typical range
Running				
Male	4.9	3.9–5.7	75	65–80
Female	3.5	2.9–4.2	65	55–70
Rowing				
Male — heavy	5.5	4.9–6.2	60	55–70
Male — light	4.8	4.3–5.1	65	55–70
Female — heavy	3.9	3.5–4.6	52	45–60
Female — light	3.4	3.1–3.8	52	45–60
Cycling — track				
Male	5.8	4.8–6.4	80	65–85
Female	3.7	3.0–4.0	63	55–70
Cycling — road				
Male	5.4	4.4–6.2	75	65–85
Female	3.5	3.0–4.0	63	55–72
Kayaking				
Male	4.8	4.4–5.2	60	55–65
Female	3.1	2.8–3.5	50	45–55
Soccer				
Male	4.6	4.0–5.2	60	55–65
Female	3.1	2.8–3.5	50	45–55

Measurements are expressed in both absolute (L/min) and relative (mL/kg × min) values (Australian Institute of Sport).

Anaerobic threshold

The anaerobic threshold (the point at which lactic acid begins to accumulate in the blood faster than it can be removed) can be estimated in the laboratory by asking the athlete to complete a series of tasks, each lasting three to five minutes, at progressively increasing workloads. Oxygen uptake and heart rate are monitored throughout the test to assess the athlete's physiological responses to the increasing workload. A capillary blood sample is drawn from the fingertip or earlobe after each effort and analysed for lactic acid concentration.

From the measurements of blood lactate levels, the tester prepares a lactate–workload graph that shows a typical rise in lactate as velocity (as in running and swimming) or power output (as in cycling and rowing) increases. The tester can then check the lactate graph for evidence of improvement, plateau or deterioration in the lactate–velocity or lactate–power output relationship of the athlete. A rightwards and downwards shift in the lactate–velocity or lactate–power output curve shows improved endurance fitness, while a leftwards and/or upwards shift shows a deterioration.

A break point in the lactate–velocity curve, which represents the anaerobic threshold, can be determined by computer-based mathematical analysis. Once the power output or velocity, lactate, heart rate and oxygen uptake at the anaerobic threshold have been determined, the tester can determine the training zones for that athlete. For example, the coach can use this information to prescribe training intensities below, at and above the anaerobic threshold of the athlete being tested. Many different training zone systems have been devised, most of which prescribe training zones using heart rate, perceived effort and training paces. Testing should be undertaken on a regular basis to ensure that training zones are adjusted to produce the appropriate physiological response.

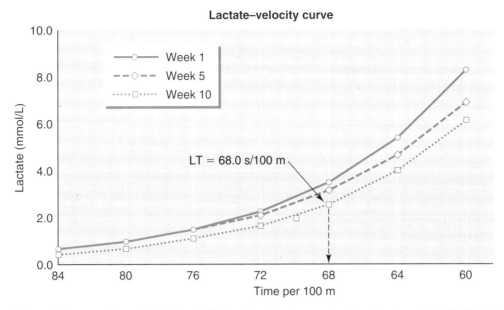

Lactate–velocity curve

Lactate–velocity curve for an Australian Institute of Sport swimmer showing the characteristic rightwards and downwards shift improvement in endurance fitness over a ten-week period. The estimated anaerobic or lactate threshold (LT) swimming speed in week 10 (68.0 seconds per 100 m) is also shown (Australian Institute of Sport).

Economy

In addition to measuring VO$_2$ max and the anaerobic threshold, some sports have established tests of economy (how efficiently an athlete uses oxygen). These tests are useful for athletes who compete in prolonged endurance events such as the 42 km marathon, road cycling, cross-country skiing and triathlon. Economy or efficiency is best calculated from direct measurements of oxygen uptake in the laboratory, although some sports use field-based measurements of heart rate and blood lactate concentration for the same purpose.

In the laboratory, athletes complete a series of submaximal three to five-minute workloads on their preferred measuring machine. The tester will often assess economy and the anaerobic threshold in the same submaximal test. It is important to be cautious when interpreting these measurements, as variations in physiological responses may also reflect an athlete's poor or inefficient technique. Residual fatigue and depletion of muscle glycogen may also influence results.

Field-based tests for endurance

The most common field test for endurance fitness is the multistage shuttle run or beep test. This test involves a series of 20 m sprints (between two set of cones) that increase in pace in time with a beep sounded by a tape recorder. Subjects continue running until they can no longer keep in time with the beeps on the tape.

The test is easy to administer, gives a valid and reliable estimate of endurance fitness (predicted VO$_2$ max) and is used by a large number of team and individual sports. Typically about 8–12 athletes are tested at one time and each test takes about 15 minutes to complete. Coaches and team staff must carefully monitor the athletes to ensure they are keeping in time with the tape and making the 20 m line at each end.

Other running-based tests of endurance fitness include tests of fixed time, such as the 12 or 15-minute run (in which subjects are required to run as far as possible in the nominated period of time), or a fixed distance (for example, the 1.6 km or 4.0 km time trial), in which subjects have to complete the distance as quickly as possible. Sports such as swimming (2000 or 3000 m for time; 30-minute distance trial), rowing (2000 m time trial) and road cycling (30-minute distance trial) also use fixed-time or fixed-distance endurance tests.

Some coaches make use of local conditions and have athletes complete a nominated route (using, for instance, a local beach or country road) as a measure of fitness. These tests require a reasonable degree of fitness and pacing to achieve the best possible result, and are better suited to more experienced athletes.

TESTS FOR MUSCULAR STRENGTH, POWER AND ENDURANCE

Three different types of tests can be used to measure muscular strength, muscular power and muscular endurance: isometric, isokinetic and isoinertial (isotonic). These types of tests reflect the various types of muscle contractions. Isometric (that is, 'constant length') contractions generate force without a change in muscle length; isoinertial (or 'constant external load') contractions involve either muscle lengthening or contraction; and isokinetic (or 'constant tension') contractions maintain a constant tension throughout the range of motion.

Muscular strength

Isometric testing in the laboratory is the most appropriate means of assessing maximum strength. An example of an isometric contraction is generating force in a rugby scrum without moving any part of the body. Although isometric contractions are not easy to find in many sports, this type of testing is useful to complement measurement of dynamic or isoinertial strength in the weight-room.

Isokinetic strength testing is mainly used in injury rehabilitation and requires specialised equipment where control of joint acceleration is particularly important. Isokinetic dynamometers (specialised laboratory instruments that measure force) are used to maintain the velocity of muscle contractions throughout a variety of movement tasks (for example, knee flexion and extension).

Most sporting actions are isoinertial in nature, and therefore isoinertial contractions should form the basis of strength testing. Isoinertial dynamometry involves weight room-type lifting tasks (bench press, chinning, squat, bench pull and leg press) during one or more repetitions (repetition maximum, or RM, is the maximum possible load that can be lifted for the designated number of repetitions). Other tests include the number of repetitions completed and velocity of body weight resistance exercises, the height attained with vertical jumping (standing, countermovement and drop jumps), and distances that various objects of known mass can be thrown.

Muscular power

The majority of sporting actions require muscular power. Olympic-style lifting tasks (for example, the clean and snatch) can be used, but maximum-load weight room tasks, such as the bench press or squat, may be inappropriate for athletes without high levels of explosive strength or power. The vertical jump test has been widely used in many sports as a measure of explosive leg power. The traditional vertical jump is calculated as the difference between the height reached by the subject in a standing position and that reached during a maximum upward jump.

Some sports use a variation of the vertical jump involving a 5 to 10 m run-up to assess athletes' ability to perform a more sports-specific running vertical jump. Vertical jump testing can be performed against a wall or by using commercially available slat or vane style apparatus, such as the Yardstick or Vertec.

Muscular endurance

Strength testing does not usually involve assessments of the muscular endurance of athletes, and endurance qualities are generally measured by testing aerobic and anaerobic power and capacity (as discussed earlier). Muscular endurance testing usually assesses athletes' ability to resist peripheral muscular fatigue, usually by counting how many repetitions athletes can manage before they can't complete one. A proportion of the athlete's 1 or 3 RM or body mass (for example, 50%) is used as the resistance in tasks such as the bench press or leg press.

TESTS FOR POWER, SPEED AND AGILITY

Many individual and team sports are based on power, speed and agility, and training programs focus heavily on the development of these markers of fitness. In recent years coaches have moved away from laboratory-based assessments of anaerobic power and capacity (cycle ergometry) towards field-based measures of speed (light gate testing) and agility (sports-specific agility tests). Light gate testing involves using specialised equipment in which a photoelectric timing device accurately measures the time taken to complete short sprint and agility tasks.

Power

Traditional laboratory measurements of anaerobic power have included cycle ergometry tests, such as the 10 and 30-second maximum effort tests and the Wingate test (a 30-second maximum effort where power outputs are calculated on five-second intervals). Power is measured in watts and expressed per kilogram of body weight. The highest power output recorded for athletes is taken as the peak rather than the average power output, while their anaerobic capacity is shown by how much their power declines from the start to the finish of the test.

Power testing using a cycle ergometry test

(National Sports Information Centre)

Speed

The most popular field test of speed is the 20 m light gate sprint test, in which athletes perform two or three maximum-effort sprints from a standing start. The coach records all sprint times electronically and split times are taken at the 5 m and 10 m marks. Some sports use a 30 or 40 m variation of this test. Athletes take the starting position, with the front foot up to the starting line. After a signal that the light gates are set, the athlete starts when ready. The light gates will start timing automatically as the athlete passes through the first light gate. Split times (5 and 10 m) and the total 20 m time are recorded.

Agility

Agility is the ability to change direction in a sports-specific fashion at the highest possible speed. The ability to change direction at speed

Typical values for the 20 m sprint test recorded at the Australian Institute of Sport and the South Australian Sports Institute

Sport	Group	5 m sprint time (s)	10 m sprint time (s)	20 m sprint time (s)
Australian football	Male (under-19)	1.09 (0.97–1.26)	1.81 (1.66–2.03)	3.05 (2.86–3.12)
Basketball	Female (senior)	1.04 (1.05–1.31)	1.95 (1.81–2.14)	3.38 (3.10–3.59)
	Male (senior)	1.05 (0.89–1.14)	1.81 (1.59–1.92)	3.12 (2.84–3.35)
Cricket	Female (senior)		2.07 (1.90–2.30)	3.52 (3.20–3.90)
	Male (AIS)		1.76 (1.75–1.79)	2.99 (2.88–3.07)
Softball	Male (under-19)	1.04 (0.96–1.15)	1.79 (1.66–1.95)	3.09 (2.89–3.33)
	Female (under-19)	1.16 (1.06–1.30)	1.98 (1.80–2.19)	3.43 (3.15–3.79)
Netball	Female (senior)	1.16 (1.09–1.27)	1.98 (1.87–2.13)	3.40 (3.19–3.60)
	Female (under-21)	1.15 (1.06–1.30)	1.96 (1.85–2.16)	3.37 (3.17–3.61)
	Female (under-17)	1.23 (1.08–1.52)	2.05 (1.89–2.37)	3.49 (3.04–3.93)
Soccer	Male (under-18)	1.08 (1.02–1.12)	1.79 (1.71–1.89)	3.02 (2.90–3.15)
	Female (national)	1.16 (1.12–1.23)	1.96 (1.89–2.04)	3.32 (3.19–3.47)

Measurements are shown in seconds as a mean with the range in brackets (Australian Institute of Sport and South Australian Sports Institute).

is important in most court and field sports. While the generic 20 m sprint test is used to assess athletes in many sports, agility tests tend to be more sports specific. Many different agility tests have evolved to simulate the movement patterns of a particular sport or sporting activity.

Examples of agility testing include the basic or modified 505 agility test, the run-a-three test in cricket and specific agility tests for basketball, tennis and Australian football. The 505 agility test is a valid and reliable test that attempts to measure an athlete's agility (see illustration below). The maximum effort test involves a 5 m out-and-back sprint, where the initial acceleration is followed by deceleration before a quick change of direction and a final acceleration back to the start. An electronic timing system is used to accurately measure the total time taken to complete the test.

The 505 agility test

Equipment
light gates, dual beam, 0.01 second resolution
measuring tape
masking tape and/or cones
indoor non-slip surface

Preparation
Using the measuring tape and masking tape, mark out the points of the course.
Set up the timing lights at the 5 m mark to form a 'gate' approximately 2 m wide.

Procedure
Sprint from the starting line through the start gate, turning at the turning line with either the left or right foot and then accelerate back through the stop gate.
Three trials are completed (Ellis et al 2000).

The coach of an under-18 representative football team was keen to employ some fitness testing for players preparing for the national championships. The coach spoke with the fitness coach of the senior club, and together they approached the state association for a copy of the latest testing protocols. They decided on the following fitness tests:

■ body size (height, body mass, skinfolds)
■ endurance (20 m shuttle run)
■ speed and acceleration (20 m sprint test)
■ explosive power (standing vertical jump), and
■ agility (running agility test).

No strength testing was conducted, as the players had only just started a weights program in the gymnasium. The players were tested at the start of the representative training (April) and then again three weeks before the national under-18 championships in July. The testing sessions were conducted on the same days as the senior club's testing to simplify the whole process.

CONCLUSION

There are many opportunities to obtain advice on testing and access to the appropriate facilities and resources. By exploring the local sporting organisation and club network, coaches can share information and resources when they want to expand and develop their training and testing programs. A good way they can start is by becoming involved with leading teams and athletes in their local area and applying this knowledge and experience to their own coaching. Coaches of senior athletes may see benefits in testing for identifying strengths and weaknesses in an individual athlete's profile. Coaches of junior athletes,

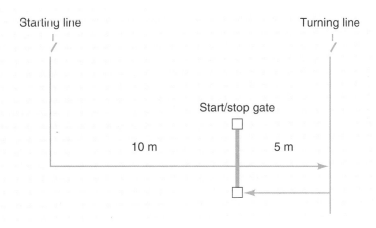

Schematic of 505 agility test course

however, should focus more heavily on instruction and skill development, and explore testing when the athletes are starting to make the transition to senior levels of the sport.

COACHING TIPS

- Regularly test athletes to monitor their progress and determine the effectiveness of the training program.

- Standardise the test environment to ensure valid and meaningful results (that is, try to test the same athlete, at the same time of day, on the same day of the week, using the same test).

- Use tests that closely match competition conditions. If possible, use minor or local competitions to test athletes under the pressure of real competition.

- Teach parents and other support personnel to assist with testing.

FURTHER READING

Abernethy, PJ, G Wilson and P Logan (1995) Strength and power assessment: issues, controversies and challenges. *Sports Medicine* 19: 401–17.

Australian Coaching Council (1998) *20m Shuttle Run Test* (CD ROM). Canberra: Australian Coaching Council.

Australian Sports Commission, Gore, CJ (ed) (2000) *Physiological Tests for Elite Athletes.* Champaign, IL: Human Kinetics.

Ellis, LB, P Gastin, S Lawrence, B Savage, A Buckeridge, A Stapff, D Tumilty, A Quinn, S Woolford and W Young (2000) Protocols for the physiological assessment of team sport players. In: *Australian Sports Commission*, CJ Gore (ed), *Physiological Tests for Elite Athletes.* Champaign, IL: Human Kinetics, 132–35.

Foster, C (1989) Physiologic testing: does it help the athlete? *Physician and Sports Medicine* 17: 103–10.

Fricker, P (1991) *Medical Screening of Athletes: The Pre-Participation Medical Examination* (Technical Notes series no 1). Canberra: National Sports Research Centre, Australian Sports Commission.

MacDougall, JD, HA Wenger and HJ Green (1991) *Physiological Testing of the High Performance Athlete.* Champaign, IL: Human Kinetics.

Norton, KI, and T Olds (1996) *Anthropometrica.* Sydney: University of New South Wales Press.

CHAPTER 8

COACHING ATHLETES AS INDIVIDUALS

Geraldine Naughton

(National Sports Information Centre)

INTRODUCTION

This chapter focuses on coaching to include the needs of all individual sportspeople. It looks at growth, development and maturation, and the special sporting needs of young and older athletes, women, athletes from diverse cultural backgrounds and people with disabilities.

THE LIFESPAN

Issues of growth, development and maturation challenge coaches of many athletes. If coaches understand these processes better, they can ensure that they provide activities that are appropriate to the levels of development of the athletes concerned.

Growth refers to increase in physical size of the body.

Maturation refers to the speed and timing of the transformation of a person into a mature state.

Development refers to the sequence of changes in the ability and potential of a person over time.

The human lifespan can be divided into eight chronological (or age-based) stages. The stages begin at conception and move through to older adulthood. However, it is important to note that, from a coaching perspective, the real ages of athletes may not necessarily be the same as their performance ages.

Stages of the lifespan

Period	Estimated age range
Prenatal life	conception–birth
Infancy	0–2 years
Childhood	2–10 years
Adolescence	10–20 years
Young adulthood	20–40 years
Middle adulthood	40–60 years
Older adulthood	over 60 years

COACHING CHILDREN

Why children should play sport

Some coaches believe that the most important part of coaching young athletes is taking fundamental responsibility for the prevention of long-term injuries by ensuring that athletes' technique is correct. Other coaches believe that the main value of early sporting experiences is in the personal, social and emotional benefits.

Vern McMillan, the director of strength and conditioning at the Victorian Institute of Sport, has identified postural dysfunction in many adolescent golfers and fervently believes that 'postural function through proper technique is pivotal to a young athlete's longevity and sporting success' (Naughton 1999c).

Stages of child and adolescent growth

Children go through identical growth stages and sequences. Infancy precedes childhood and childhood precedes adolescence. The speed and timing of these changes create vast differences among and within young athletic squads. Some young athletes experience puberty early and others do not experience it until their mid-adolescent years. In addition, some athletes can take months to mature after puberty, while others can take several years.

John Stathis, from the Strathmore Aquatic Swimming School in Melbourne, believes that 'up until around 13 years of age children can gain a lot of social and personal values from being part of a training squad. They can learn to relate to a different group of friends, develop time-management skills and increase their sense of belonging' (Naughton 1999).

Development in childhood and adolescence

Coaches should think about which activities are developmentally appropriate. The fundamental movement skills are those regarded as important for lifelong enjoyment of physical activity, for example, running, leaping and jumping. These also incorporate the 'ballistic' skills, such as throwing, kicking and striking, and 'reception' skills, such as trapping, stopping and catching.

Movement skills usually mature quickly with practice, but there is a big difference between crude early skills and those of a highly skilled performer. Movement, or motor skill, has various components that mature at different rates. For example, visual motor coordination is the ability to track and judge when and how to intercept an object. A five to six-year-old child can track an object, such as a ball, when it moves in a horizontal plane. By about eight to nine years of age, children can track a ball moving in an arc.

Theoretically, children can develop sports skills once they have acquired the fundamental movement skills. Development of these skills is highly individual, as it is dependent on the ability, capacity, experiences and attitude of the participant. Children often develop decision-making ability in sports towards the end of the primary school years, but by then they will also have a vast array of other abilities. Some children read play very naturally and others require more strategic coaching.

(National Sports Information Centre)

Young children have less refined skills than adults.

The nature of training and the expectations of children's performance outcomes must change with the developmental stages, as the potential for learning and movement efficiency improves. For example, practices may involve games using imaginative activities with younger children, minor games in small groups with pre-adolescents and more complex drills with adolescents. Checking with young participants to be sure that they understand what is expected of them before they perform an activity is a good idea at any age.

Early and late development

Early maturation may be an advantage in sports requiring anaerobic power and speed. However, this advantage may be temporary, as other children may not take long to catch up. Early maturation is a disadvantage in some sports, such as female gymnastics and figure skating. The disadvantage for early maturing females in aesthetic-based sports is that the weight gained is predominantly fat. The additional weight can not only interfere with the streamlined pre-adolescent body image, but can be extra mass to be carried and controlled during performances.

Early childhood development (ages 4–6)

Physical characteristics	Physical activity attributes	Psychosocial characteristics	Implications for coaches
Slower growth than in infancy	A wide variety of fundamental movements developed and refined	Egocentric and feel that their ability matches their effort	Maximise opportunities for gross motor play
Gains of about 5 cm/yr in height and 2.3 kg/yr in weight	Gross and fine movement patterns developed with play	Creative and imaginative and thrive on opportunities to show initiative	Challenge children's creativity and initiative
	Skills develop at different rates	Growing independence	Include activities for all large muscle groups and both sides of the body

Pre-adolescent development (ages 6–10)

Physical characteristics	Physical activity attributes	Psychosocial characteristics	Implications for coaches
Slow physical growth	Physical skills refined from fundamental to specialised	Improved socialisation skills — generally happy to comply	More opportunities for skill refinement — teach and encourage practice
Bone and tissue change gradually	Improved reaction time and visual perception	More willing to share and enjoy responsibility	Small groups first, before moving to larger groups
Limb growth is greater than growth in the trunk		Increased awareness of fair play	Encourage involvement in a variety of modified sports

Adolescent development (ages 10–20)

Physical characteristics	Physical activity attributes	Psychosocial characteristics	Implications for coaches
Growth spurt begins around 10 years in females and 12 years in males.	Moving from generalist sports skills into stronger specialised interests	Some adolescents become very aware that their effort may not match their ability.	A balance is required between cooperation and competition.
Growth spurt takes about 4.5 years and results in rapid increases in height and weight. Rates of development are vastly different in terms of when puberty starts and finishes.	Increased effort given to fitness and skill refinement	Some adolescents' participation is dependent on how they regard their own physical ability.	Set and provide constructive feedback for individuals' contributions. Allow for different maturing rates and matching heights and weights during training sessions and drills.
Weight gain in males comes largely from increase in muscle mass and height. In females it is largely due to increases in fat and height.	Great individual differences partly resulting from differences in maturation rates	Often participate to belong, to master and to have fun. Competition may not be important for some adolescents.	Provide social opportunities, make training fun and allow athletes some choices in what they do.

Adam began puberty at 11 years of age, and was fully developed by the age of 13. He was junior badminton champion of his state between the ages of 11 and 14. When he reached 15, he found that friends whom he'd always defeated in the past were suddenly able to beat him. Adam was not used to this and became very disillusioned about his ability. Within one year, Adam had completely withdrawn from all sporting activity.

Coaches should encourage and develop alternative skills, sports and physical activity so that, when the early-maturing child's advantage and motivation to excel in one particular position or sport begin to decline, he/she will have other options for physical activity. Coaches should encourage children to be good generalists in physical activity during childhood: rather than concentrating on one sporting or physical activity, they should experience and learn a variety of activities.

Coaching a late-developing child can be a challenge in some sports. Smaller late-developing children who play many of the popular team sports in Australia are sometimes clearly inappropriate opponents for their much larger and more powerful peers who have developed earlier. Under these circumstances, coaches should think about setting goals for each child that are within the child's control. Examples of this strategy include aiming for personal best times, applying predetermined sporting tactics, or making consistent interception efforts.

Recognising the achievement of personal goals by athletes is one way the coach can increase young athletes' perceived physical competence (feeling good about what they can do) despite the outcome of the competition. Coaches can also emphasise the value of the friendship and the feeling of belonging that can grow out of team or group activity, as these can also become strong incentives for young people to continue to participate in sport, regardless of their stage of development. During training sessions coaches who are sensitive to the different stages of development can incorporate drills and activities that neutralise size differences between young athletes.

Mixed competition

The sizes of young athletes depend on their stages of development as well as their genetic make-up. During mixed competitions that include young males and females, the issue of equality is often raised by coaches. Before puberty, girls and boys are so similar in size that there are very few reasons to restrict

mixed competitions. During and after puberty, the female is likely to be disadvantaged when competing against her male peers (at a similar stage of development) in sports that require strength, power and speed. This is partly the result of differences in the size and function between the sexes, and males' greater active muscle mass.

Some young female athletes may not feel any disadvantage in participating in mixed competitions and should ideally have the right to choose the type of competition in which they participate. Mixed competition for young people may also be very good for fulfilling social and cultural goals in communities. Coaches should have different expectations of performance for each sex, especially for activities requiring strength and power, for athletes in mixed competitions.

The fitness of young athletes

In general, girls don't perform as well as boys at the earliest age that the data can be collected during laboratory and field-based tests for endurance. Biological differences between pre-adolescent boys and girls are not large enough to explain this, and sociocultural differences and expectations are thought to be contributing factors.

Depending on the starting level, endurance training can improve aerobic performance at any age. However, there is a markedly greater improvement in the aerobic performance of males following puberty compared with the improvement made before puberty. This improvement is sometimes explained using the trigger hypothesis, which attributes this substantial increase in responsiveness to aerobic training to the triggering of the male adolescent growth spurt. The growth spurt results in greater heart and lung capacity, improved oxygen-carrying capacity because of increased amounts of haemoglobin in the body, an increased active muscle mass, and changes in hormonal activity during the adolescent years. Females appear to respond to aerobic training in the same way before and after puberty, although much more research is needed in this area.

Strength differences between males and females are apparent from three years of age. These differences are more substantial from puberty. Muscle mass in males accounts for 42% of body composition by five years and increases to 54% by the age of 17. Within the same time span, the muscle mass of females increases from 40% to 42.5%. Improvements in muscle size and function that accompany resistance training in adolescent males are assisted by hormones such as testosterone and human growth hormone, so adolescent males are likely to show greater absolute strength gains than adolescent females. The best training program for young athletes, and the extent to which gains from resistance training can affect the sporting performances of the young, are yet to be determined.

Heat and young athletes

Exercising at any age generates heat. Heat loss happens differently in children and adults. Children generally maintain the same core temperature as adults. This characteristic alters, however, with fitness, body composition, body size and state of acclimatisation. Young people who are fit, lean, hydrated and acclimatised generally cope very well during exercise in the heat. Children are thought to compensate for not losing as much heat through sweat as adults do by losing more heat through radiation and convection.

COACHING OLDER ADULTS

Many of the diseases and disabling conditions associated with ageing can be prevented, postponed or improved with regular physical activity.

Why older people should remain active

Regular exercise provides physiological, psychological and sociocultural benefits that combine to help prevent injury and retain independence in older adults. Reports show that older people who do aerobic exercise have a reduced incidence of cardiovascular disease, because their blood pressure and the levels of more harmful blood fats are reduced. For non-athletic older people, aerobic training should engage large muscle groups (walking, swimming and cycling) at mild to moderate intensity (intermittently or continuously) at least three times each week for 30 minutes or more. Engaging in physical activity more than three times each week will provide greater health benefits at any age.

For older sportspeople, the incentive to participate in sport may shift from competitive success to opportunities for social activity, and so coaches of older athletes often develop social networks to inspire athletes to keep participating. Older beginners in a sport may be embarrassed or unsure of techniques, as well as being afraid of injuring themselves, so careful planning for gentle progression in programming can also help to keep people involved. When coaches design the exercise program, they should plan to teach older participants to monitor their own progress.

Individual and realistic goal setting by the coach will demonstrate the vast array of abilities and potential that can be developed within a group of older participants. Programming for older participants in any sport should be based on what the athletes can do and not on what they 'should' be able to do at their age. A well-trained 65-year-old can perform better than a sedentary 25-year-old

How children regulate heat

Characteristics of children	Implications for coaches
Larger body surface area to body mass ratio	Can be an advantage to children under moderate conditions as they can lose heat more quickly Can result in children gaining more heat when the environmental temperature reaches or exceeds the child's core temperature of 37°C, so coaching should be substantially modified or cancelled under these conditions
Lower sweating rate	Coaches should encourage children to remove unnecessary layers of clothing that could prevent heat loss through radiation and convection, rather than evaporation for cooling.
Slower acclimatisation	Children may take longer to get used to hot weather. They may need more rest, less training and greater encouragement to drink at the start of hotter weather.
Poor at drinking without being prompted	Children may need to be educated and reminded to drink water before, during and after exercise.

Older athletes benefit from involvement in sport.

(National Sports Information Centre)

in aerobic power, strength and flexibility. Even strength training programs in frail and elderly people aged over 80 have resulted in improved muscle size and strength. Such training programs have also reported improvements in the general wellbeing of the elderly as a result of exercise participation.

Other coaching considerations for older athletes include:

■ they may require longer warm-ups and recovery

■ because of the higher risks of poor thermoregulatory control during exercise in hot and cold conditions, particularly in untrained athletes, they should avoid exercising in environmental extremes, and

■ their coaches should consider focusing on low-cost and convenient programs.

Although the results are not conclusive, the training recommended is **dynamic** (exercises where the limbs move through a range of motion) rather than **isometric** (exercises where the limbs remain fixed against a resistance at the one angle). This sort of training with older people should involve programs that begin with one to three sets of 12 to 15 repetitions involving large muscle groups (legs and trunk), before including the smaller muscle groups (arms). Regular weight-bearing activity in old age can also improve bone health, as can both aerobic and strength training, particularly in postmenopausal women. This reduces the risk of osteoporosis (thinning of bone density) and improves postural stability.

Medications can complement or complicate the way active older adults respond to training. For example, some drugs prescribed to lower blood pressure may produce a faster response to exercise training than when exercise alone is prescribed. Some other drugs, such as beta blockers (medication sometimes used for heart problems), lower the heart rate and can therefore mask the true or desired exercise heart rate, although those who take them still make training improvements. Athletes, medical practitioners and coaches should work collectively to maximise training opportunities for athletes who depend on prescribed medicine. Successful coaches of ageing athletes must ensure that they maintain athletes' physical, psychological and social wellbeing.

COACHING FEMALE ATHLETES

Comparisons in exercise performance between adult males and females are difficult to make. It is impossible to find groups of male and female athletes who are similar in aerobic power, body composition, training status and hormonal levels. There are, however, some reports that when females and males are matched for age, training status, and event results, aerobic power expressed per kilogram of lean body mass is similar between males and females. Other researchers are critical of these types of reports, as the females who participate are not likely to represent the majority of female athletes.

Depending on the starting level, similar percentage improvements can be expected from aerobic and resistance training in males and females. The improvement at the end of training may still, however, be lower in females than males. Disappointingly from a female perspective, when males and females are placed on a similar weight loss regime, the males are able to lose more weight. All of these physiological responses mean that the expectations imposed on the female athlete are different from those placed on the male athlete.

At maturity and compared with male athletes, females athletes:

- have about 10% more body fat
- have about 20% less lean body mass
- perform with about 15–30% lower aerobic power
- have fewer sweat glands
- can have about 23% lower haemoglobin (the oxygen-carrying component in blood)
- can have about .5–1 L less blood
- have smaller hearts
- have less lung capacity
- have up to 20 times less testosterone
- have 6–40 times more oestrogen than males, and
- have up to three times more progesterone than males.

Hormones and the female athlete

Menstruation

There is still a lot to learn about the way the female reproductive system is regulated throughout life. **Primary amenorrhoea**, delayed onset of the first menstrual period, is linked to intensive training, genetics, and the fact that lean females tend to choose sports such as gymnastics and athletics, which overtly or covertly welcome lean-bodied young athletes.

How strongly the menstrual cycle influences performance is still being debated. Some reports show better aerobic and anaerobic performances in the middle of the follicular phase compared with the luteal phase while other researchers do not support this. The following table outlines the suggested theoretical links to the menstrual cycle, but they do not apply to all athletes.

Pregnancy

Moderate activity during pregnancy can provide the health benefits associated with exercise at any stage of life. The safest forms of activity appear to be non-contact and non-weight bearing, and exercise where athletes are not lying on their backs. The need to avoid getting too hot during exercise in pregnancy suggests that swimming is an ideal way to maintain or increase fitness. Pregnant athletes must ensure that they eat and drink enough to accompany moderate exercise during pregnancy. How quickly women resume sport after pregnancy depends on individual needs.

Joanne Metcalfe returned to play in the Women's National Basketball League three months after giving birth to baby Kayla. Having the baby meant that everything had to be organised and prioritised differently. Her exercise program became very focused on rehabilitating those muscles that needed repair, stabilising and strengthening after the birth, before starting an intensive pre-season program. She felt that 'without the support network of family and friends, the hard work that it took to return to the WNBL would not have been possible' (Naughton 1999a).

Phases of the menstrual cycle and implications for coaching

Phase	Characteristics	Coaching suggestions
Menstrual flow (early follicular phase)	Ranges between 3 and 7 days and may be psychologically difficult	Not a good time for peaking in highly stressful performances
Mid and late follicular phase (days 6–13)	Mid-follicular = low oestradiol and progesterone Late follicular = peak oestradiol	A good time for peaking in performances without excessive fatigue — coaches may like to schedule time trials or testing sessions during this phase
Ovulatory phase (days 13–14)	Can increase core temperature by .5°C	
Luteal phase (days 15–28)	Progesterone peaks late in the phase (about day 21), and is linked to increased ventilation, increased body temperature and water retention	High volumes of training may be very fatiguing for athletes during this phase, when some athletes can feel and perform at their worst

(National Sports Information Centre)

Female athletes have different physiological capacities to males.

Menopause

Coaches should take the time to educate themselves about menopause, so that they can recognise the signs and symptoms. They should also ensure that they communicate with athletes so that the training loads and programs of menopausal athletes can be adjusted to help cope with the physiological and psychological stresses that are likely to occur. Menopause:

- occurs in most women between 48 and 53
- results in a reduction in circulating oestrogen, progesterone and testosterone
- results in reduced relative fertility, and
- may be accompanied by hot flushes, night sweats, vaginal dryness, depression, irritability, forgetfulness and fatigue.

CULTURAL DIVERSITY

It is vital that coaches understand how the cultural backgrounds of the athletes with whom they work can affect sporting activity, and how sport can affect athletes' cultural needs. Coaches and sporting organisations should avoid making generalisations about the skills and abilities of any group, and should be prepared to make allowances for cultural differences. For some groups, family obligations take a particularly high priority (for example, Indigenous Australian peoples), and some have religious restrictions on participation (for example, female Muslim athletes). Coaches should also consider that diverse cultural or religious needs may also extend to the nature of food presented at events, the availability of a quiet room for prayer times, the kind of changing facilities provided for participants and other special needs.

In some sports, undesirable behaviour by players, coaches and spectators may be linked to historical conflicts between teams' or individuals' ethnic groups. Sometimes the differences between rival towns, regions or states can also cause problems. In such situations, the coach may need to develop strategies to cope with any potential conflicts before they emerge.

Michael is the coach of a soccer team that has strong ethnic ties. Another team in the competition also has strong connections to an ethnic group. Unfortunately, the two ethnic groups have a long history of conflict overseas. Often, when these two teams play each other, there is conflict among the spectators from both teams. This often spills over on to the field, and affects the performances of the teams.

Michael worked closely with the competition organisers to deal with the problem, devising strategies to overcome it. The competition organisers arranged mediation between the rival clubs, and increased security at the matches. Michael and his team spent time discussing the issue, and established some simple rules for player behaviour during these types of incidents. The players agreed not to taunt opposing players and spectators, even if they were provoked. A meeting of parents and likely spectators was also called to discuss the expectations of the players and spectators. A post-match meeting was held to discuss the success of these strategies.

Indigenous athletes

The success of many of Australia's Indigenous athletes has helped to make sports organisers and coaches more aware of the need to develop the sporting potential of this population. Moving from remote communities to train in big cities can make young athletes feel powerless and isolated, as strong family and community links are fundamental to Indigenous Australian cultures.

Coaches and sporting organisations have helped Indigenous athletes develop their skills without having to leave their communities by initiating sports development clinics for Indigenous people within their own communities, and taking well-known Indigenous athletes to remote communities to encourage sporting pursuits in young people. Such programs are culturally appropriate

ways of promoting healthier lifestyles in remote communities, and of fostering development among those who demonstrate exceptional sporting skills.

National sporting bodies that recruit young Indigenous athletes from remote or rural communities should also be prepared to be generous in supporting such athletes' needs for time and financial assistance to travel home regularly. Some national level sporting clubs have relocated family members to provide ongoing support for their young Indigenous athletes. The Australian Sports Commission has compiled a very useful resource to support Indigenous sporting programs (see the Further reading section of this chapter).

(National Sports Information Centre)

Olympic gold medalist in hockey and Olympic sprinter, Nova Peris-Kneebone

Susan is the coach of a successful athletics squad in Perth who works to identify talented Indigenous athletes. On several occasions, the more promising athletes have moved to Perth to train with Susan. For these athletes, the transition to city life and a more intense training schedule has often proved difficult and in most cases the athletes returned home or dropped out of the squad within 12 months. To address this situation, Susan has worked with a local Indigenous regional sport liaison officer to find out how she can create an environment for Indigenous athletes that will better suit their needs.

Strategies that they have implemented are:

- providing a family support structure for athletes moving from regional areas to the city (for example, arranging for them to live with an extended family or friends)

- educating/supporting the parents and family left behind, so that they know the athlete is being looked after and that the move will benefit the athlete's sporting career in the long run

- setting up a peer support system with successful Indigenous athletes in Perth from other sports

- ensuring that the training program incorporates lots of group sessions to enable interaction and support between the athletes

- meeting regularly with the athletes to discuss their training programs, personal needs and other lifestyle issues, and

- where athletes do not wish to move to Perth, setting up a series of regular visits by Susan to the athletes in their home towns, and/or visits by the athletes to Perth.

COACHING ATHLETES WITH A DISABILITY

Marius Ghita, 1997 Paralympic Coach of the Year, says, 'We all have a disability, some people are small, tall, divorced, have an old car like mine or talk with a strong accent. Again, like mine! What is normal anyway? I treat all people the same as myself. I don't make allowances or excuses and I don't see the disability. I can't see that Neil does not have a leg. When I came to Australia I found out that I am the same class as people who have a disability because I am from a different country. They call me a NESB [from a non-English-speaking background]. However, I did not come here to speak, but to make a difference!' (*Sports Coach* 1998).

Good coaching comes with understanding of individual performance needs, performance potential and the communication skills required to coach each athlete. From this perspective, athletes with a disability offer the coach the same challenges as able-bodied athletes. Every athlete is a unique individual: a good coach will make adjustments to accommodate the special needs of all athletes. With good sports-specific knowledge, and a commitment to treat all athletes equally and fairly, all coaches can coach athletes with a disability.

Isabel had been riding horses for most of her life. When she moved from the country to the city she decided to look into riding competitively. She made some inquiries and decided to approach Debbie, who was a very successful coach at the local equestrian club. Isabel went out to one of the training sessions and, because she liked the way that Debbie was coaching the other riders, she approached Debbie and explained that she was a competent rider and that she was keen to start riding competitively. Isabel also mentioned to Debbie that she had an amputation just below the hip.

Debbie was a little taken back and said, honestly, that she had never coached anybody with a disability before and really didn't know much about it. Isabel explained that she had a modified saddle that had been specially made for her, but that everything else was pretty much the same. Debbie said that she was keen to try to coach Isabel and learn a little about her condition as they worked together.

Coaches who want to work with athletes with a disability should follow the following formula:

- assess what the athlete can do and how they perform the skills and movements of a particular sport or activity
- compare the athlete's movements to the way those movements are performed by able-bodied athletes, and

(National Sports Information Centre)

Coaches of athletes with a disability adapt skills to suit the athlete.

■ make necessary adaptations to the athlete's skill in order to maximise their performance within the rules of competition.

Coaches should realise that although the 'usual' way of performing the skill may be the best starting place from which to work out how athletes with a disability can best perform that skill, the way they finally perform the skill may be quite different from the way it is 'usually' performed. Coaches may have to try many different movements until they find one that suits the individual athlete. Athletes with a disability can be great sources of information for a coach and are usually experts on issues such as how specific tasks may be modified to suit their ability.

Although the physical fitness and basic motor skills of people with a disability are generally poorer than those of their able-bodied peers, research has shown that this has been primarily because of lack of opportunity to participate in physical activity programs, rather than any physiological factors. Athletes with a disability generally have the same, or very similar, responses to training as their able-bodied peers, providing they have no health-related complications.

Consequently, they can usually train to similar levels of intensity as their able-bodied peers. Their performances, however, may be inhibited by factors related to mechanical efficiency in terms of distance travelled or time taken (for example, an athlete with paralysis of one limb would take longer to travel a course than some other athletes). Where this occurs, training loads should be adjusted accordingly to prepare the athlete physiologically.

It is important to concentrate on the 'functional ability' of the athlete. Coaches should be aware that a lack of skill does not necessarily indicate the lack of potential ability. Australian athletes with a disability have been very successful and one of the main factors in that success has been the connection of dedicated athletes with coaches who have good sports-specific expertise.

The Coaching Athletes with Disabilities (CAD) scheme was developed to demystify and simplify the field of sport for people with a disability by educating coaches about the needs and processes for including such athletes. The CAD scheme aims to develop specific skills relevant to coaching athletes with a disability and more information on this scheme can be obtained from the Australian Sports Commission (see Further reading section).

CONCLUSION

In summary, coaches should consider the individual characteristics, and understand the limitations and potential, of all athletes working with them. They should remember that some people in their sixties can run marathons and others may not be able to participate in sport at all. Athletes' abilities and potential are more important than their chronological age and other people's expectations. Coaches should also aim to achieve a holistic understanding of the physiological, sociocultural and psychological needs of athletes of all types. Coaching people of any age and background should be a positive and rewarding experience for both the coach and the athlete.

COACHING TIPS

■ Track the rate of growth and development of athletes as a guide to prescribing appropriate training and competition programs.

■ Be aware of the early developer who might succeed in the short term, but find winning harder when others increase in size and strength.

■ Be patient with the late developer who may be overwhelmed in the early stages, but improves rapidly later.

■ Understand that athletes with a disability are primarily athletes. Place the focus on what they can do, rather than what they can't.

■ Consider the physical, psychological and social factors involved with the range of different athletes you coach (for example, children, females, older athletes or athletes from different cultures).

FURTHER READING

For Australian Sports Commission resources on the Coaching Athletes with Disabilities scheme, contact the Australian Sports Commission, PO Box 176, Belconnen ACT 2616, email DEP@ausport.gov.au.

Australian Sports Commission and the Aboriginal and Torres Strait Islander Commission (1999) *Indigenous Community Sport Better Practice Models*. Canberra: Australian Sports Commission and the Aboriginal and Torres Strait Islander Commission.

Chan, K-M, and L Micheli (eds) (1998) *Sports and Children*. Hong Kong: Williams and Wilkins Asia Pacific.

Daly, J, and W Ey (1995) *Don't Stop for Menopause: A Guide for All Active Women*. Canberra: Australian Sports Commission.

Daly, J, and W Ey (1996) *Hormones and the Female Athletic Performance*. Perth: Women's Sport West and the Australian Sports Commission.

Gallahue, DL (1993) *Developmental Physical Education for Today's Children*. Madison, Wis: Brown and Benchmark.

Malina, RM, and C Bouchard (1991) *Growth, Maturation and Physical Activity*. Champaign, IL: Human Kinetics.

Naughton, G (1999a) Interview with J Metcalfe, 1 November.

Naughton, G (1999b) Interview with J Stathis, 1 October.

Naughton, G (1999c) Interview with V McMillan, 7 October.

Shephard, RJ (1998) Aging and exercise. In: TD Fahey (ed), *Encyclopedia of Sports Medicine and Science*, Internet Society for Sports Science, <http://www.sportsci.org>, 7 March 1998.

Sports Coach (1998) CAD chat. *Sports Coach* 20(4): 34.

PREPARING THE ATHLETE

CHAPTER 9
PRINCIPLES OF TRAINING

Frank S Pyke

(National Sports Information Centre)

INTRODUCTION

The most consistently successful sports training programs use a systematic approach to develop athletes. To do this, coaches must have an intimate knowledge of the requirements of the sport and the attributes of individual athletes so that they can prescribe suitable programs for them.

First, coaches must identify the technical, tactical and psychological skills, as well as the elements of fitness, that are needed in the sport. They must then assess the individual strengths and weaknesses of the athletes in the program, using a variety of tests. When they have evaluated the athletes' performance profiles, they can then prescribe training programs that meet the requirements of the event or game. This is how training plans are prepared. Coaches and athletes are more likely to have success if they use planned individualised fitness programs, rather than haphazard, communal methods, where outcomes are left to chance.

A number of accepted training principles have evolved, based on scientific evidence and coaching experience. These include the principles of overload, recovery, reversibility, specificity and individuality. They provide the framework on which coaches should base their recommendations for training programs.

OVERLOAD

In order for athletes' fitness to improve, their bodies must be subjected to training loads beyond that to which they are normally accustomed. Whenever athletes are subjected to a training stimulus that causes a degree of strain or fatigue, their bodies will reorganise to cope with the extra demands. As athletes become fitter, their bodies gradually adapt to repeated and progressively higher workloads. The most perplexing problem confronting a coach is determining the right amount of overload to apply as a training stimulus. It must make the athlete's body work hard enough to create strain and so force it to adapt to the new conditions, but it must not be excessive, exhausting the body and stopping it from adapting.

In the graph on page 102 that shows hypothetical responses to three different training loads, we can see that the ideal stimulus induces fatigue and creates a need for the body to adapt. However, if the athlete trains too hard (overtraining), fatigue prevents the body adapting any further and the athlete becomes chronically exhausted. On the other hand, if the training stimulus is too weak, there is no need for the body to adapt and performance doesn't improve.

Overload can be prescribed using the volume and frequency of training, as well as the intensity of the load. The degree to which the body adapts depends on how these variables are managed, as well as the initial fitness level of the athlete. Coaches applying progressive overloads to train athletes should consider the following points:

- Training should begin slowly and progress gradually. Sudden increases in volume or intensity can be counterproductive, particularly after a period of reduced load.

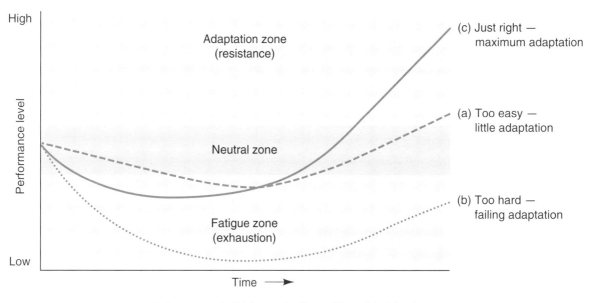

Performance of athletes under three different training loads

The graph shows:
- High / Low (Performance level, y-axis)
- Time → (x-axis)
- Adaptation zone (resistance)
- Neutral zone
- Fatigue zone (exhaustion)
- (c) Just right — maximum adaptation
- (a) Too easy — little adaptation
- (b) Too hard — failing adaptation

■ The volume and/or intensity of training should be elevated in weekly steps, but not by more than 10% per week.

■ Training stress should be cyclic, with harder sessions or periods alternating with easier ones.

Coaches should recognise the potentially negative effects of emotional stress, poor diet, lack of sleep, a long journey and environmental stressors, such as high altitude and hot weather, on athletes' capacity to adapt to training. In these circumstances athletes have the symptoms of overtraining (see above), but training is not the only cause.

Phases of training — periodisation

The organisation of a training program into phases and/or cycles is sometimes referred to as the periodisation of training, and includes alternating work and recovery cycles during different phases of the season. Training for endurance includes aerobic or base training (high volume, low intensity) during the non-competitive or off-season, followed by a gradual transition to high-intensity specific-speed or power training, before the load is finally tapered to freshen the athlete for competition.

When athletes are training for speed, their base training phase is usually shorter than it would be if they were training for endurance, and it is then followed by speed–endurance and high-quality speed phases, leading up to competition.

Cathy Freeman is the Olympic 400 m sprint champion. Her event requires sustained speed involving a mix of speed and endurance. During the early phases of training after a lay-off, her coach Peter Fortune prescribes high-volume, low-intensity training, such as 6 km runs over hilly terrain. This is interspersed with weight training, circuit training using body weight as the load, and Swiss ball training for the development of core body strength and stability.

Cathy Freeman

(National Sports Information Centre)

As Cathy's fitness improves, the intensity of her training gradually increases. Speed work (starts, acceleration runs and flying 50 m sprints) is incorporated to prepare for the domestic season from January to March, when she competes mainly in 100 and 200 m events.

From April to June, lactate tolerance work (to build Cathy's tolerance to lactic acid build-up in the body) forms a progressively larger part of her training as she prepares for the international season. Both the volume and the intensity of training are kept high during the early competition period, then the workload is reduced in August for the major events in late August and September.

While periodising training loads works most effectively in individual sports where a personal best performance is required on a specific day, it is also important in team sports. During the pre-season period, the volume and intensity of a team's training can be cycled just as it is in individual sports. In the competition season it is more difficult for teams to adhere to prearranged phases of training, but coaches should plan around factors such as the quality of the opposition, the breaks between matches, and travel requirements and education or work commitments, rather than just responding to weekly results (see chapter 18, An Integrated Approach to Planning, for more information on periodisation and program planning).

RECOVERY

The overload that determines the effectiveness of a training stimulus is linked closely to the allowances made for recovery between training efforts, sessions or cycles. Hard training without sufficient recovery produces fatigue rather than optimum performance. Athletes need recovery time to adapt to the stress of training, so the coach must plan recovery time and recovery activities. The speed of an athlete's recovery from heavy training can reflect the effectiveness of his or her training program.

Coaches can ensure that athletes don't get too tired by skilfully manipulating training loads. They can facilitate this by reducing the workload in the last phase of a training session or at the end of a weekly cycle. Also, alternating hard, medium and lighter work sessions helps athletes adapt to training loads by balancing work and recovery time.

If athletes train once a day and follow an appropriate cycle of hard and easy training

sessions, it is usually possible for them to recover completely in 24 hours. For example, one or two days of easy training should be included in a seven-day cycle. If athletes do two or three weeks of heavy training, they should then do a lighter week to ensure that they recover adequately.

When athletes train two or three times a day, recovery is more difficult. Light sessions act as preparation for recovery from the main, specialised training session. It is important for athletes to avoid closely spacing long sessions of intensive work, and to use low-intensity efforts to allow the neuromuscular system to recover. Athletes take longer to recover from running work, which tires them more than activities such as cycling and swimming.

Diet is important in the recovery process. Athletes need more protein, the key nutrient in tissue building and repair, after prolonged intensive efforts or in response to heavy strength training and muscle-building programs. They can obtain this by simply eating more, and don't usually need protein supplements.

Muscle glycogen reserves (energy stored in the muscles) can become depleted after successive days of hard endurance training and this creates chronic fatigue. If athletes eat more carbohydrates, the rate at which muscle glycogen is replaced increases. By elevating the percentage of carbohydrate in their diet from 50 to 70%, athletes can completely restore glycogen levels in 24 hours, rather than taking up to twice this time.

It is also important during the recovery period to replace the fluid lost in sweating. Both fluid and fuel replacement should occur immediately after training and competition. The success of tapering or peaking schedules, where both the volume and intensity of training is reduced during the lead-up to an important competition, shows why athletes need to recover or unload from hard training.

Olympic swimmers such as Michael Klim and Daniel Kowalski taper their training load from 100 km to 40 km per week during the last five weeks before a major competition. Generally, they do the same types of training during this period, but less of each. For example, anaerobic threshold work at heart rates approximately 20 beats below maximum might take up to 60 minutes a week during hard training, but only 15 minutes a week towards the end of the taper period (see chapter 10, Endurance Training, for information on anaerobic threshold training).

At the same time, interval training to improve the oxygen carrying capacity of the blood (VO_2 max) will be reduced gradually from 30 minutes to 8 minutes per week. The rate at which the workload is reduced depends on each individual and the number of races in which they will swim during the meet. The reduction improves the strength and contractile power of the athletes' muscles, as well as the efficiency of movement.

Coach Buddy Portier says that there are no hard and fast rules about tapering. The coach must be flexible and judge how each swimmer is responding to the taper, both physically and psychologically. Having a good eye for this is all part of the art of coaching.

The recovery process is assisted by a number of other strategies.

Passive rest

It is important for athletes to develop good sleeping habits to help their bodies adapt to training. If sleeping is difficult they should try relaxation techniques (muscle relaxation, breathing exercises, meditation, reading or listening to relaxing music) and avoid caffeine, alcohol and high-protein meals before going to bed.

Active recovery

Light exercise and stretching at the end of a training session help the body remove lactic acid and retain joint mobility after it has cooled. Team game players often use swimming pools for active recovery sessions, because they can exercise without the impact forces involved in other sports. Yoga is another useful method of active recovery.

Many athletes follow a simple six-step recovery regime following training or competition.

1. Drink and eat
   - Start restoring fluid and energy levels within the first five minutes after exercise with a sports drink, light sandwiches or fruit.
   - Stretch lightly while the muscles are warm and keep moving to prevent the blood pooling in the limbs and help remove lactic acid.

2. Stretch and shower
   - Continue to rehydrate and refuel during the first ten minutes of recovery and stretch the muscles in a warm shower.
   - Alternate between hot and cold water in the shower every 30 seconds for three to five minutes.

3. Continue recovering
   - During the 60–90 minute period after exercise have a meal and keep drinking fluids.
   - Use a relaxation technique or music to unwind.

4. Unwind in the evening
   - Relax in the evening by listening to music, reading a book or watching television, shower or bath to relax the muscles and stretch and self-massage, especially the legs.

Michael Klim

(National Sports Information Centre)

5. Prepare for sleep
- Immediately before going to bed use relaxation skills, such as visualisation or breathing exercises, to switch off for the day.

6. Morning check
- Check your resting heart rate and body weight to monitor hydration.
- Think about how you feel and plan your training for the day accordingly.

Physical therapies

A wide range of physical therapies is available to assist recovery. These include water therapies, such as alternate hot and cold showers, ice baths, high-pressure water jets, spas and flotation tanks.

Sports massage is a frequently used recovery technique that aids blood flow, relaxes muscles and reduces the feeling of fatigue. Self-massage of particular muscle groups is a viable alternative to a professional massage.

Psychological therapies

A number of psychological therapies are used successfully to relax athletes and facilitate recovery. These include meditation, imagery and visualisation, and direct the thought processes of athletes towards calmness and relaxation. Light entertainment, such as listening to music, watching a video, reading a book or visiting a park or an art gallery, can also provide a relaxing diversion from hard training and facilitate recovery.

Both overload and recovery training should be part of a periodised training plan. This plan should be flexible enough to accommodate the differences in the capacity of individual athletes to cope with training. It is essential that coaches obtain feedback from athletes about their physical and psychological wellbeing, to optimise their adaptation to training. Athletes must learn to monitor these responses and, in the process, develop a capacity to manage their own training and performance.

OVERTRAINING

Some coaches and athletes believe that improvements in performance are directly related to the amount of work done during training. However, experience shows that, at the upward limits of training, there comes a point where more training results in less improvement. Moreover, there are many cases where athletes who have been subjected to excessive training loads have suffered physical and psychological problems.

The symptoms of overtraining appear in three general stages — psychological, performance and physiological breakdown. The first sign of overtraining occurs in the form of mood changes, shown by increased levels of mental fatigue, tension, irritability, depression and disinterest. Coaches should ask athletes how they feel, monitor their sleep patterns and appearance, and gauge their overall interest in training.

(National Sports Information Centre)

Use of recovery therapies

If hard training continues, a deterioration in performance soon occurs. First, athletes alter their technique to try to maintain their performance, but then performance deteriorates. Movement patterns that initially looked smooth and efficient now appear strained and costly.

The final point of breakdown is in the physical and physiological areas. Symptoms include chronic joint and muscle soreness and stiffness (swimmer's shoulder, jumper's knee, Achilles tendonitis), increased heart rates and energy use, head colds, allergic reactions (compromised immune system), occasional nausea, headaches and decreased appetite and body weight. Coaches may gauge athletes' state of fatigue by asking them to record their own heart rate before they get out of bed each morning. Overtraining often elevates the resting heart rate.

If the coach has access to more sophisticated laboratory services, overtraining can be detected from changes in blood variables. These might include lowered concentrations of red blood cells, haemoglobin and iron, and increased concentrations of muscle enzymes resulting from physical damage to the muscle fibres. During periods of hard training, coaches should watch for any of the signs of overtraining and be prepared to either suspend training for a few days or lower the workload until it's clear that the affected athlete has recovered. See chapter 17, Medical Considerations in Sport, for more information on treatments for overtraining.

These symptoms make it clear that coaches should place a high priority on rest and recovery to achieve the best conditioning process. While it is obvious that too little training will not bring about the desired results, the negative effects of too much are often ignored. Coaches must try to find the middle road for each athlete.

REVERSIBILITY

The principle of reversibility is essentially that 'if you don't use it, you lose it'. This principle is relevant for understanding the detrimental effects of enforced bed rest as the result of illness, restricted movement as a result of injury, detraining between competitive seasons and changes in the training prescription between training cycles.

Several scientific studies have examined these effects. Three weeks of complete bed rest have been shown to reduce endurance fitness by as much as 25%. After two weeks of inactivity, well-trained distance runners have shown decreases in endurance capacity of between 5 and 9%.

Coaches of wheelchair athletes, such as Paralympic champion John Lindsay, must understand the unique circumstances that surround disability. Life can sometimes be much more complicated for these athletes and activities that are taken for granted by the able bodied may require more time and attention for athletes with a disability.

Former coach and adviser, Kathryn Lee, appreciates that, if John sustains an injury in the arms or shoulders that requires rest, it limits the way he moves around in the wheelchair and so affects the rest of his life profoundly. This leaves John's only mode of recovery as bed rest, which results in a significant deterioration in fitness. For John, it is therefore particularly important to avoid injury through attention to strengthening, stretching, massage and icing of muscles, good technique and early medical intervention should a 'niggle' arise.

Muscular strength and power are also lost during detraining. This becomes particularly noticeable when broken limbs or joint reconstructions need a supporting cast. The size and strength of the muscles deteriorate rapidly in these circumstances. Coaches should encourage athletes who are injured to maintain aspects of their fitness by using other limbs or modes of exercise. For example, footballers with ankle injuries may not be able to run, but can cycle or swim to maintain their cardiorespiratory fitness.

During the break between seasons, athletes should remain active. This will allow them time to recover from the specific demands of their own sport, but maintain fitness during the transition period. They will then enter the preparatory phase for the next competitive season at a higher level of fitness and be in a better position to make annual improvements in performance. Athletes who become inactive during the off season spend the preparatory phase of the next season trying to regain their former level of fitness, rather than building further on a well-established base.

As athletes proceed from the preparatory to the competitive phase of the season, the focus of their training usually changes. For example, in team games there may be less emphasis on endurance work and a greater concentration on technical and tactical skill development. Unless the coach is careful to combine endurance and skill training in activities such as interval skill drills, the players can sometimes lose endurance stamina during this period.

SPECIFICITY

According to this principle, the best training stimuli are those that reproduce the movements and balance of energy systems used in the sport in question. This may suggest that there is no better training than performing in the sport. However, in competition it is usually not possible to have enough trials at sufficient work intensity to obtain a fitness training effect. It is better to select parts of the race distance or intensive game situations and repeat them in training. This subjects the athlete to a higher quantity and quality of training than is possible while playing the sport.

The evidence in support of the principle of specificity is very strong, and the principle applies both to the muscle groups, and the muscle fibres or energy systems, being used.

Muscle group specificity

It only takes a small change in the position of the body during a movement to completely alter the muscle groups involved in the action. For example, when an athlete flexes an arm at the elbow joint, the stronger biceps muscle is used more with the forearm turned out, than when it is turned in. Hence more chin-ups can be done with the underhand rather than overhand grip.

Several endurance training studies have also found that non-specific training is not as beneficial as specific training. When rowers ran on a treadmill they produced more lactic acid and performed worse than runners, but the situation was reversed when both groups rowed on an ergometer. Kayak endurance performance has been shown to be enhanced by kayak training, but not by bicycle training. After a period of swimming training, a group of swimmers significantly improved their performance in tethered swimming, but their running performance did not change.

In more closely comparable activities such as cycling and running, which both use mainly leg muscles, cycling training produces gains in cycling performance that are not as noticeable while running. This is because these activities load the major muscle groups differently. Cycling tends to emphasise the buttocks and thighs, while running places a greater load on the calf muscles.

It is clear that the muscle groups involved in training should be those used in the sport to be played. Free weights used in whole body exercises such as squatting, cleaning and snatching are more sports specific than machine weights, in that they require the balance, coordination and strength needed in certain activities. Hopping and bounding exercises (plyometrics) also offer a useful preparation for sports involving jumping and sprinting.

Muscle fibre specificity

As explained in chapter 6, Physiology and Sports Performance, sprint and power athletes use high-intensity training to activate predominantly fast-twitch muscle fibres, which are capable of quickly generating high tension in muscles. Endurance athletes use low-power distance training to engage predominantly slow-twitch muscle fibres. Team game players require a mix of high and low-power training to involve both muscle fibre types.

There are some cases where non-specific activity can be beneficial: in recovering from hard training, in providing variety in training and as foundation work. However, as training focuses more on specifics further into the season, coaches should plan to use fewer unnecessary and potentially damaging non-specific activities. The major portion of the training program should by then consist of activities that are directly related to competition.

Cross-training

Cross-training involves athletes training in activities that are different to their sport. On the surface this contradicts the principle of specificity of training that we've just discussed. While a runner should not expect to obtain optimal training benefits from swimming, water-based running training may be useful in reducing the strain on a runner's muscles and joints.

Cross-training is best left to multievent sports, such as triathlon, which include different types of exercise. However, it can be used to maintain general fitness when injuries prevent athletes participating in their primary activities. It can also provide variety in training, allow recovery and prevent overuse of specific muscle groups. However, coaches should not expect cross-training alone to improve athletes' performance in their sport.

INDIVIDUALITY

Even though all of us recognise that each person is unique, the principle of individuality is not used as often as it should be, because it is much easier for a coach to adopt a communal approach and train athletes in groups. However, this does not provide the best training for each athlete in the squad.

First we must recognise that an athlete's capacity for a particular sport relies on inborn characteristics. Distance runners are born and then developed by training, as are sprinters. However, at the elite level of performance, training cannot bridge the genetic gap between these two groups of runners.

Athletes have different fitness, skill and psychological attributes, different lifestyles, different education and work commitments and different ways of responding to the training environment. It is essential that a training program caters for these individual capacities, needs and preferences in a holistic approach to athlete development.

Training responses

Some athletes respond to hard training better than others, but there is no guarantee that the most tolerant trainer is going to be the best performer. The coach must carefully monitor athletes' capacity to cope and be prepared to adjust the training program accordingly.

Athletes with a high proportion of fast-twitch muscle fibres have been shown to gain more from weight training than endurance-oriented athletes, who use mostly slow-twitch fibres. The high degree of tension created in the muscles during weight-training exercises brings the fast-twitch fibres into play. As a result these fibres expand and, because they are abundant in the muscle of sprinters, they contribute significantly to increases in muscle size.

Some athletes need longer to recover from heavy training or intense competition than others, particularly older athletes. Coaches should recognise these differences either by reducing the training load or lengthening the recovery period in athletes who show symptoms of chronic fatigue. These differences may also determine the length of the taper period before competition.

In order to help athletes enjoy training as much as possible, coaches should try to cater for each athlete's likes and dislikes. While coaches shouldn't allow athletes to work only on their strengths and ignore their weaknesses, they should encourage them to be positive about and keep firmly to a training schedule. This is easier if athletes are involved in the planning process, as it makes them responsible and accountable for their training and performance.

Olympic and world rowing champions, 'the Oarsome Foursome', presented their coach, Noel Donaldson, with the challenge of prescribing a different program for each member of the crew. He had to meet their individual training needs and tolerances as well as accommodate any injury problems.

There were significant differences between the four rowers, both in their tolerance for training and their off-water activities. Mike McKay was capable of completing the highest rowing workload, both on the water and on the ergometer. Nick Green had the lowest tolerance for high-volume and intense training early in the program, but handled it better closer to competition. James Tomkins supplemented his on-water training by riding to work and playing tennis and golf. Drew Ginn ran to training and was a keen surfer during the summer months prior to the domestic season. Both Green and Ginn had chronic back problems needing careful management and requiring specific rehabilitation exercises.

Donaldson accommodated these differences by using a variety of training types, including cycling on rollers, rowing in pairs and on ergometers, and strength and conditioning exercises. This complemented their individual lifestyles and training preferences, as well as ensuring their fitness for rowing as a team.

(Sport. The Library)

Oarsome Foursome and their coach, Noel Donaldson

Environmental tolerance

There are wide individual variations in athletes' responses to the physical environment. Their tolerance for hot and cold conditions is related to body physique and composition. While heavier, fatter individuals are more tolerant of the cold than lightly built athletes, the reverse is true in the heat. Preadolescent and veteran athletes are also less tolerant of hot conditions than young adults (see chapter 8, Coaching Athletes as Individuals). The coach should be aware of these differences when exposing athletes to training and competition in hostile and extreme climates.

Altitudinal changes and polluted environments also affect some athletes to a greater extent than others. Symptoms of mountain sickness (caused by lack of oxygen), such as headache and insomnia, can be debilitating for some people at quite moderate altitudes, whereas others can tolerate much higher altitudes (and lower oxygen levels) without experiencing problems. In the same way, some athletes experience respiratory distress in only mildly polluted air, while others are unaffected. The coach must be prepared to adapt training loads according to the way each individual tolerates the prevailing environmental conditions.

Squad training

Within a training squad there are likely to be athletes from all walks of life: some might be students, some manual labourers, some office workers and some shift workers. As the demands of athletes' working lives often compete with those of their sport, coaches should be aware of athletes' commitments to other aspects of their lives throughout the training year. These commitments may change from time to time: peak stresses for students occur at exam time, for those in business at the end of the financial year and for those in industry, near job completion deadlines. Some people cope well with these stresses, while others have great difficulty. Training loads should be adjusted to compensate for the demands imposed by life outside sport.

Training squads usually contain people with an assortment of different interests, tastes and personalities. In the heat of hard training and intense competition this can produce friction between athletes and negatively affect their performance. It is the responsibility of the coach to smooth out these aggravations and provide a training environment that is productive and enjoyable.

CONCLUSION

Each of the principles we've discussed must be properly considered by coaches who are formulating a scientifically based training program. While, collectively, these principles determine the training load appropriate for athletes, the observations and intuition of the coach, as well as the athletes' feelings, are vital in determining the ultimate training prescription. Coaches should always be aware of the need to maintain this balance between the art and the science of coaching.

COACHING TIPS

■ Remember the principles of training as SORRI (**S**pecifically **O**verload **R**ecovered athletes to stop **R**eversal of **I**ndividual performance).

■ Increase the volume and intensity of training gradually, in weekly steps.

■ Use proven recovery techniques to counterbalance the effects of training overload.

■ Watch for signs of overtraining, such as moodiness, loss of weight, interrupted sleep, and poor training and competition performances.

FURTHER READING

Calder, A (1996) Recovery. In: R de Castella and W Clews (eds), *Smart Sport: The Ultimate Reference Manual for Sports People.* Canberra: RWM Publishing.

Hawley, JA, and L Burke (1998) *Peak Performance: Training and Nutritional Strategies for Sport.* St Leonards: Allen and Unwin.

Rushall, BS, and FS Pyke (1990) *Training for Sports and Fitness.* South Melbourne: Macmillan.

Selye, H (1978) *The Stress of Life.* New York, NY: McGraw Hill.

Wilmore, J, and DL Costill (1988) *Training for Sport and Activity.* Dubuque, IA: WC Brown.

CHAPTER 10
ENDURANCE TRAINING

Richard D Telford

(National Sports Information Centre)

INTRODUCTION

Endurance training enhances the athlete's ability to continue to generate energy and minimise speed loss over distance and time. As we saw in chapter 6, Physiology and Sports Performance, the body's three different energy systems — phosphate, lactic (the anaerobic systems) and aerobic — combine in different ways to ensure that athletes have the required staying power, or **endurance**, for their sports.

Endurance athletes don't rely only on aerobic energy, as people might think. Coaches must consider all energy systems when planning endurance training programs, and adjust the emphasis on each system according to the distance for which the athletes are preparing. Any coach or endurance athlete who ignores anaerobic development is unlikely to be successful.

TYPES OF ENDURANCE TRAINING

Coaches usually describe their training programs in terms of the quality and quantity of the effort to be made, and the degree of rest or recovery needed. They describe parts of programs by talking about which specific energy systems are used for each part.

Maximum phosphate (alactic) anaerobic training

This training is designed to generate maximum power and capacity to produce energy using the phosphate energy system. The exercise takes around five seconds for alactic power training and 10–15 seconds for alactic capacity training. The rest periods between exercises must be long enough so athletes can perform maximum speed efforts each time.

Rests should be longer for faster (anaerobically trained) athletes — around one to five minutes. While this type of training produces lactic acid, especially in sprinters, it is designed to minimise acid build-up and allow time for it to be removed. As a result of this training, athletes are likely to:

- store more high-energy phosphates and associated enzymes in their muscles, so helping the transfer of energy to the muscle fibres, and
- be able to use more muscle fibres and have better neuromuscular coordination during extreme efforts.

Maximum lactic anaerobic training

A 20–30 second effort will stimulate athletes' lactic anaerobic *power* development, while a 40–75 second effort will develop their capacity to produce lactic anaerobic *energy*. The rest period must be long enough (around

15 minutes for a sprinter and five minutes for a middle-distance athlete) to allow the body to dispose of a large proportion of the lactic acid generated during the effort, so that another high-speed maximum effort can follow.

As a result of this training, athletes are likely to develop higher concentrations of the enzymes that help to produce energy, as well as higher concentrations of lactic acid in the blood (the price to pay for being bigger anaerobic energy producers). Accordingly, sprinters develop greater concentrations of lactic acid in their muscles than middle or long-distance performers, and so need longer recovery periods. Recovery periods should involve very low-intensity aerobic work that will promote the removal of lactic acid from the muscles and the blood.

Lactic tolerance training

This training challenges athletes to continue to work at high to medium intensity as lactic acid is building up in their blood and muscles. Athletes training in this way are likely to become more tolerant of high lactic acidity by using two separate processes. First, they are able to increase their ability to chemically buffer the acid. This occurs when blood concentrations of bicarbonate increase and the bicarbonate combines with the hydrogen ions (the acid) to form water. Second, athletes may possibly adapt by increasing their psychological capacity to continue to work at a higher level of discomfort. Athletes with highly developed lactic anaerobic systems can develop very high lactic acid concentrations in their tissues and blood during extreme efforts. High blood acidity levels can make some athletes feel quite ill after they've completed highly motivated anaerobic exercise, particularly repetitive exercises.

This type of training generally accompanies maximum aerobic training, because it is often associated with a considerable build-up of lactic acid as it uses up glycogen in the muscles. On the other hand, some long-distance athletes may work quite hard aerobically, but accumulate relatively low levels of lactic acid, so the combination of near-maximum aerobic training and tolerance training doesn't always occur. This is especially true in a program of high-volume endurance training in, say, a marathon runner, when glycogen stores may become quite low and so provide little scope for anaerobic energy production and associated lactic tolerance training.

It is important to distinguish between two types of lactic tolerance training.

A. Single-effort-induced tolerance work

In this type of training, the athlete exercises intensively to generate lactic acid during the first part of a single effort, and 'tolerates' it for the remainder of the effort. The athlete works hard to try to resist the tendency to slow down or lose control of technique. An example is an all-out 150 m swim, the last 75 m or so of which occurs as the acidity of the muscle increases, and similarly for the last 200 m of a 600 m run. Athletes doing this training require a long recovery period in order to be able to produce another appropriately intense effort and a repetition of this lactic acid build-up.

B. Multiple-effort-induced tolerance work

This involves a series of repeats that are not as fast, or over as great a distance, as for single-effort tolerance work. The effort is still intense, but athletes accumulate lactic acid and carry it over from one effort to the next, reducing the speed at which they can exercise subsequently.

Both these methods train the muscles to work when they contain high concentrations of lactic acid. Type A is probably more specific to the real race situation, and might well be used more as the competition season approaches, but both should be included in the program to produce the greatest psychological, as well as physiological, adaptation in the athlete. Needless to say, coaches shouldn't use these techniques very frequently, because they require intense work and more recovery time than most other categories of training.

Maximum aerobic training

Athletes using this training method work at near-maximum pace for two to five minutes, depending on their sport's requirements. Those competing in shorter races will usually train over shorter distances for maximum aerobic training. This is because sprinters — and to a certain extent, middle-distance athletes — usually generate more power and reach maximum oxygen uptake more rapidly than more endurance-oriented athletes. (Maximum oxygen uptake, or VO_2 max, is the maximum rate at which the athlete's body can transport and use oxygen.) Sprinters and middle-distance athletes also usually generate more lactic acid at any given work rate. This means that any maximum aerobic session is also likely to be a more significant lactic tolerance session as well in these athletes, and coaches must take care to allow for this.

Two to five minutes is probably ample time for most athletes to stress their aerobic system to the extreme. In my experience, some short to middle-distances athletes can achieve their VO_2 max within just one minute of commencing all-out exercise, but athletes training for longer distances usually need longer.

I said earlier that maximum aerobic training and lactic acid tolerance training often go hand-in-hand. However, the accumulation of lactic acid in maximum aerobic work can be retarded by building up the speed gradually over the distance. This can occur, for instance, in a 400 m 'acceleration' swim, in which the athlete gradually increases speed over the first 300 m, to swim the last 100 m as fast as possible. For a 1200 m run, athletes increase the speed over the first 800 m, with a near all-out final 400 m.

Anaerobic threshold training

The anaerobic threshold is the highest level (usually measured in speed or percentage of VO_2 max) at which athletes can perform before lactic acid accumulation is detected in the bloodstream. This corresponds with an accumulation of hydrogen ions in the muscles, and, in turn, interference with muscle contraction mechanisms that leads to fatigue (see chapter 6, Physiology and Sports Performance, for more information on anaerobic threshold). When athletes exceed this threshold, their bodies are no longer removing lactic acid from their blood at the same rate as it's being produced, so they must slow down (or work at a lower level) in order to restore that equilibrium and avoid exhaustion.

Anaerobic threshold may be a useful concept around which training intensities can be planned, but coaches should be aware that lactic acid is produced during all forms of training, and is even being produced by our bodies as we sit and read this chapter. It is not as though the anaerobic system is switched on at a certain exercise intensity, but more that we have a greater proportional use of anaerobic energy as intensity increases. Lactic acid is often removed (lactate can re-enter the energy production pathways or it can be used for glycogen resynthesis) as fast as it is produced, so that blood measures during low intensity and so-called steady-state exercise give the impression that little or no lactic acid is being generated. The lactic acid concentration of blood corresponding with the anaerobic threshold is around 3–6 millimoles per litre (mmol/L), this level varying from one athlete to the next.

If an athlete has an anaerobic threshold corresponding to a steady whole-blood lactate concentration of, say, 5 mmol/L, then he or she should, in theory, be able to hold this lactate concentration (and the level of exercise at which it is achieved) for around 30 minutes or more. The concentrations of lactic acid that can be tolerated vary enormously from athlete to athlete.

In effect, anaerobic threshold or simply 'threshold' training is high-quality aerobic training without the added stress of excessive anaerobic training. In the well-conditioned athlete who is working steadily, the heart rate is generally within 20 bpm (beats per minute) of maximum heart rate, but it is not in the 'hurtful' zone. This type of training should form a significant part of the programs of middle and, especially, long-distance athletes. Threshold training, in particular, benefits athletes by developing their aerobic system function, especially control of lactic acid accumulation at and around the threshold speed. This speed is often close to race speed for the longer distance athletes, so it is race specific as well. Threshold training benefits athletes in similar ways to maximum aerobic training, but it has the advantage of training the aerobic system without developing large amounts of lactic acid.

While athletes could, in theory, train at close to anaerobic threshold speed for 30 minutes or more, this can be difficult in the middle of a hard week of training. Consequently, coaches often split these training distances to help control lactic acid build-up, or simply to allow a partly fatigued athlete to train close to the desired speed. For example, 1600 m may be swum as eight 200 m legs, with short recoveries of ten seconds between each. The breaks help to control the swimmers' lactic acid concentrations, but athletes will also find it beneficial to complete an occasional unbroken swim, where lactic acid levels must be controlled without the breaks. Coaches of runners sometimes use a similar procedure to split an extended training run into segments, with runners doing a series of, say six 1 km repetitions with a 30-second jog recovery.

A classification of training

Types of training	Heart rate (bpm)	Duration	Maximum blood lactic acid (mmol/L)	Perceived exertion	Typical workout and guide to speed for middle-distance athletes	
					Swimming	Running
Maximum phosphate (alactic) anaerobic	160–180	5–15 s	3–5	Fast but comfortable	10 x 25 m at max training speed for distance, 60–90 s rest between	10 x 75 m at max training speed for distance, 60–90 s rest, jogging, between
Maximum lactic anaerobic	180–190	20–75 s	15–20	Very hard	6 x 125 m at max training speed for distance, 4–5 min rest between	6 x 400 m at max training speed for distance, 4–5 min rest between
Lactic tolerance A	190–200	75–120 s	8–12	Hurtful	6 x 150 m at max training speed for distance, 2–3 min rest between	4 x 600 m at max training speed for distance, 4–6 min rest between
Lactic tolerance B	190–200	60–120 s	6–8	Hurtful	12 x 75 m at 90–95% of max training speed for distance, 20–30 s rest between	6 x 300 m at max training speed for distance, 30 s rest between
Maximum aerobic	190–200	2–5 min	6–10	Hard work	6 x 300 m, build up to max effort over last 100 m, 2–3 min rest between	3 x 1200 m, build up to max speed over last 600 m, 5–7 min rest between
Anaerobic threshold	170–180	15–30 min	3–5	A little uncomfortable	4 x 800 m at close to max training speed for distance, 1 min rest between	3 x 10 min at max training speed for distance, 1 min rest between
Low-intensity aerobic	120–150	5 min–2 hr	1–3	Comfortable	Easy 2000 m	Easy 20–30 km

Training workouts inevitably involve two or more types of training. However, each type of training is distinguished here so that coaches can vary the emphasis on them systematically. While swimming and running have been used as examples, the types apply equally well to sports with similar training principles (for example, rowing, canoeing, skiing and cycling). Note: max(imum) training speed refers to the speed corresponding to the athlete's best effort over the entire set. It differs from an all-out effort or a maximum effort in that the athlete has to control the effort to some degree to enable repetitions at near equivalent speeds. It also differs from personal best race speed in that the athlete is not in a tapered state, and so a maximum training effort will not be as fast.

Low-intensity aerobic training

This is long, slow distance work. It can be used for warm-up or cool-down, or recovery between intense sessions. However, when it is used as a training stimulus, long slow swimming or running is likely to help by enhancing athletes' ability to use fat as fuel and so saving their glycogen supply, and gradually developing strength in connective tissues such as bones, ligaments and tendons. The heart rate is usually 120 to 150 bpm when the athlete is swimming or running in the upper zone of low-intensity aerobic training. The blood lactic acid level is likely to be around 1–3 mmol/L, and sprint athletes usually have higher values than distance athletes, even at very low intensities.

Coaches from different sports can often pick up useful ideas from each other. For example, as a coach of middle-distance and distance runners and a former coach of Australian rules football, I have found the circuit training done routinely by footballers to be a useful inclusion in the weekly program of runners. Such variety of work, involving partner activities, sprints in different directions interspersed by stretching and strength work, all incorporated into a half-hour session, has proved valuable. On the other hand, the swimming practice of starting each repetition at the same time (for example, working on cycles of 100 m swims every two minutes) is useful when transferred to running. It allows runners of different abilities to begin each effort together, although they run at different speeds. This helps novice or less able runners lift their performances, as well as fostering a sense of teamwork.

PRACTICAL METHODS OF ENDURANCE TRAINING

The practical methods of endurance training include:

- long-distance training
- fartlek training
- interval training, and
- time trials.

Using these methods, coaches can ensure that they achieve the right balance of endurance work for each event or sport. In other words, these training methods are the tools with which coaches can implement the types of training outlined in the previous section.

Long-distance training

This can be divided into:

- long easy distance, and
- long solid distance training.

Long easy distance work is relaxed low-intensity training of the aerobic energy system. It is an important part of endurance training, particularly for sportspeople involved in the long endurance events, but also, over shorter distances, for recovery. This training may take from half an hour to three hours for the already well-conditioned sportsperson, and is often best performed in a group of similarly motivated athletes.

Long solid distance work is more stressful, and can be divided into 'constant effort' or 'constant speed' work. In constant effort

(National Sports Information Centre)

To achieve the best performances in rowing events over 1000 to 2000 m, a mix of aerobic and lactic tolerance training is ideal.

training, the heart rate remains relatively stable as the pace is maintained on flat portions and, in the case of cycling, running and skiing, reduced up the hills, and increased down hills. Constant speed work involves easier work on the flat sections, but this pace is maintained as much as possible up hills and emphasises hard hill training.

Fartlek training

Fartlek (from the Swedish for 'speed play') training involves efforts of varying intensity and duration interspersed within a generally relaxed framework of easy running, cycling, skiing or rowing. The session is designed by the participant during the exercise and according to feel, but sometimes the training will be structured to a certain degree. An athlete might pick out a landmark ahead and decide to surge to that point. On other occasions the athlete might just accelerate or ease back whenever he or she chooses. Sometimes there can be a general plan: the athlete might, for instance, have a general theme to put into operation within the fartlek session, such as 'eight hard efforts of around 20 or 30 seconds'.

Fartlek is useful because it reduces the stress of a structured session in which specific targets are attempted. The session can then be very strenuous or relatively easy, depending on the general wellbeing of the athlete. While coaches can give general instructions, athletes should control fartlek training. They can then substitute a fartlek session for a session on the track or in the pool, to facilitate recovery if they are beginning to feel a little 'flat' during an intensive period of structured training. At the beginning of the training build-up, fartlek is useful for introducing speed work before the structured and more precisely controlled work starts.

Interval training

Interval training involves efforts of varying intensity interspersed with recovery periods of different lengths. It is usually distinguished from repetition training, which involves a more complete recovery period, but here repetition training is treated as a subset of interval training.

Interval training is the basic working tool for the coach, because it is so versatile that it can involve all the types of training discussed above. The way athletes use the energy systems can be manipulated by varying the length and intensity of the effort, the length of recovery time, the type of recovery, the number of repetitions, the number of sets of repetitions, and the frequency of these sessions per week.

Some examples of interval training sessions designed to meet the requirements of each of the types of training are set out for running and swimming in the table earlier in this chapter. Coaches must use knowledge of the energy requirements of the event, and the fitness and stage of development of athletes, in designing workouts. An example might be a 200 m swimmer whose current requirements are:

- maximum aerobic training
- anaerobic threshold training, and
- lactic tolerance B training.

For maximum aerobic interval training, the coach could use six 300 m swims, building up in the first 100 m, swimming strongly for the middle 100 m, with an all-out effort for the last 100 m. The athlete recovers with a very relaxed 100 m. The build-up prevents early accumulation of excessive lactic acid in the muscles, and the 300 m distance is enough to enable the athlete to achieve VO_2 max. This assumes that the swimmer is well prepared and has recovered from prior training. The active recovery facilitates the dispersal of much of the lactic acid from the muscles before the next effort.

An example of anaerobic threshold interval training is a set of four 600 m swims at a speed that is around the swimmer's fastest *over 2000 m* in a tapered state (in the classification of training table I have referred to this as 'max training speed', as a swimmer in the middle of hard training is likely to have to work very hard to swim consistently at threshold speed in repeated efforts with short rests). The recovery should be long enough to enable this speed to be repeated: for a well-conditioned swimmer, one minute should be enough. As a swimmer's aerobic fitness level increases, so will the threshold speed.

An example of a lactic acid tolerance B interval session for a swimmer is 20 x 50 m at about 90% of maximum training effort, with 30 seconds' recovery at the end of the pool or 25 m active recovery. In this session the lactic acid accumulates in the muscle and blood during each effort. The recovery period is only long enough to allow partial removal of lactic acid, so that each later work period becomes progressively more difficult as lactic acid builds up, but not excessively so.

Time trials

If athletes can improve the power and/or capacity of each or some of the components specific to their event, then they can also perform better in their events. For example, 5000 m runners may use maximum aerobic work, anaerobic threshold work, tolerance work and even alactic speed work as components of their programs, but certain physiological and psychological adaptations are necessary to put all these improvements together for the actual event. This can be done with a time trial, in which an athlete runs as fast as possible over a distance usually similar to, but sometimes not the same as, the official race distance (athletes often like to preserve their efforts over the actual race distance for the real competitions).

This is very demanding work, and the athletes should be thoroughly prepared and partially tapered to meet such demands. It can often help to have other runners pace the athlete for part of the time trial, or at least offer encouragement and race like conditions. Running at the over-threshold pace required of such a trial bridges the gap between normal training and racing. However, the absence of race tactics and the psychological stresses to be found in important races distinguishes the latter from time trialling. For this reason, athletes performing in an important meet after a long spell from competition should always be given preparatory races, and if these are not available then time trials simulating races are essential.

There are many different combinations of training that will lead to success for any individual. This is illustrated by two of Australia's finest ever marathon runners, Lisa Ondieki and Nickey Carroll. Lisa emerged from a background of 400 m junior hurdling, while Nickey, following a junior career in tennis, tried ultra-marathons and then marathons.

The differences in their backgrounds showed in their training. Lisa enjoyed carefully timed interval training on the track, whereas Nickey prefers to do all her training, including her interval work, off the track in the forests, and has little interest in precise measures of her speed. Nevertheless, both athletes followed the basic principles of completing long runs each week, as well as shorter and longer interval work. Both recognised the importance of increasing their endurance as well as their threshold speed.

(National Sports Information Centre)

Lisa Ondieki

ENDURANCE TRAINING FOR TEAM SPORTS

Energy considerations

In preparation for the more vigorous team sports, aerobic endurance training forms the basis of fitness work. The aerobic system is the energy system most easily influenced by training, as it can be modified more than the anaerobic system. Further, aerobic endurance is important in most team sports, especially in those sports or positions of play that require continuous high levels of energy output.

Aerobic endurance is also a very important attribute of the player who relies on intermittent energy bursts interspersed with active recovery periods, because the rate of recovery depends, in part, on the aerobic system (to remove lactic acid). In the highly active team sports, repeated high-speed efforts also need anaerobic energy. This is produced predominantly by the phosphate (or alactic) system (where efforts of just a few seconds are required).

The lactic anaerobic endurance level may also be occasionally tested when athletes are asked for second and third efforts in quick succession. Generally speaking, the type of endurance required for repeated short efforts comes from the ability to tolerate the increase in muscular and blood acidity, which can be developed in training similar to the lactic tolerance B training. So endurance for team sports must develop the aerobic system, as well as the phosphate anaerobic and lactic tolerance systems.

In the 1970s, the Western Australian Sheffield Shield cricket team instigated a well-constructed fitness program and achieved considerable success on the field. Apart from their superior physical fitness, some of their success may have resulted from the psychological advantage of knowing that they were more professionally prepared than their competitors. The Victorians took note of this in the late 70s and they too enjoyed success at that time.

Now, all Australian teams recognise the value of being in good physical condition, and this is one of the reasons that the Australian test team is one of the finest ever. Team members have sufficient endurance and specific fitness to ensure that their skills do not deteriorate in times of physical challenges, such as longer innings, bowling spells and fielding time, particularly on hot days.

(National Sports Information Centre)

Team sports require aerobic endurance to produce energy and assist recovery.

Practical methods of endurance training for team sports

There is room in every team player's program for some distance, fartlek and interval training, and these methods are best introduced in this order. The distance work is essential to prepare the body for some of the more specific work to follow and it is important to increase the training load progressively (for more information on this see chapter 9, Principles of Training).

Fartlek work is useful in the pre-season preparation of team players, and has its place in season as well. The players can be grouped according to their levels of aerobic fitness. Athletes also appreciate a choice of training venues, and a forest or beach can be a welcome relief from the competition arena. Fartlek can be used as a forerunner to the more specific stages of training.

Interval training is the most important method of endurance training for ball game players, because it can be structured to meet the requirements of the particular stage of training and the specific requirements of the sport. Following longer periods of steady running and fartlek running, interval training provides a new, more formal dimension to training, as times are recorded and players become more aware of their relative fitness levels. Typical interval workouts for a soccer player might be:

- ten 300 m sprints, with a two-minute, very slow jog recovery. This type of session can be performed at speeds that engage the aerobic system predominantly (with only moderate lactic acid accumulation), but the rest periods mean that the athletes can run faster than they would if they were exercising continuously. The session is therefore more specific to the actual game than a longer slower run. Faster aerobic work of this type is certainly recommended, and this type of session is important in developing the ability to tolerate and remove the moderate levels of lactic acid that have been produced in the muscle. Other sessions might include:

- 16 x 200 m sprints with a one-minute jog recovery (the speed is such that quality can be maintained fairly well as the set progresses. Consequently this session is, again, to a large degree aerobic, with anaerobic and tolerance features, and at a speed more specific to the game than a long slow run.)

- 25 x 100 m sprints with a 45-second jog recovery (lactic acid accumulation can be avoided if the speed is kept well under control), or

- 30 x 50 m sprints at maximum speed with a 60-second jog recovery. The emphasis here is on phosphate or alactic anaerobic endurance and the ability to repeat such efforts. This type of training also partly uses the lactic anaerobic system, however, and even an aerobically well-conditioned athlete will accumulate lactic acid as the session progresses. Recovery time in this session can be adjusted to prevent athletes accumulating excessive lactic acid and losing speed.

It is obvious that, by varying the duration, speed, recovery and time, coaches can develop an infinite variety of interval training workouts, according to the athletes' stages of training and the requirements of the sport.

Interval skill drills, modified games and practice matches

Those players and coaches who have participated in pre-season training without specific ball drills and simulated games know that running on its own can't give athletes adequate match fitness. For this reason it is essential that specific drills, modified competition, and finally match practice are all used in preparing for the first competitive game. By using these techniques, the specific muscle group coordination involved in twisting, turning and making bodily contact can be introduced gradually.

The astute coach can then continue with forms of interval training, working on the energy systems by manipulating aspects of the drill, for example, the number of players in the drill, its duration and the area in which the drill is performed. When, for example, a three-minute handball drill in Australian rules football is conducted in an area of 20 by 20 m, it will provide predominantly alactic work, short and sharp. A similar drill in a 30 by 30 m area, when the receiver of the ball must run at least 10 m with one bounce, adds a different dimension to the exercise, and has the potential to deploy more aerobic and lactic anaerobic energy.

Coaches of high-energy team sports should be careful not to overstress players with lactic anaerobic efforts. Excessive training that increases acidity in the muscles and blood can lead to overtraining symptoms and possibly illness or injury (see chapter 9, Principles of Training, for more information on the symptoms of overtraining). Experienced players are unlikely to allow themselves to develop high

(National Sports Information Centre)

Team sports players can benefit from interval training.

levels of lactic acid in most ball games, because they know that this will probably detract from their skill and ability to play consistently throughout the full course of the game.

OTHER TRAINING CONSIDERATIONS

High-volume training

Coaches who ask all athletes to participate in a long high-volume aerobic build-up before a more specific training phase can risk limiting the athletes' anaerobic capacity. This is probably because some of the fast-twitch muscle fibres, those that respond quicker and with greater force (see chapter 6, Physiology and Sports Performance, for more information on muscle fibres), may adapt to such training by increasing their ability to produce aerobic energy at the expense of anaerobic power. While this may be good for endurance athletes, too much emphasis on high-volume endurance training may compromise the explosive speed of the fastest athletes. The coach may or may not want this outcome.

Swimmers or middle-distance runners approaching the pre-competition phase of their program may have a lower anaerobic fitness level than they do at the beginning of the high-volume aerobic training because of this effect. Given that anaerobic capacity improvements are important for the success of these athletes, coaches must ensure that training that occurs just before competition retrains the anaerobic system to the required standard.

A young swimmer was very disappointed to miss selection in the Australian team because she finished third in the trials. Her time was well below her best, which was even more disappointing considering she had put much more effort and dedication into her training over the last year.

The Australian team went away without her and, being quite despondent about her 'failure', she did not train at all for two weeks. Then she was asked to race in a local meet, and reluctantly agreed. When she began to warm up she felt a lot better than she expected, so she decided to try to swim as fast as she could in the race, just for fun. To everyone's amazement, she swam faster than she did in the trials, and fast enough to have earned a place in the Australian team, had she managed it in the trials. The lesson she learned was that, after a very long build-up of endurance work and high-intensity training, the pre-competition and taper periods may also need to be longer.

Coaches should remember that high-quality training sessions can also be compromised if the athlete is trained too intensely or too long beforehand. Residual fatigue and inadequate recovery may prevent the athlete from exercising hard enough and contributing enough anaerobic work to the training effort.

Adaptation to endurance training is often more difficult for the developing athlete than it is for an athlete with a large training base. Regan, a promising 16-year-old rower in his school's senior eight crew, told his coach that he was feeling tired all the time. The coach had introduced a daily monitoring procedure for his rowers and he could see that Regan's morning resting heart rate had climbed to ten beats above his normal resting state, and that he was experiencing poor sleep.

The coach wanted to keep Regan training with the team, as they had an important regatta in four weeks, but Regan began to lose weight rapidly, and lost 2 kg in three days. This was the result of training hard, studying for year 11 exams at the same time, and having a growing body that could not cope with all of these demands at once. Regan may have exhausted his glycogen supplies, and may have also been partially dehydrated.

The coach wisely took heed of the set of warning signs and rested Regan for three to four days until his resting heart rate returned to normal, his weight had stabilised and his sleep quality had improved. Then he implemented a graded active recovery program, starting with a light training load at 20% of effort, then building up to 80% over the next ten days. Regan recovered well enough to undertake all the training sessions for the last week before the regatta, and compete successfully without experiencing any illness or injury.

Environmental influences

Since the 1968 Olympic Games were held in Mexico City at an altitude of 2350 m, sports scientists have tried to answer the seemingly simple question of whether training at medium altitude for periods of a few weeks produces better sea-level performances in middle and long-distance events. Amazingly, and despite many studies, the answer is still unclear.

Many athletes who normally don't live at altitude have performed exceptionally well after training at moderate altitude for periods of three to four weeks. However, many other elite athletes who have not trained at altitude have also performed very successfully. Exposure to reduced ambient air oxygen levels over long periods stimulates non-athletes' bodies to make more red cells.

Scientists agree that, if they could show that athletes who did short-term altitude training also produced more red blood cells, it would be very strong evidence that altitude training benefits sea-level endurance performance. However, the majority of published studies involving elite athletes have not yet shown that altitude training increases the number of red blood cells in highly trained athletes.

What does seem to be emerging is that the regime of 'living high — training low' (that is, sleeping and living at higher altitudes and training at lower altitudes) seems to be more effective than living and training continually at altitude. The 'live high — train low' regime allows the athletes to train normally, with the full quota of atmospheric oxygen, while gaining advantage from sleeping in hypoxic (low oxygen) conditions. But is there an advantage for elite athletes who then compete at sea-level venues?

Recently, some laboratories (including the Australian Institute of Sport's [AIS] physiology group) have suggested that any advantage for athletes might relate to their increased ability to buffer lactic acid after the 'live high — train low' regime. The AIS group used motel-like sleeping quarters with a lowered oxygen concentration (the Altitude House), but the athletes trained outside in normal conditions during the day. In my opinion, the jury is still out on the benefits of altitude training for elite athletes. However, there seems little doubt that training in a pristine mountain environment, with a highly motivated group of fellow athletes, can add a valuable dimension to training, whether or not it gives athletes other advantages.

The scientific evidence in support of heat acclimatisation for competition in hot conditions is very clear. Endurance athletes are at a serious disadvantage in hot or humid conditions if they do not allow themselves time to adjust. Unless this occurs, they will not sweat as easily during exercise and will therefore run the risk of overheating. There are also other physical adaptations and certainly psychological adaptations that occur to allow an athlete to perform well in the heat.

The scientific evidence suggests that it only takes ten days of regular training in the heat to improve the sweating response and stabilise the circulatory adaptations (see chapter 17, Medical Considerations in Sport,

for more information on preventing heat problems in athletes). Coaches should ensure that they allow time for this to occur before competition, but also bear in mind that training in hot and humid conditions before competition can also be too prolonged. The acclimatisation process is very much an individual concern, which shows how important it is for coaches and athletes to value individual experience when planning training.

CONCLUSION

With careful planning, coaches can ensure that endurance athletes are properly prepared in each stage of their training program. By considering which combination of the energy systems they want to develop at each stage, and by referring to the principles and examples of training outlined in this chapter, they can develop the optimal combination of power and capacity for specific endurance performance.

COACHING TIPS

- Include endurance training in the preparation phase for most sports.
- Consider the physical requirements of the sport and the needs of the individual athlete to determine the types and methods of endurance training used.
- Make endurance training less boring by varying the training venue, incorporating group activities and including skill work where appropriate.
- Structure interval training for teams to mimic the specific endurance requirements of their sport.
- Carefully monitor young athletes' adaptations to endurance training.

FURTHER READING

Hawley, JA, and L Burke (1998) *Peak Performance: Training and Nutritional Strategies for Sport*. St Leonards: Allen and Unwin.

Martin, DE, and PN Coe (1997) *Better Training for Distance Runners*. Champaign, IL: Human Kinetics.

Shephard, RJ, and PO Astrand (eds) (1992) *Endurance in Sport*. Oxford, UK: Blackwell Scientific Publications.

CHAPTER 11
SPEED, STRENGTH AND POWER TRAINING

Warren Young

(National Sports Information Centre)

INTRODUCTION

Speed, strength, power are important for the movements necessary in many sports. For example, the speed and power produced by the muscles significantly contribute to success in sprinting, jumping, throwing, hitting, kicking and punching movements.

In the past decade tremendous advancements have been made in the understanding and application of the training required to develop speed, strength and power. Weight training is now used in many sports, and strength and conditioning has emerged as a growing profession. Today many coaches use strength and conditioning specialists to help with the physical preparation of athletes. However, not everyone has access to such assistance, and so all coaches should have a sound background in designing conditioning programs.

Coaches must ensure that they and their athletes are appropriately experienced before undertaking weight training and other speed, strength and power activities. Athletes must have appropriate levels of fitness to undertake specific activities, and they must be taught to use safe and correct techniques.

DEFINITIONS

Speed

Speed is the distance travelled divided by the time taken to travel it, so the shorter the time taken to cover the distance, the greater the speed of the movement. Some sports' actions require very fast movements of limbs, such as punching in combat sports, while others involve total body speed, such as sprinting. The following discussion will focus on running speed — important in many sports — but the same principles apply to the speed of body parts (arms or legs, for instance).

There are four types of running speed.

- maximum speed
- acceleration speed
- speed–endurance, and
- change-of-direction speed.

Maximum speed

Maximum speed is the highest speed an athlete can reach. Most do so after 30 to 60 m of straight sprinting from a stationary start, and in a shorter distance if they start from a running start. Maximum speed is relevant to many track and field events, such as sprints, hurdles and horizontal jumps, and to field sports, such as football and soccer.

(Duane Hart/sportingimages.com.au)

Sprinters must have good maximum and acceleration speeds.

Acceleration speed

In sports that require relatively short sprints (that is, less than 30 m) from a stationary start, the athletes don't reach maximum speed, and so their **acceleration speed** or ability to increase speed rapidly is more important. This applies to most team sports and especially sports such as netball, basketball or tennis, where the play takes place in a relatively confined area.

Speed–endurance

Speed–endurance is athletes' ability to sustain maximum or near-maximum speed and withstand the effects of fatigue. It is important when either sprints are relatively long (for example, greater than 60 m), or when the rest interval between sprints isn't long enough for

the athlete to replenish energy stores. The 200 and 400 m sprint events are typical examples of long sprints, whereas repeated sprints with less than a minute's recovery are common in many team sports.

Change-of-direction speed

While track events involve sprinting in a straight line, many team sports require rapid changes of direction, either to evade or chase an opponent. The ability to change direction at high speed in team sports or racquet sports is very complex and can be thought of as **agility**. Agility performance is influenced by many perceptual and motor performance factors, including **change-of-direction speed**, which is discussed here.

Strength

The strength of a muscle group can take two forms:

- maximum strength and
- strength–endurance.

Maximum strength

Maximum strength is the maximum force that can be generated by a muscle group. It can be either absolute maximum strength or relative maximum strength. **Absolute strength** refers to the maximum force produced or the maximum weight that can be lifted, and **relative strength** refers to strength relative to the body weight of the athlete (absolute strength divided by body weight).

In the example depicted on the next page, the shot-putter has the greater absolute strength, but the high jumper has the greater relative strength, because of his or her smaller body weight. This is to be expected, since the main resistance to the throw in the shot-put is the weight of the shot, but high jumpers must project their whole bodies into the air.

The relative importance of types of speed

	Maximum speed	Acceleration speed	Speed— endurance	Change-of-direction speed
Tennis	1	3	NA	3
Basketball	1	3	2	3
Rugby	3	3	3	3
100 m sprint	3	3	2	NA
400 m sprint	3	2	3	NA

The relative importance of each of the four types of speed is rated on a three-point scale: 3 = very important, 2 = some importance, 1 = minor importance and NA = not applicable.

Absolute and relative maximum strength for two athletes

	Shot-putter	High jumper
Maximum weight lifted in half squat (kg)	250	200
Body weight (kg)	100	72
Absolute maximum strength (kg)	250	200
Relative maximum strength	2.5	2.78

Strength–endurance

When a high level of muscular force must be applied for a relatively long time under conditions of fatigue, **strength–endurance** (or muscular endurance) is the important quality. For example, in rowing in the single scull, the force applied to the oar handle is around 40–50% of maximum strength, and has to be sustained for several minutes, so both strength and endurance are necessary. Strength–endurance is also important in wrestling, where an athlete may have to sustain a forceful hold for a long time.

Power

Power is the rate of performing work (or force multiplied by speed). Since strength refers to the maximum force produced, power can also be described as strength multiplied by speed, so a powerful or explosive movement is one that involves relatively fast and forceful actions. **Reactive strength** is the ability to quickly change from an eccentric muscle action (when the muscle lengthens or stretches) to a concentric muscle action (when the muscle shortens). Athletes with reactive strength can react quickly as their muscles stretch, so they can quickly shorten them to propel the body in the desired direction.

A good example of reactive strength is the jump to spike in volleyball. After the short approach run, the legs are planted to begin the take-off. Flexion (a decrease in the angle of the joint) occurs at the hips, knees and ankles as the body descends. During this time, the leg extensor muscles (gluteals, hamstrings, quadriceps and calves) stretch or lengthen and therefore contract eccentrically. Then the same muscles begin to shorten or contract concentrically, causing the legs to extend and the body to rise. This eccentric–concentric or **stretch–shortening cycle** (SSC) of muscle use is typical of jumping and many other sports movements.

Power–endurance

Power–endurance allows athletes to sustain powerful contractions or maintain power output when fatigued. Sprint cycling or a 100 m swimming event are examples of sports that need power–endurance.

(Duane Hart/sportingimages.com.au)

High jumpers have greater relative strength than many other athletes because they have to launch their whole bodies into the air.

RELATIONSHIPS BETWEEN SPEED, STRENGTH AND POWER

Speed qualities

Athletes can be relatively good at acceleration speed, but not at reaching a high maximum speed or at speed–endurance. Athletes trained in straight sprinting do not necessarily use their sprinting speed when they need change-of-direction speed or agility in team sports. Conversely, the players that appear fast on field are not always the best athletes in straight-line sprints.

Maximum strength and strength–endurance

The greater the resistance (the force that must be overcome to achieve the movement) encountered by athletes in a sport, the greater the contribution their maximum strength makes to their strength–endurance. For example, if a rowing stroke requires a force that is 40% of the rower's maximum strength, then maximum strength also significantly influences that athlete's strength–endurance performance. If the force requirement of the sport was only 25% of maximum, training for maximum strength to develop strength–endurance would be less important.

In this example, both rowers apply the same proportion of maximum strength to the oar (40%), which causes an equal rate of fa-

Differences in the strength of rowers (in kg)	Rower A	Rower B
Absolute maximum strength in rowing position	250	150
Average force exerted on oar per stroke (40% of max)	100	60

tigue. If both athletes have the same stroke distance and complete the same number of strokes in the race, because rower A produces the greater force, he will also produce more total work (force x stroke distance), and therefore have the advantage in performance.

Power, reactive strength and power endurance

Since power is strength (force) multiplied by speed, both factors contribute to power output. However, when the external resistance is relatively high, the resulting movement is relatively slow and large muscular forces can be produced. In this case, strength contributes more to the power output than does speed. Conversely, a relatively light resistance can be moved faster, but with less force, and therefore this activity can be said to be speed-dominated.

(Warren Young)

Elite lightweight rowers applying maximum strength to the oars

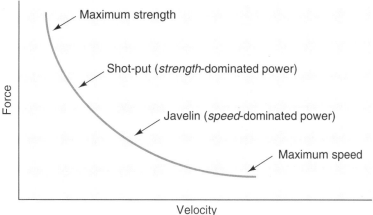

The relationship between force and velocity in a muscular effort

The shot-put event is an example of **strength-dominated power**, since shots weigh 4 or 7.26 kg, and are thrown at a velocity of no more than 15 m/s, but the javelin throw is an example of **speed-dominated power**, because javelins weigh 600 or 800 g and can be thrown at around 30 m/s.

The relationship between power and reactive strength was discussed earlier. While it is possible for an athlete to possess similar levels of each, they are different and are developed differently in training.

There are many complex relationships between all these physical qualities. An athlete with a high level of one quality won't necessarily have a high level of another, probably because they are influenced by different neuromuscular and biomechanical mechanisms. There are two important practical applications of the relationships between the qualities.

1. Because they are so specific, training to develop one quality will not necessarily be useful in developing another. Coaches must understand the relative importance of the various strength qualities in their sports, so they know how much emphasis to place on training them. If they train athletes for power, for example, but their sport is more influenced by reactive strength, they won't achieve the best results.

2. Because there is sometimes a strong connection between, for example, strength, power and strength–endurance, training can be organised so that some qualities are trained to serve as a base for the development of others. Because strength is a part of power, maximum strength is usually developed by coaches before power and reactive strength, which in turn provide a base from which to develop the speed qualities.

TRAINING METHODS FOR SPEED, STRENGTH AND POWER

Speed

Maximum speed is best developed by reducing the training emphasis on the acceleration phase, and using a 'flying' start. For example, speed is gradually built up over 30–50 m and, when maximum speed is reached, it is held for a short distance, such as 20 m. Maximum running speed equals stride length (m) multiplied by stride frequency (strides/s), which are not only influenced by the neuromuscular qualities of the working muscles, but also by technique.

Training for maximum speed should include technical drills to achieve increases in stride length and frequency. Examples include running slowly with a high knee lift (thigh horizontal or higher) to develop stride length, and the performance of 'butt' kicks to improve leg recovery speed and the development of stride frequency.

Acceleration speed is developed by isolating the characteristics of the acceleration phase in sprinting. This includes maximum effort running from a stationary position, either standing or a crouch, or from a slow walk over relatively short distances. An important feature of acceleration running is a distinct forward lean, which encourages a backward pushing movement of the legs. This action can be encouraged by sprinting against a substantial resistance (see resisted sprinting on the next page).

Both acceleration speed and maximum speed training should be performed in an unfatigued state (that is, before other training), and fatigue should be avoided throughout the session to allow the nervous system to operate at its best. Coaches can check whether athletes are making a *complete* recovery between sprints by monitoring whether they can maintain times from one repetition to the next. Coaches often make a mistake in team sports training by allowing athletes to sprint in a fatigued state, either because they didn't have enough rest or because they were sprinting at the end of a long training session. This can interfere with the development of acceleration or maximum speed.

An Australian rules football coach wanted to train athletes' maximum speed, but couldn't afford the time to perform ten 20 m flying sprints with several minutes' rest between efforts. He solved the problem by incorporating some non-fatiguing drills between sprints (for example, handball or kicking for accuracy). These activities didn't interfere with the sprint training and helped to make good use of training time.

Resisted and assisted sprinting

Using resistance with sprinting (**resisted sprinting**) allows more force and power to be produced than training with no resistance. An athlete can add resistance during running by:

- towing a sled along the ground
- towing a parachute that produces air resistance
- running up a hill or stairs, or
- wearing a weighted vest or belt.

When considering which of these methods to use, coaches should give thought to the nature of the resistance. For example, pulling a sled involves a resistance that is essentially horizontal, but a weighted vest resists the vertical motion of the body. While the first method resists the pushing movement of the driving leg, the second would increase the stretch load placed on the leg extensor muscles when the foot strikes the ground, and target reactive strength.

Assisted sprinting is any method that assists the forward motion of the runner and allows the athlete to move faster than is normally possible. The purpose of this training is to attempt to break an individual's maximum 'speed barrier', by forcing the neuromuscular system to fire at levels not possible with previous maximum efforts. This overspeed sprinting can help athletes achieve significant increases in stride frequency and in the speed at which the nerves fire in the leg muscles. An athlete can be assisted by:

- being towed by a partner attached to an elastic or inelastic cord
- sprinting on a treadmill
- running with an assisting wind, or
- sprinting down a slight decline (approximately 2°).

(Duane Hart/sportingimages.com.au)

Rugby league players accelerating to their maximum speed

Enough assistance should be provided to increase speed by only up to 5%, but in practice this can be very difficult to control. Excessive speed increases may lead to:

- an increased risk of injury resulting from the higher stresses placed on the musculoskeletal system, or from accidents, and
- significant changes to sprinting technique, such as overstriding, which could negatively affect performance.

Coaches should restrict assisted training to athletes with more than one year's experience in sprint training, and should use these techniques only at low volume, such as one session per week.

Speed–endurance training involves athletes in maximum or near maximum sprints that are either long, with several minutes recovery, or short, with correspondingly shorter rests between efforts. The first approach would be suitable for a 200 or 400 m runner, while the second would be more specific to the demands of many team sports. Both methods require athletes to sprint in a fatigued state. Note that a combination of these speed training methods could be used to perform up to four sessions in a training week.

Athletes can develop change-of-direction speed by running as fast as possible while changing direction in ways similar to the way they do while playing their sport. All relevant directions should be included, so the athlete doesn't develop any weaknesses. The signal to change direction can be initiated by either reaching an obstacle, such as a cone or another player, or by a visual or sound signal from the coach. Players should notice how they decelerate, accelerate and position their bodies to achieve quick movements.

Since the running techniques for straight sprinting and change-of-direction sprinting are different, the drills used to encourage the development of stride length, such as high knee lifting, are not suitable for change-of-direction speed. Sports equipment and decision-making drills can also be introduced to simulate game conditions and improve overall agility.

Strength

Maximum strength

There are two distinct training methods for developing absolute maximum strength:

- **hypertrophy**, which increases the size or cross-sectional area of the muscles, and
- **neural methods**, which are designed to increase the capacity of the nervous system to activate the existing muscles.

Although more muscle generally equates to greater strength, it will also usually produce an increase in body weight, so coaches must ask themselves whether athletes can afford to gain body weight. If the athletes have reached the optimum weight for their sport or have trouble 'making weight' in sports involving weight divisions, the answer will be no. In this case, hypertrophy methods should *not* be used. If an increase in muscle mass and weight is desirable, as it is in a developing junior footballer, hypertrophy methods can be used.

If relative maximum strength is more important and an increase in body weight is not desirable, neural methods should be used. **Extensive** (higher repetitions, lower weight) and **intensive** (lower repetitions, higher weight) hypertrophy methods should be used for strength–endurance and power sports respectively, because they develop different sorts of muscle fibres. Slow-twitch fibres are well suited to resisting fatigue, but develop force relatively slowly, and fast-twitch fibres contract relatively fast and so are advantageous for power sports (see chapter 6, Physiology and Sports Performance, for more information on muscle fibre types).

Neuromuscular fatigue is acceptable for hypertrophy training, but should be avoided

Program variables for training acceleration speed, maximum speed and speed–endurance

	Maximum speed	Acceleration speed	Speed–endurance	
Intensity	95–105%	100%	95–100%	
Interval length	10–20 m	5–30 m	20–30 m	120–300 m
Rest between intervals	Complete (3 min +)	Complete (3 min+)	30–90 s	5–8 min
Start method	Flying	Stationary, slow walk	Not applicable	
Base qualities	Power and aerobic	Strength and aerobic	Speed and aerobic	
Frequency (sessions/week)	2	2–3	2–3	

Program guidelines for training maximum strength

	Hypertrophy	Neural	
	Extensive	Intensive	
Sets	3 +	3 +	3 +
Repetitions	12–20	6–10	2–6
Load (RM*)	12–20	6–10	2–6
Rest interval (min)	2	2–3	Complete (3+)
Frequency (sessions/week)	2–3	2–3	2–3
Duration of program (weeks)	4–5	3–4	2–4
Developments produced	Increase in size of slow-twitch fibres (mainly)	Increase in size of fast-twitch fibres (mainly)	Neural with minimal growth in muscle size
Example of application	Absolute strength for heavyweight rower	Absolute strength for shot-putter	Relative strength for sprinter

*RM means 'repetition maximum'. A 10 RM load means a weight that can only be lifted 10 times and no more. A 20 RM load can only be lifted 20 times, and so on.

with neural methods. One way coaches can minimise fatigue is by organising exercises in their programs so there aren't consecutive exercises that involve the same muscle group.

Peripheral neural fatigue from either neuromuscular or hypertrophy training can last several hours and result in a marked reduction in power output the following day. Underwater massaging of the fatigued muscle groups speeds up recovery from this sort of fatigue. The Australian Institute of Sport netball squad uses a spa and contrast plunge pool after such sessions to help recovery. As the squad trains at least twice a day, it is important that its members recover well, so they can train hard at each session.

The athletes start with three minutes in a warm spa (39–40°C) with the water jets massaging large muscle groups of the thighs, buttocks, and lower legs. Then their bodies are submerged up to the neck in a cold plunge pool (10°C) for 30 seconds. The whole process is repeated three to five times. Light massaging techniques, such as the jostling or shaking of large muscle groups, can be done in the spa.

Strength–endurance and power–endurance methods

There are four conditioning modes suitable for training strength–endurance and power–endurance:

- own-body weight exercises
- weight training
- circuit training, and
- resisted sports movements.

Since very heavy weights are not needed for strength and power–endurance training, these qualities can be trained with **own-body weight** exercises, such as push-ups. The advantage of using body weight as the resistance is that little or no extra equipment is required and training can be conducted almost anywhere. However, the disadvantages are:

- the resistance cannot be precisely set, progressively increased or measured. For example, a relatively large number of repetitions must be performed to achieve a strength–endurance effect. Many developing athletes would be unable to achieve this in an exercise such as a chin-up, and
- the choice of exercises is limited.

As a mode of conditioning, weight training generally does not suffer from these drawbacks. **Circuit training** is a system in which athletes use their own body weight, and/or weights, to develop strength/power–endurance. They perform one set of an exercise, then have a brief rest, then perform a set of a different exercise. This procedure is continued until one set of several exercises has been performed, which is one circuit, and the entire circuit is then repeated.

Athletes can induce fatigue of the muscles by performing a relatively high number of repetitions, such as 30 or 40 seconds of work, and/or by performing consecutive exercises involving the same muscle group. An advantage of circuit training is that a relatively large group of athletes can be trained at one time and it is time-efficient.

Another way to train for strength/power–endurance is to perform the sports movement with added resistance, but to execute a high number of repetitions to produce muscular fatigue.

Program guidelines for strength–endurance or power–endurance training

Sets	2 +
Repetitions	30–50
Load (RM)	30–50
Rest between sets (min)	0.5–2
Frequency (sessions per week)	2–4

Two ways a rower can train for strength–endurance are by performing three to four sets of 30 repetitions with a two-minute rest between sets using:

- weight training, for example, seated row and leg press, and

- power strokes in the boat, for example, by using a tube to add water resistance to the boat.

The obvious advantages of the on-water training method are its specificity to the sport and the convenience of training with little equipment at the usual training venue. The advantage of the weight training exercises is that they fatigue specific muscles, such as those in the upper body, that can't be worked as intensively in the boat. The optimum development might be achieved by using a combination of both methods.

Power

Weight training

Weight training can be classified as either heavy or light-load training.

The heavy method is similar to weight training for maximum strength, except that it emphasises attempting to move the weight as fast as possible during the concentric or raising phase of the lift. Although the heavy load doesn't allow the bar to move very fast, this strategy is used to generate a high nerve input to the working muscles, so that the relevant nerves learn to activate these muscles more quickly. For example, if the squat exercise was being performed, the bar would be lowered under control until the bottom position was reached and the athlete would then attempt to raise it as fast as possible, until the body was fully extended.

The light method uses a load of around 30% of maximum strength, because this allows a greater bar speed and is roughly the load that will generate the highest mechanical power output. Some exercises are explosive by their nature, whichever power development method is used. For example, the power clean and power snatch, which are adaptations of the Olympic weight-lifting lifts, must be performed explosively because of the need to generate enough vertical bar momentum to complete the lifts. Exercises involving jumping or throwing are also explosive, especially if the distance jumped or thrown is monitored.

Explosive weight-lifting

(Duane Hart/sportingimages.com.au)

Heavy and light-load weight training methods for power development

	Heavy	Light
Sets	3–6	3–6
Repetitions	2–5	5–8
Load	2–5 RM	30% 1 RM
Rest between sets	Complete	Complete
Tempo	Explosive concentric	Explosive concentric
Choice of exercise	Explosive by nature	Explosive by nature
Frequency (sessions per week)	2–3	2–3
Physiological objective	Nerves learn to activate muscles more quickly	Mechanical power output is increased

Both weight training methods have advantages and disadvantages, which the coach must weigh up when prescribing power training. The heavy-load method may be more appropriate for the development of strength-dominated power, and the light-load method might be more suitable for training speed-dominated power. Lifting a heavy load in an explosive way causes very high muscle forces and may increase the risk of injury, so this method is more appropriate for athletes with strength training experience.

The major weakness of the light method is a large deceleration phase as the weight is raised. For example, in the bench press, if a high bar speed is generated early in the lift, the bar will also have to be quickly slowed down (decelerated) in order to bring the bar to a stop. The slowing down of the bar is achieved by 'switching off' the muscles and allowing the bar's momentum to complete the lift. As this can occur quite early in the lift, the muscles are not overloaded effectively for much of the range of motion. Many of the non-weight training methods overcome this problem.

Non-weight training

While weight training is quite versatile, it is very difficult to simulate sports movements in the weight room. Non-weight training methods are often included to make the exercise more specific to the athlete's sport and include those listed in the table below.

When extra resistance is added to any sports movement, the athlete's motion will be altered to some extent. Coaches must monitor the technique used by athletes with these methods to ensure that they don't learn faulty movement patterns as a result. This can be achieved by:

- adding only enough resistance to help training, but not enough to interfere with technique
- limiting the amount of this type of training, so that it makes up a relatively small proportion of the total training, and
- always practising skills under normal unresisted conditions over the same period as the resisted training.

Plyometrics

Resistance exercises involving the stretch–shortening cycle (SSC) of muscles are called plyometrics. An example of a plyometric exercise is the depth jump or drop jump. In this exercise, an athlete drops from a predetermined height, such as from a stool, and at ground contact the downward momentum of the body forces the legs to bend or flex at the

Non-weight training methods

Non-weight training method	Example
Fluid resistance (air or water)	Swimmer towing a bucket in the water
Weighted sports equipment	Golfer swinging a weighted golf club
Medicine balls	Tennis player throwing a ball as in the service action
Plyometrics	Long jumper bounding

hips, knees and ankles, producing a stretching of the leg extensor muscles. Then, without any pause, the athlete rebounds as explosively as possible and the legs extend as a result of a shortening of the leg extensors. The higher the drop height used in this exercise, the greater the stretch load placed on the leg muscles.

This and other plyometric exercises are especially useful for the development of reactive strength, because the athlete must quickly reverse direction after actively stretching the muscles. Many sports contain SSC activities, including running and jumping. Likewise, in a golf swing, the muscles that rotate the trunk are actively stretched as the club slows down near the end of the backswing, and then shorten to initiate the downswing.

Some advantages of plyometrics include that they:

- are explosive in nature and therefore develop power
- are especially valuable for training reactive strength
- are often highly sport specific
- are without a significant deceleration phase during muscle shortening, and
- require little if any equipment.

Coaches should remember that plyometric exercises are one conditioning tool available to the coach, but they aren't relevant to all sports. Cycling and the upper body movements in swimming don't need any reactive strength, but high jumpers do, because they place significant stretch loads on their take-off legs.

These are some guidelines for plyometric training using jumping exercises.

- Plyometrics require athletes to have a sound level of muscular and skeletal strength.
- Athletes should try to minimise the pause between the stretching and shortening phases of the exercise.
- Coaches should also monitor the use of correct technique.
- Coaches should ensure that athletes completely recover between exercises to prevent neuromuscular fatigue and deterioration of technique.
- Athletes should progress from double to single-leg exercises. Generally single-

support exercises involve high loading to each leg and are technically more complex.

- Since jumping exercises can involve high-impact forces, athletes should use shock-absorbing shoes and a ground surface. Running shoes and a wooden or rubberised floor, or firm grass, are ideal. However, a thick gymnastic mat or a sandpit are too shock absorbing, and can significantly alter the timing and nature of the exercises.
- Coaches should emphasise plyometrics after strength training.

Examples of lower body plyometric exercises, in order according to intensity (forces applied to body), include:

- hopping for speed (least intense)
- drop jumps from a 30 cm height, emphasising rebound height
- speed bounding (bounding for distance and speed)
- hurdle or box jumps with short contact times
- bounding for distance in zigzags, and
- bounding for horizontal distance by alternating left and right–leg take-offs (most intense).

Penny Williams is a tennis coach who wants to give her players some suitable plyometric exercises. She first analyses the explosive movements in the sport, including forehand and backhand drives and lunging to return a drop shot, then plans the exercises.

The players throw a 2 kg medicine ball with a sideways slinging action. The muscle stretching is produced when the players quickly withdraw the ball as though completing a backswing, or by catching the ball from a partner's throw. The forward swing is done as quickly as possible with no pause after the backswing, and the ball is thrown as far as possible. Throws are performed to both sides to account for forehand and backhand shots, and to discourage muscle imbalances.

A plyometric lunge involves starting with the feet in a forward–backward split position and jumping as high as possible. When the athletes land, they allow their legs to bend to a typical lunge position and then quickly extend them into the next jump. They alternate legs in the air so the opposite foot lands in front. Five sets of five to eight repetitions are performed for both of these exercises.

Needs analysis: the importance of physical qualities for 100 m sprint running

Speed		
Acceleration speed	3	
Maximum speed	3	
Speed–endurance	2	
Strength	*Lower body*	*Upper body*
Absolute maximum strength	1	1
Relative maximum strength	2	2
Power	*Lower body*	*Upper body*
General	3	3
Reactive strength	2	1
Power–endurance	1	1

3 = very important, 2 = some importance, 1 = minor importance

PROGRAM DESIGN

There are many factors to consider when incorporating speed, strength and power into a conditioning program: the principles of training, program guidelines and other factors listed in this chapter. In addition, training must be planned so that those qualities that are most important for success reach peak levels at the time of the most important competitions, a process known as **periodisation** (see chapter 18, An Integrated Approach to Planning, for more information on periodised planning). To illustrate the design of a 12-month periodised program, I have used the example of an 18-year-old junior female national level 100 m sprinter (see table). The first step is to conduct a needs analysis as shown above, to determine the most important qualities in the sport.

The planner has noted that:

- there is a single annual peak for the national championships in late March, and all other competitions throughout the season are not considered important
- the athlete has a training age of 3–4 years, and
- since the athlete has not reached her optimum body weight, an increase in muscle mass is desirable.

The annual plan

The year is divided into phases that all have a different training emphasis (see table on opposite page). The objective of the competition phase is to maintain and refine all qualities. It is relatively short, to maximise the time available for development, but long enough to

A one-week program for a junior 100 m sprinter

Day	Session	Quality trained
Monday	Sprints with weighted vest (6 x flying 10 m) Speed-bounding (6 x 30 m)	Reactive strength
Tuesday	Block starts (2 sets of 5 x 20–30 m)	Acceleration speed
Wednesday	Maximum sprints (2 sets of 5 x 20 m with flying start)	Maximum speed
Thursday	Weight training for power	Power
Friday	Rest	
Saturday	Club competition (100 m, 400 m and 100 m relay leg)	Acceleration speed, maximum speed and speed–endurance
Sunday	Weight training for power	Power

Simplified yearly plan for training the speed, strength and power of a junior 100 m sprinter (track and field)

Months	April	May	June	July	Aug	Sept	Oct	Nov	Dec	Jan	Feb	March
Phases	Transition		General preparation			Specific preparation			Pre-competition			Competition (at end March)
Training emphasis	Mental and physical recovery		Endurance base, hypertrophy, strength			Acceleration speed, maximum strength, power			Maximum speed, power, reactive strength			Maintenance
Acceleration speed												
Maximum speed												
Speed–endurance												
Hypertrophy												
Maximum strength												
Power												
Reactive strength												
Power–endurance												

allow athletes to refine their competition practices and tapering. The shading (see the yearly plan on page 135) indicates the quality that is emphasised, but not necessarily trained exclusively. For example, power could be trained throughout the entire year, even though the emphasis on it varies at different periods.

The base qualities are emphasised first and then the most important qualities are emphasised as the competition peak approaches. For example, the athlete's muscle mass is increased using hypertrophy methods before maximum strength and power training occurs. Training strength qualities and endurance in the same program produces only moderate gains in both. One way of preventing this is to emphasise them at different times, for example, first concentrating on hypertrophy while endurance is maintained, and then reversing the emphasis.

The general preparation phase is the time to address any musculoskeletal deficiencies. This might require certain muscle groups to be selectively targeted. In many sports, the development of trunk or **core stability** is emphasised at this stage. For example, if the lower back and deep abdominal muscles can stabilise the core while sprinting, the leg muscles can produce propulsion more effectively. If they can't, inefficient technique and an increased risk of injury can be the result.

Exercises for core stability

Exercise type	Example
Free weights, such as barbells and dumbbells	Dead lift with light weights
Static holds	Prone hold (push-up position emphasising posture)
Unstable conditions	Single leg squat Swiss ball sit-up

This program slightly emphasises the athlete's power and maximum speed and fits with the annual plan for December. Note that the three club races are considered to provide a training stimulus for acceleration speed, maximum speed and speed–endurance. The example illustrates the speed, strength and power-related qualities only. Other performance factors that have to be integrated into the program include technique, flexibility, endurance and mental skills.

CONCLUSION

Training for speed, strength and power should be carefully planned based on the specific needs of each athlete. Coaches should appreciate that many of these training methods involve relatively large muscular forces and intense efforts, so they should ensure that they teach and supervise safe exercise technique, to minimise the risk of injury.

COACHING TIPS

- Understand that speed is an important element of most sports — the types of speed required will vary with each sport.

- Teach young athletes to develop speed, strength and power without compromising skill and technique. Get the technique right, then add speed.

- Understand that speed is dependent on an ability to relax, rather than just effort — the faster athletes want to go, the more relaxed they must be.

- Encourage athletes to use body weight as their training load, so that they don't have to buy expensive equipment, and try the big five: push-ups, chin-ups, dips, body-weight squats and sit-ups.

FURTHER READING

Draper, JA, and MG Lancaster (1985) The 505 test: a test for agility in the horizontal plane. *Australian Journal of Science and Medicine in Sport* 17(1): 15–18.

Mayhew, JL, FC Piper, TM Schwegler and TE Ball (1989) Contributions of speed, agility and body composition to anaerobic power measurement in college football players. *Journal of Applied Sport Science Research* 3(4): 101–06.

Mero, A, and PV Komi (1986) Force-, EMG-, and elasticity–velocity relationships at submaximal, maximal and supramaximal running speeds in sprinters. *European Journal of Applied Physiology* 55: 553–61.

Young, W, M Hawken and L McDonald (1996) Relationship between speed, agility and strength qualities in Australian rules football. *Strength and Conditioning Coach* 4(4): 3–6.

Zatsiorsky, VM (1995) *Science and Practice of Strength Training*. Champaign, IL: Human Kinetics.

CHAPTER 12
FLEXIBILITY TRAINING

Victor Popov

(National Sports Information Centre)

INTRODUCTION

In sport, one of the factors that limits or determines performance is flexibility. The range of motion available to joints, muscles, tendons, connective tissue and nerves can affect athletes' performances by influencing their technique (positively or negatively) or helping to cause injury. Every sport or event has a specific flexibility requirement determined by the skills involved in playing that sport or event. Each athlete has an individual requirement for flexibility training, based on factors such as inherent levels of flexibility and training history.

Coaches should consider the flexibility requirements of the sport or event they are coaching, appreciate the individual requirements of athletes under their care, and devise effective ways of training to improve and maintain flexibility. This will help to produce the best performances and reduce the risk of injury. Athletes should also understand the importance of flexibility training, and it often falls to coaches to educate and motivate athletes to stretch effectively.

THE ROLE OF FLEXIBILITY IN PERFORMANCE

Types of flexibility

Flexibility has two components: static flexibility and dynamic flexibility. **Static flexibility** refers to the range of motion through which a muscle or joint can be taken and then held by a slow and forceful movement. It is limited by the structure of bones, joints and muscles and by muscle tone. Static flexibility can be seen as the limit of passive motion.

Dynamic flexibility describes the range of motion that is used when the body is moving, and can be seen as the limit of active motion. Dynamic flexibility is limited by static flexibility, nervous system function and coordination. Static flexibility limits dynamic flexibility because the body, in movement, can not exceed the passive limits of joint and muscle range without being injured. Dynamic flexibility is most important in high-speed movement, and so good dynamic flexibility is essential in sport, and is the major goal of flexibility training.

Flexibility and technique

Range of motion can be a limiting factor in the execution of a skill. Hurdlers need good hamstring flexibility to be able to lift their lead legs to clear hurdles. Swimmers need good shoulder internal rotation to achieve an effective 'catch' in the first part of their stroke. Javelin throwers and baseball pitchers both need good external rotation of their throwing shoulders to set up the cocking position to throw. Cyclists need hamstring and gluteal flexibility to be able to achieve an effective riding position.

Hurdlers have specific flexibility needs.

(National Sports Information Centre)

ibility, or the ability of athletes to use their available range of motion. Video feedback sessions with athletes help to point out flexibility problems and show their effect on skills, and are a very effective way of motivating athletes to improve flexibility.

Alex Popov, one of the greatest swimmers of all time, demonstrates his fantastic back and shoulder flexibility, which gives him an extremely effective technique. When Alex and other elite swimmers stretch on the pool deck before competition, it is easy to see how dynamically flexible they are. Gennadi Touretski, Alex's coach, uses rhythmic, dynamic, total-body calisthenic exercises to develop this type of flexibility.

Flexibility and injury prevention

Inadequate or excessive range of motion can lead to injuries. Lack of range of motion (or **hypomobility**) is often more obvious because of the technique changes it causes than excessive range of motion (**hypermobility**), but both can lead to injury. Swimmers with either too little shoulder internal rotation, or too much, are inclined to develop shoulder injuries.

Hypomobility often leads athletes to use positions or movements that they don't have the flexibility to achieve easily, thus resulting in repeated stress on structures and, eventually, to an overuse injury. Impingement injuries of the shoulder in swimming are an example of this. They occur in swimmers who have inadequate shoulder internal rotation but, as a part of training, repeatedly put their shoulders into internal rotation, thus causing jamming up of tendons in the front of the shoulder.

If these athletes do not have the required range of motion of the muscles or joints mentioned, then ideal technique is not possible, and performance will be negatively affected. Conversely, if an athlete has a specific range-of-motion problem that cannot be changed, then the coach may have to consider varying the ideal technique to allow that athlete to achieve his or her potential.

It is important for coaches to know when athletes have a flexibility problem that is hindering the way they perform their skills, and video analysis of technique can help to do this. This analysis is really looking at dynamic flex-

Alex Popov, demonstrating back and shoulder flexibility.

(National Sports Information Centre)

Overuse injuries in running can also be linked to lack of flexibility. Calf tightness is one of the causes of a range of injuries, including shin soreness, Achilles tendonitis and calf strains. A hamstring tear that occurs in a footballer's leg while he is kicking the ball is an example of a traumatic injury related to lack of flexibility. Muscles taken suddenly beyond their available range may tear or strain. Good hamstring flexibility is essential for an Australian rules footballer, as kicking is an integral part of the game, and kicking involves regularly taking the hamstring from a shortened to a near full lengthened position. Sometimes, in trying for extra distance in a kick, a footballer follows through too far and takes the hamstring beyond its available range, leading to a tear or strain.

Hypermobility may lead to difficulty in controlling or stopping movement. Swimmers who have excessive shoulder rotation can develop problems around the shoulder because the joint moves around too much while they swim. In this case, tendons or the joint capsule can be pinched or otherwise compromised repeatedly, leading to injury.

A rugby front-row forward with a long and mobile neck would be at risk of injury in a scrum, and it would be unwise for someone with excessive neck mobility to choose to play in this position. Gymnasts, who strive for extremes of spinal flexibility in order to execute some of their skills, often suffer from stress fractures in their lower backs (see chapter 5, Functional Anatomy, for more information on stress fractures). These stress fractures may be caused by repeated overextensions of the lumbar spine.

Flexibility and muscle performance

The way muscle is structured affects its performance. Muscles have a certain amount of stretchiness, just like a rubber band. This is caused by the way the muscle is structured: it has a contractile component (the actin and myosin proteins that are involved in contraction) and an elastic component (tendons, fascia and other connective tissue that hold a muscle together). It is the elastic component that gives muscles stretchiness, which is important in their performance, as many dynamic movements in sport involve the sudden stretching and then contraction of a muscle. This stretch–contraction is called the **stretch–shortening cycle** (SSC).

An example of this is the action of the hamstring in sprinting. As the thigh or upper leg moves forward in the sprinting action, the lower leg is rapidly extended, and the hamstring contracts to slow the lower leg down and to stop the knee locking out just before the foot hits the ground. The hamstring works hard in this phase, but it is still lengthening (contracting eccentrically), and all the tendons and connective tissue of the hamstring are stretched. Then the hamstring begins to contract and shorten (concentric contraction), as it works to extend the hip and propel the body forward. The SSC is more effective if the hamstring is stretchy like a

a   b

(National Sports Information Centre)

When footballers kick, their hamstrings (a) change very quickly from very short or contracted (b) to very long or stretched.

rubber band, and less effective if it is stiff. Flexibility training helps to reduce the stiffness of a muscle, and thus affects its performance.

Muscle stiffness is not the only factor affecting the SSC. Nervous system function and activation are equally important, and certain types of stretching may negatively affect neuromuscular function. For example, strong and sustained static stretches may inhibit a muscle's ability to be 'switched on' to the maximum if they are done immediately before power or maximum strength activities. Coaches should consider this in planning a warm-up for a power event. The role of stretching in warm-up is discussed later in this chapter.

ACQUIRING FLEXIBILITY

Structures involved

Various body structures can limit range of motion. Joints, muscles, tendons, connective tissue and nerves can all be involved in flexibility, and all require different types of stretching. For example, to stretch an ankle joint into dorsiflexion (lifting the toes), you must first take the calf muscles off stretch, and then place a shearing force through the ankle. This is very different from a gastrocnemius muscle stretch, done with an extended knee, but also with the ankle dorsiflexed. To stretch the soleus muscle or the Achilles tendon, ankle dorsiflexion is coupled with knee flexion.

Ballistic (swinging or bouncing) movements are needed to stretch connective tissue effectively. To stretch nerves, athletes' must place their bodies in specific positions in relation to the anatomy of the nerves and the spinal cord. It is important to be aware that all of these various structures may limit range of motion, and coaches and athletes should know and understand how to stretch them separately. A thorough knowledge of anatomy, especially about where the muscles are attached to the bones, is essential for this.

Principles of stretching

Athletes must stretch to be flexible. The basic principle of stretching is taking the structure to the end of its current range of motion, and then taking it a little further. The body's soft tissue structures are pliable, and if a stretch stimulus is applied long enough and often enough, the range of motion will be increased. There are inherent risks in stretching: injury can result from excessive or over-vigorous stretching. As a general rule, stretches should be taken to the point of stretch, rather than the point of pain. As with most rules, there are exceptions. Nerve stretches have to be uncomfortable to be effective.

The more highly trained an individual, the more likely they are to handle vigorous stretching. Post-surgical or post-injury stretching is also often painful, but should be programmed and supervised by the appropriate health professional.

There are several principles of muscle stretching that are commonly observed:

- Athletes should try to avoid pain while stretching, especially if they are untrained.
- To increase flexibility, athletes should do three to five stretching sessions per week.

Gastrocnemius stretch   **Soleus stretch**

(Victor Popov)

■ Stretching appears to be more effective if it's done after general physical activity or an increase in body core temperature (because warmth increases the pliability of collagen and fibrin, the proteins that make up most soft tissue structures).

■ When athletes are doing static stretches for muscles, they should hold them for more than ten seconds, the time needed to overcome the protective or reflex mechanisms that protect the body against overstretching.

The muscles of the body can be divided into two types — postural and phasic. **Postural muscles** tend to be slower acting and are used in maintaining the positions of joints (for example, lateral abdominal muscles), while **phasic muscles** (for example, hamstrings) are more dynamic and faster acting. Postural and phasic muscles each respond best to different types of stretching.

Types of stretching

Stretching can be categorised as either:

■ static

■ ballistic

■ dynamic, or

■ proprioceptive neuromuscular facilitation (or PNF).

Each category of stretching has its place in the flexibility program.

Static stretching takes a structure to the end of its range of motion and holds it there for a period of time. Muscles, nerves, joints and tendons can be stretched this way. Holding time for static stretches varies from 30 seconds to a few minutes, depending on the structure being stretched. Athletes can tolerate longer static stretches after activity, when their body core temperature is higher, and the nervous system is relaxed. Static stretches are very safe if the athlete and coach are careful to avoid stretching to the point of pain.

Ballistic stretching is repeated swinging or bouncing into the end of the range of a movement. Connective tissue and tendons are stretched this way, as ballistic movements initiate the stretch reflex in a muscle, causing the contractile part of the muscle to be activated. Ballistic stretching carries a greater risk of injury than static stretching, because it is less controlled. It is important, however, to include ballistic movements in a flexibility program

(especially for high-level athletes), as ballistic movements form an important part of most sporting activity. As ballistic stretches are also an essential part of most warm-up routines, coaches should closely supervise athletes who are less experienced or trained during this phase of warm-up. Ballistic stretching should be done following a warm-up, or towards the end of a warm-up, just prior to skill drills.

Dynamic stretching refers to a combination of movement and static holds, where the athlete reaches the end of range of a movement deliberately and slowly, holds it briefly and then releases it. Nerves, joints and connective tissue can be stretched this way. Often athletes do dynamic stretches into a position that approximates one they use in their sport, and various structures are stretched together.

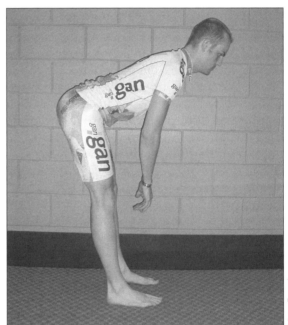

(Victor Popov)

Cyclists have to achieve a flat and low body position to be aerodynamic. By dynamically stretching into the position shown above, they stretch the posterior structures of their legs and strengthen their lower back muscles, making aerodynamic positioning easier. This type of stretching achieves many purposes, and so is good value for time.

Proprioceptive neuromuscular facilitation or **PNF stretching** refers to a group of techniques that use neuromuscular mechanisms to improve the range of motion. These techniques were mainly developed from research into neuromuscular development problems (such as minimal cerebral dysfunction or MCD). Techniques for PNF stretching use reflexes or responses that affect muscle tone.

A contract–relax (CR) stretch involves taking a muscle to the end of its range, then isometrically contracting that muscle against resistance, before then relaxing and stretching the muscle further. The isometric contraction results in a reflex lowering of muscle tone, which facilitates the subsequent stretch.

Contract–relax antagonist–contract (CRAC) is another PNF technique, in which a contraction of the muscle that works opposite (the antagonist) to the one being stretched is added to the end of a CR stretch. Some research that has compared different stretching techniques (mostly over a few weeks or months) indicates that PNF stretching is the most effective way of stretching muscle.

Programming of stretching

Flexibility training should be programmed into a training plan just like any other part of preparation. In long-term planning, flexibility goals should be identified and achieved during the preparatory phase of training. Changing flexibility patterns will affect skill levels, so the competition phase is not the time when a coach or an athlete should aim to improve flexibility.

Flexibility can be lost during hard training or injury time, so important flexibility parameters should be monitored and restored during recovery phases of training, and enough stretching should be programmed into regular training to maintain the ideal range of motion. Remember, each sport and each athlete has specific flexibility needs, so coaches must individualise flexibility training for each athlete where possible. This can only be achieved if coaches know each individual athlete's flexibility patterns.

An individual's flexibility patterns are determined by musculoskeletal screening, which forms part of many national, state and club programs. The flexibility component of screening involves standardised flexibility tests of appropriate muscles or movements, and should be followed up with a flexibility program that helps the athlete reach established goals. It is useful to rescreen athletes at various times through the year to monitor their flexibility, as it is a dynamic quality that changes with training.

On the following page is a standardised screening protocol as used by the Queensland Academy of Sport (QAS) swimming program. The testing is administered by QAS physiotherapists and mirrors the national screening program. These tests (for example, hip extension) are done in standardised ways and can be administered by any sports physiotherapist. All of the test movements are of some use in swimming, and have normal or desired ranges that should be achieved by swimmers. Each sport needs its own specific screening protocol. A screening program such as this is only worthwhile if any problems found are managed, and the athletes are rescreened after a time to check that appropriate ranges are being achieved (courtesy Queensland Academy of Sport).

There are variations in flexibility with sex and age. Generally, females tend to be more flexible than males. This is probably a result of the hormonal differences that make males generally stronger than females. During pregnancy, a woman's joint flexibility is increased by the presence of relaxin, a hormone that increases relaxation of ligaments to facilitate childbirth. As people age, biochemical changes occur that affect the quality of the collagen (the protein that gives soft tissue its elasticity) in their bodies. The collagen tends to become less flexible: wrinkles are one of the external signs of this, and reduced flexibility is an internal sign. These age and sex variations are only generalisations, and there are exceptions to these rules. As with other physical characteristics, flexibility (or lack of it) also seems to be an inherited trait.

The younger people are when they start flexibility training, the easier it is for them to achieve and maintain flexibility. Ballet dancers and gymnasts are two groups of athletes who develop great flexibility, as it is required by their disciplines. Coaches often have to develop fun ways to incorporate flexibility training into the programs of other young athletes, to achieve better results and avoid the boring nature of stretching.

During a training session, stretching should be included as part of warm-up, and part of cool-down. I suggest that athletes warm up as follows:

- start with general whole-body activity to raise body temperature
- move on to static stretches, followed by PNF stretches and dynamic stretches
- then do some gentle, but sport-specific, drills or exercises
- follow this with ballistic stretching of specific muscles
- move up to higher speed and higher skill drills, and
- then the competition or the main part of the training session.

QUEENSLAND ACADEMY OF SPORT

Physiotherapy Screening:
Range of Motion Assessment

	Left	Right
Name:		
Date:		
Physiotherapist:		
Combined elevation		
GH internal rotation		
Abduction with internal rotation		
Hip extension		
Hip internal rotation		
Tibial external rotation		
Hip internal rotation + tibial external rotation		
Hip flexion		
Thoracic rotation		
Chest expansion		
Ankle plantar flexion		
Straight leg raise		

Injury record: Training days lost in last 3 months:

Description of recent injuries:

Comments:

QAS screening form

143

This is a very general list, and some parts may be left out, depending on the desired result of the warm-up. The role of stretching in warm-up is to prepare for the training session or competition to follow. This list gradually increases the intensity and complexity of stretches to match the increase in nervous system activation required to go from a 'cold' to a performance state.

A general principle of warm-up is that the time required to warm-up is inversely proportional to the duration of the training session or event, and directly proportional to the intensity of the training session or event. So a 100 m sprinter (short duration, high intensity) warms up for a longer time than an iron-man triathlete (long duration, low intensity).

Stretching in cool-down is done to aid recovery and help to maintain or improve flexibility. Some good research exists to show that training soreness is not directly helped by stretching, but flexibility losses can definitely be reduced by post-training stretching. Cool-down stretches can often be held for a longer duration, and be taken further into range because of the elevated body temperature and post-training nervous system relaxation.

Coaches of junior athletes often have limited time for training, and so have to integrate different stretching components throughout the session. For the teacher who has a session lasting 60 minutes, with a class of 20 to 25 children, there are some easy ways to accomplish this.

The first five minutes can be taken up with a light game with balls or suitable equipment, as an activity to warm up the muscles, and help the children focus on the training to come and have fun with other children. This type of warm-up is also a useful way to stretch actively and prepare mentally for the session. After the warm-up game, they should do a few light static stretches (six seconds) of, for example, calves, quadriceps, and hamstrings. This is an ideal opportunity to give instructions for the next part of the session.

The training part of the session may last up to 40 minutes and then warm-down takes ten minutes. Reducing the intensity of movements in this ten-minute period serves as a form of active recovery and can incorporate some active and static stretches. Each static stretch should be held for ten seconds and repeated twice. A fairly comprehensive stretching routine should then be completed over the final five-minute period.

As previously mentioned, injury may be a direct result of a lack of flexibility, and often stretching forms an important part of the rehabilitation process after injury. The goal of rehabilitative stretching is often to improve flexibility beyond the pre-injury level, thus helping to prevent reinjury.

To improve specific flexibility or range-of-motion problems, athletes may have to stretch regularly outside the training environment. This may be in therapy sessions, or as a regular evening stretching session. Coaches should encourage athletes to stretch at home each evening, which can be a good way to wind down, as well as work on flexibility problems. Remember though that, in these 'cold' stretching sessions, all stretches should be done gradually and gently to minimise any injury risk.

Stretching technique

The technique of stretching is as important as the programming. Coaches and athletes can only develop efficient technique if they know the anatomy of the structure to be stretched and understand its relationships to surrounding structures. Effectively stretching nerves or muscles that cross more than one joint involves positioning a number of joints carefully to make the best of the stretch. A sciatic nerve stretch, in which the position of the head, spine, hips, knees and ankles all affect the stretch, fully elongates this nerve with maximum spinal flexion and ankle dorsiflexion and inversion. Stretching the rectus femoris (the most commonly injured part of the quadriceps muscle group

(Victor Popov)

Sciatic nerve stretch

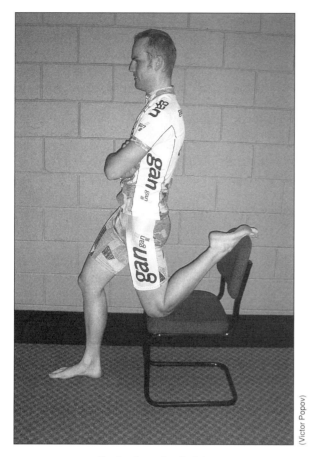

Rectus femoris stretch

(Victor Popov)

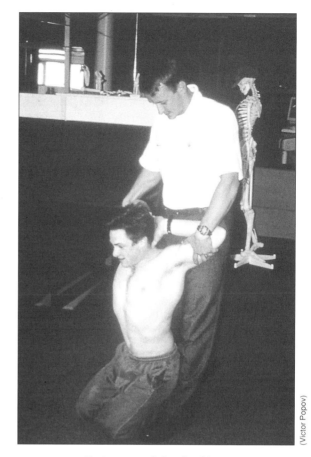

Partner stretch for shoulders

(Victor Popov)

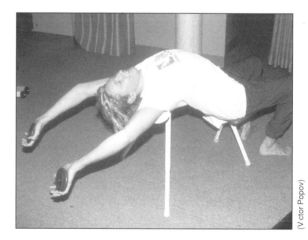

A stretching chair for the thoracic spine

(Victor Popov)

in kicking sports) involves extension of the hip, flexion of the knee and posterior pelvic tilt to achieve maximum stretch. If any of these components are missing, the stretch is less effective.

Partner stretching is a very useful technique for a number of reasons. Flexibility training is often more interesting and athletes more compliant if partner stretching is part of the training process. Certain stretches are more effectively done and PNF techniques are more easily achieved with assistance. Coaches and partners should take care that partner stretching doesn't push too far and cause injury. It is essential that coaches set guidelines and ensure that good communication is established between partners about how far to stretch.

Certain stretching equipment can help with flexibility training. The 'chair' for stretching thoracic spines, while also stretching front shoulder structures, can be seen on pool decks all over the country. It is a very convenient way of regularly stretching these important parts of the body for swimmers.

Specific stretches

When coaches are trying to develop a specific flexibility program for an athlete, it is important that they remember that any structure can be stretched more than one way, and sometimes structures need to be stretched in a variety of ways to achieve the desired result. There are three ways of stretching the hamstring at the back of the thigh. The first stretch is a neural stretch for the sciatic nerve (which can affect hamstring length). The second is a stretch in which tilting the pelvis forward pulls the beginning (or origin) of the hamstring (on the pelvis) away from its end (below the knee on the tibia). The third stretch of this sequence pulls the end of the hamstring away from its origin. All three stretches should be done to improve posterior thigh flexibility. This particular sequence also seems to be very effective in achieving hamstring flexibility.

Coaches can find stretches described in many available resources, but in planning the individual program they should consider factors such as how much time is available, how flexible the athlete already is, and what the sport requires in terms of flexibility. In

a

b

Three hamstring stretches: for a neural stretch, see sciatic nerve stretch on page 144; (a) pelvic tilt stretch; (b) pulling the hamstring away from its origin

planning group stretching (for example, at a team warm-up), coaches should allow time at the end of the group session for individuals to do any other specific stretches they need.

Massage and flexibility

Massage is very important in reducing tissue tightness and helping to increase range of motion, and so as part of a regime for gaining flexibility. Although the scientific research in this area is not extensive, enough anecdotal evidence exists to suggest that massage should be used regularly in recovery. This can include self-massage, as well as formal massage sessions.

Massage aims to reduce tone in muscles, as well as helping to increase the pliability of connective tissue structures. Both of these effects can be better achieved with regular use of massage, the frequency of which will vary with training load and proximity of competition.

MULTITASKING

Time allocated for flexibility training can also be used to achieve other goals. In team situations, communication skills can be fostered and a team-building atmosphere can be developed in stretching sessions. Individuals within a team may be designated by the coach to run stretching sessions, or the responsibility for the session may be shared by the group, with the players each 'leading' a stretch until the program is complete.

Self-responsibility may also be promoted using flexibility training as a tool. A coach may take an athlete through a regular stretching routine, and initially supervise each session. The coach may then stop supervising the stretch (gradually or suddenly), and may instead give the responsibility for this aspect of preparation to the athlete. In this situation it is important for the coach to occasionally monitor these sessions to ensure that they are effective. The extent to which athletes can be responsible for themselves is sometimes (but not always) a function of age, so children often need closer supervision.

Some forms of psychological training may also be done during flexibility training. Athletes can practise visualisation and relaxation techniques while stretching and, once routines are well established, the time can also be used for tactical discussions or race planning.

CONCLUSION

Flexibility training should be seen as an integral part of the training process. Ideally it should be individualised, monitored and developed as the athlete progresses. Coaches should appreciate the principles, methods, reasons and techniques of stretching in order to ensure that this aspect of preparation is effectively done by athletes in their care.

COACHING TIPS

- Encourage athletes to do flexibility exercises to increase their range of movement and hence improve technique, efficiency and performance.

- Stretch muscles when they are warm.

- Incorporate different types of stretching into different parts of a training session, for example, ballistic stretching towards the end of the warm-up and static stretching at the end of a session.

- Use the team stretch period to focus on team strategies or game analysis.

FURTHER READING

Alter, M (1998) *Sport Stretch*. Champaign, IL: Human Kinetics.

de Castella, R, and W Clews (eds) (1996) *Smart Sport: The Ultimate Reference Manual for Sports People.* Canberra: RWM Publishing.

Hutton, RS (1992) Neuro-muscular basis of stretching. In: PV Komi (ed), *Strength and Power in Sport.* Oxford, UK: Blackwell Scientific Publications.

McKean, M (1999) A review of research on stretching. *Network* July: 50–52.

Rushall, BS, and FS Pyke (1990) *Training for Sports and Fitness.* South Melbourne: Macmillan.

St George, F (1989) *The Muscle Fitness Book.* Brookvale: Simon and Schuster Australia.

Taylor, D (1990) Visco-elastic properties of muscle tendon units: the biomechanical effects of stretching. *American Journal of Sports Medicine* 18(3): 300–09.

Walker, B (1998) *The Stretching Handbook: Your Guide to Avoiding Sports Injury and Improving Athletic Performance.* Robina Town Centre: Walkerbout Health and Leisure.

Wilkinson, A (1992) Stretching the truth: a review of the literature. *Australian Journal of Physiotherapy* 38(4): 283–87.

CHAPTER 13
PERFORMANCE PSYCHOLOGY

Sandy Gordon

(National Sports Information Centre)

INTRODUCTION

'There is nothing wrong with saying to yourself "I don't want to do all that mental training stuff"! But there is something wrong with thinking you will get to the top without doing it. You will never reach the top without developing your mental strength' (Orlick 2000).

This chapter explains the principles of some mental skills that are useful to coaches, as well as showing coaches how to teach these skills. As the above quote suggests, athletes who are never taught mental skills will never reach their true potential, and coaches who

are not skilling their athletes mentally are simply not coaching properly.

Performance profiling

Performance profiling is a procedure coaches can use to both identify the training objectives of mental skills for athletes and make it easier for athletes to keep to their mental skills training. Coaches who use performance profiling benefit in several ways:

- It creates a visual display of the athletes' evaluations of their specific mental skills (strengths and weaknesses).
- Athletes, as well as coaches, identify the qualities required for consistent performance.
- Athlete self-assessments can be matched with coaches' at different times in a season.
- Priorities are established for mental skills training.
- Training progress is measured.

As an example, coaches could simply ask athletes to rate themselves against a list of fundamental mental skills or qualities required for top performances in their sport (from 0 = very poor to 10 = very strong). These can be compared with the coach's ratings of each athlete and both coach and athlete can discuss any discrepancies. Athletes could also be asked to rate themselves 'currently' and 'ideally', or pre-season self-ratings could be compared with later assessments early, in the middle, or late in the competitive season.

Both the coach and athlete then have a picture of training priorities for the athlete's mental skill development, which can then be integrated into daily or weekly coaching plans.

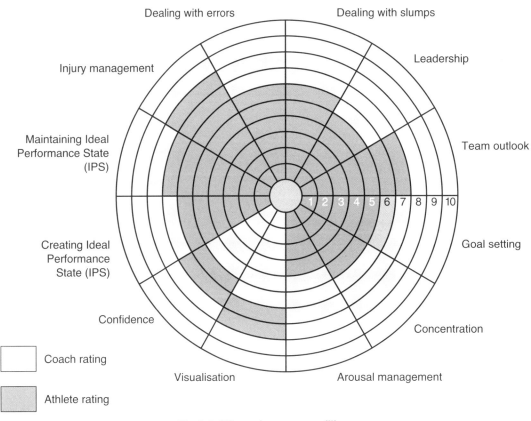

Mental skills performance profiling

Coach rating

Athlete rating

Principles of teaching mental skills

Sport psychology consultant to a group of coaches: 'Let's consider the importance of mental skills training in sport. Can anyone estimate what percentage of their sport is psychological or mental?'

A coach responds confidently: 'I'd say my sport is about 80 to 90% mental'.

Consultant: 'That's interesting. So what percentage of your normal practice time do you think you spend on teaching or coaching mental skills?'

Coach: 'Hmm' (embarrassed silence).

Mental skills training is a developmental process that begins with simple familiar examples and gradually develops, with practice and good instruction, to apply to complex and unfamiliar situations. Individualised programs should be set as early as possible and, because the quality of effort required by both coach and athlete is the same for learning and acquiring *physical* skills, similarly they can expect problems keeping to the *mental* training program. Since coaches are the most powerful influence in all learning they must be positive models of the skills being taught.

The first step in developing mental skill practice plans is to decide on learning objectives, taking into account the diversity of ma-

turity and ability levels likely to be present even in the most stable clubs and teams. These are best stated simply and conservatively. The total time for each drill should also be stated. Coaches should then prepare a simple and concise explanation or script of the drill in their own words. A good clear explanation can often set up an effective practice and learning experience.

Key teaching points should be presented to athletes, and coaches should segment the activities they will use to make them easier to absorb. Before the athletes move on to another part of the coaching session, it is critical that what they practised and learned is summarised. They should be left in no doubt what the objective was, why it was relevant, what they can practise on their own, and when the next session will take place.

Coaches should also plan for equipment and space required. Whether an inside or outside venue is needed for the sport, coaches should ensure that learning happens in the natural setting where athletes perform (that is, in the pool, on the field or on the court) and, ideally, without distractions. While, at more advanced levels of mental skill development, some distraction (or even a lot) can be desirable, it is seldom helpful at the introductory stage and should be avoided if at all possible.

Application example: Sample concentration skills practice plan for soccer

Learning objective

To improve concentration when shooting, keeping shots low and on target

Total time: 15–20 minutes

Explanation

In a shooting situation there are only two critical cues to pay attention to in the act of shooting: first, planting the non-kicking foot beside the ball, and second, striking the ball smoothly and with poise. If players are thinking about any other cues at this critical moment they are not concentrating.

Key teaching points

Beginning

Illustrate what happens when the foot is planted correctly (head is down, knee over ball, ball kept low), and composure is maintained (firm strike, kept on target). Introduce cue words to emphasise critical cues (for example, 'plant', 'there') and immediately reinforce/correct initial efforts using phrases such as 'pay attention to . . .', 'remember the critical cues' and 'smooth'.

Middle

Work unopposed/opposed drills (once mental skill is achieved).

End

Before moving on to the next step, summarise what's been done so far.

Equipment or space required

Goal area, one ball each, two feeding positions

Next steps

1. As above, but ask players to identify critical cues before starting.

2. Athletes should move from spending less time opposed to more time opposed.

Comments

Look for: initial preoccupation with results (that is, scoring a goal).

Expect: all players to treat practice as if it were a technical drill.

Tell them: 'Focus on what you are thinking about as you practice; pay attention to the critical cues', that is, 'plant' and 'smooth'.

Finally, coaches should plan the next steps in the learning process, which may be required immediately by certain athletes. Both fast and slow learners must be catered for even in a 10–15 minute drill. Coaches can record anticipated problems and teachable moments (when pupils are likely to respond correctly or appropriately). Responses to awkward questions can also be handled more effectively with preparation.

GOAL SETTING

Goal setting is a planning, organisational and evaluative tool that helps athletes of various ages and competency levels perform better. It influences performance directly by focusing athletes' attention on important elements of the skill they are performing, mobilising their efforts, prolonging their persistence, and fostering the development of new learning techniques. Goals also influence performance indirectly by affecting athletes' psychological states and such factors as confidence levels, anxiety and satisfaction. A correctly implemented goal-setting program also helps athletes to:

- make training more challenging
- foster pride, self-satisfaction and self-confidence
- become more committed and motivated
- become measurably more successful
- develop psychological maturity
- prevent problem behaviours
- become more effective leaders
- become better communicators
- cope better, and
- have more empathy for others.

Principles

Goal setting involves a step-by-step process of achievement, starting from a baseline level of performance in one of six different goal areas: physical, technical, tactical, mental, behavioural and environmental.

There are several basic goal-setting principles for both individuals and teams. Problems include:

- convincing athletes to actually set goals
- not setting specific goals
- setting too many goals too soon
- setting outcome versus performance goals (because performance goals are controllable but outcome goals, such as winning a game, are not)
- not adjusting goals when they have or have not been achieved, and
- not arranging goal-setting evaluation and follow-up procedures.

Understanding and anticipating these problems will help coaches to both reduce the negative effects and perhaps circumvent them altogether.

Principles of goal setting

	Individual goals
Set	• specific goals in measurable and behavioural terms
	• difficult but realistic goals
	• short and long-range goals
	• goals for practice and for competition
	• positively worded, as opposed to negatively worded, goals
Identify	• individual personality and motivational needs
	• strategies to achieve goals
	• target dates for goal attainment
Record goals	• write goals in a diary or log book — 'ink it, don't just think it'
Provide	• ways to evaluate goals
	• support for goals by recruiting coach, team-mates, family and friends to help
	Team goals
Establish	• long-term goals
	• then, short-term goals (paths to long-term goals)
Involve	• all members of the team (players, coaches, support staff)
Monitor	• progress toward goals
Reward	• progress toward goals
Foster	• team confidence related to team goal achievement

Application example: Sample goal setting sheet for volleyball

Goal: To improve my hitting out of the back court, position four

Type: Technical   Date set:

To achieve this goal (answer all six questions):

1. What do I have to do?
   - Be more assertive/decisive in swinging at the ball
   - Develop a more appropriate spatial relationship with the ball
   - Develop a more dynamic approach/take-off

2. How am I going to do this?
   - Practise hitting from the back court more often myself (as opposed to drills with others)
   - Develop a drill to improve 'spatial relationship' specifically
   - Develop a drill to automate a dynamic approach

3. How can I measure improvement?
   - Objectively — six out of 10 (60%) → eight out of 10 (80%)
   - Subjectively — feedback from coaches/team-mates and video of self

4. Who can help me achieve this goal?
   - Coaches
   - Team-mates whose ability in this area I admire/respect

5. How will I know I have achieved it?
   - See 3 (when I am achieving 60–80% consistently and without conscious thought)

6. How will I prevent myself from achieving this goal? What excuses will I use?
   - 'Too difficult', 'I can't' and 'she'll be right'

Coaches can adapt this example to suit each athlete, and can also prepare a similar goal-setting form on which athletes can plan general and less specific sports goals, which can be used before the season starts by both teams and individuals.

CONCENTRATION

Coaches and sport commentators often define concentration and sport intelligence as the ability to pay attention to the right things at the right time. Consequently there are three aspects of the art and science of concentration:

- focusing on the relevant cues
- staying focused, and
- being aware of changes as they happen.

Like other technical, tactical, and physical skills, concentration can be learned and developed with practice, patience and persistence. An athlete's ability to concentrate is not finite. It can always be improved with training, and even small increments of improvement over time can dramatically improve performance.

After three consecutive poor fielding performances in Pura Milk Cup matches (formerly Sheffield Shield) in 1998, Alex, a relatively inexperienced first-class cricketer, told his sport psychologist that he had problems concentrating at the critical moment (the point of delivery). According to Alex and his captain, the problem seemed to be worse when he was moved from in-field (for example, gully) to out-field positions (for example, deep extra cover).

The psychologist devised a strategy to improve Alex's awareness of concentration lapses at the point of delivery that involved filling Alex's left trouser pocket with paper clips at the beginning of each session of play. Subsequently, during each two-hour session, if Alex noticed that he was not focusing at the point of delivery, he moved one paper clip to the right pocket. At the end of each fielding session his concentration lapses were tallied. Within one game this exercise helped restore the player's concentration to where it should have been at the point of delivery. Objectively measuring the number of perceived concentration lapses effectively channelled Alex's energy towards achieving a mental (versus technical) goal each session.

Principles

1. Selective attention at critical moments

Athletes must learn what to focus on, as well as when and how to focus. Various types of concentration are appropriate for specific sports and activities. **Attentional focus** can have two dimensions: width (broad or narrow) and direction (internal or external).

A broad attentional focus allows an athlete to perceive several things in a rapidly changing sport environment simultaneously, as does a soccer player dribbling the ball up the field. A narrow attentional focus occurs when athletes respond to one or two cues only, as does a golfer lining up a putt. An external attentional focus directs attention outward to an object, such as to an opponent's movements in tennis. An internal attentional focus is directed towards thoughts and feelings, as a high jumper does when preparing for a jump.

Where no pressure or difficulty exists (at training or practice) athletes can usually combine width and direction of attentional focus. However, when pressure or difficulty occurs (during competition), attentional problems can occur. To teach appropriate attentional focus, coaches can ask athletes in specific sport roles to, first, identify the critical moments in their sport and, second, to identify the critical attentional cues at each critical moment.

2. A present focus

Because the mind often wants to replay previous events during a contest, or worry about what might happen ahead, it is vitally important for athletes to stay focused in the present. In addition to focusing on irrelevant past or future events, they can also become either self or other-aware, instead of task-aware. Neither self-awareness (such as thinking 'I'm not playing well' or 'I'm tired') or other-awareness (such as thinking 'my opponent looks awesome' or 'the umpire is incompetent') are appropriate strategies during performance.

On the other hand, task-awareness — often described as mental toughness — facilitates a more appropriate and present focus, and is simply the athlete's response to the question, 'what is it that I have to do right now, to play well?' Coaches can teach athletes to stay in the present by training them to be task-aware.

3. Minimise periods of peak concentration

Because extended periods of concentration can lead to premature mental and physical exhaustion, athletes need to develop techniques to switch up (at critical moments), switch down (between critical moments) and

(National Sports Information Centre)

Athletes must learn to refocus quickly.

switch off (at appropriate times) during competition. Switching channels of concentration (up, down, off) during training and competition will help athletes both conserve energy expenditure and re-energise. Coaches can teach pre-performance routines to help athletes both minimise periods of peak concentration and maintain their task-awareness and present focus.

4. Refocusing plan

Often the mark of fully prepared athletes and teams is their ability to bounce back and refocus during periods of distraction. Sources of distraction may be non-game related (such as personal problems at home or interpersonal problems with other players) or game related (such as pain, fatigue, mistakes made, the score or the stage in the game). By preparing refocusing plans to deal with distraction and difficult periods, athletes are not thinking negatively, they are thinking ahead.

Application example: Sample pre-bowling routine for cricket

When does your bowling spell begin and how do you respond to it?	1. When game begins, study the batsmen 2. Establish my plan — visualise it happening 3. Keep my body ready — relaxed, loose
What do you do when called upon?	1. In the over before, warm up, rehearse action and consider field placings 2. Click plan in 'deeper and deeper'
What do you do when you are up?	1. Work out run-up carefully 2. Bowl two or three deliveries to a team-mate 3. Check field placings with captain
What do you do at the crease?	1. Visualise line and length 2. Pick a target area to bowl at
What is your pre-delivery routine?	1. Behavioural — stretches and relaxed breathing 2. Mental — visualise each delivery
At the point of delivery what will you pay attention to?	1. Target, target, target!

AROUSAL AND ANXIETY MANAGEMENT

While arousal refers to the general physiological and psychological activity of athletes at a particular moment, ranging from when they wake in the morning (low arousal) to when they compete (high arousal), anxiety refers to a negative emotional reaction to arousal at that time, and feelings of nervousness, worry and apprehension. **Cognitive anxiety** is the degree to which athletes ruminate, worry, or have negative thoughts about an event. **Somatic anxiety** concerns the moment to moment changes in physiological activity during an event, for instance, sweating, increases in heart rate, breathing and muscular tension.

The coach of a male hockey team referred a talented but very temperamental forward to a sport psychologist to discuss the number of green, yellow and red cards the player was receiving during state league games. The player, Andre, readily acknowledged he had a temper problem and often overreacted to what he thought of as incompetent officiating and illegal play.

Typical thoughts in the heat of the moment included 'Does this official have parents?', 'I'll get you back for that!', and subsequent feelings included anger and uncontrollable rage. Andre understood that he left his opposition player unmarked, leaving his team significantly disadvantaged. During discussions he realised that a more appropriate thought in both circumstances would be 'Where's the ball?' and that, if he smiled through his gum-shield, his anger would subside (because smiling reduces the tendency to anger) so he could focus more quickly on playing the game.

This cognitive and behavioural strategy was practised at training and it worked immediately during games simply because Andre's thoughts became task versus other oriented, and he channelled his energies more productively.

Principles

Coaches can help athletes understand the factors that affect the arousal–performance relationship by asking them to identify:

- a particularly stressful situation in their sport
- their typical thoughts about this event (what do they think?)
- their typical emotions and physical reactions to this event (how do they feel?), and
- how they typically react (how do they behave?).

What coaches and athletes will learn from this exercise is that how an athlete thinks about a situation is usually the starting point of a chain reaction that ultimately leads to overly aroused states and unhelpful levels of anxiety. In other words 'how you think' becomes 'how you feel', which explains 'how you react or behave'. Some measure of management over anxiety soon becomes evident when athletes realise that they always have control over how they think. Often what was previously seen as a threat, or something to avoid, soon becomes less threatening (for example, a challenge) and something to approach enthusiastically.

Application examples

Enhancing self-awareness of arousal and coping skills can be achieved by asking athletes to identify their **Ideal Performance State** (IPS). In the table on the top of the next page, female athletes show how they create and sustain their IPS for basketball, based on recollections of best-ever performances. Coaches can adapt this method to suit their sports or simply ask athletes to identify a 'best-ever performance' and to recall how they felt and what they did on the day, night, morning or afternoon before the game.

This introductory arousal management mental skills practice plan for young netballers can be integrated within a normal training plan.

Sample arousal mental skills practice plan for netballers

Learning objective

To improve the players' awareness of their physical and mental arousal levels

Total time: 10–15 minutes

Explanation

Arousal is the intensity level of behaviour. Common physiological responses include a racing heartbeat, tense muscles, and butterflies, whereas thought processes are characterised as including distracted attention, negativity and a sense of lack of control. Different times associated with sporting performance (night before, warm-up, after event) are associated with different arousal levels.

Key teaching points

Beginning

After they have warmed up for two minutes, ask players to take their pulse, note their breathing, sweating and muscle feeling. Following a two-minute

155

Ideal Performance State pre-game plan for women's basketball players

Goals	Actions
What feelings do you want to attain and maintain before the game?	**What will you do and how will you do it?**
Physically	
• relaxed, loose • energised, strong, fit • 'pleasantly fatigued?' • alert, charged	• physical warm-up: starting when I wake up in the morning • technical warm-up: practise skills • nutrition — eat well
Mentally	
• task oriented, focused • belief in my ability to perform my job in team • organised/prepared • focused on my strengths	• visualise the job to be done • affirmations: 'I can do . . .', 'I am an excellent . . .' • prepare for distraction(s)
Emotionally	
• determined, read to compete • apprehensive, eager to play • happy, 'let's play ball' • 'relaxed awareness' • composed, poised	• convey support and enthusiasm • smile a lot, 'it's show time!' • tell jokes

rest restart the drill but increase the difficulty so that players' stress/arousal levels are elevated. Tell players that the number of dropped balls will determine who gets to play in the next game. After two minutes, stop them to take notice of their bodily functions. Discuss physical changes between the two states and make them aware that these are their stress signs.

Middle
After they have performed another drill, ask players to note their concentration, what they are saying to themselves and how they feel about the drill. Restart the drill, but beforehand inform them that the number of mistakes will be recorded and after training they will be given some form of punishment, such as push-ups or shuttle runs. After two minutes, ask players to note their thought processes again and compare them with the previous ones. Discuss the changes between the two mental states and make them aware that these are their stress signs.

End
At the next session, practise match or real competition, players are to watch for and note down their stress signs. They may occur the night before the game, the morning of the competition, on the way to the venue, when entering the stadium, in the changing room, during warm-ups, just before the event, at the start, during the event or at the finish.

Equipment and space required
Regular training facilities and equipment

Next steps
Determine each player's ideal arousal level for optimum performance.

Comments
Note, team selection for the next game should not really be decided by the number of dropped balls in the drill, and carrying out the punishment is optional. After the drill, clarify this with the players!

(National Sports Information Centre)

The netball coach helps players to monitor their arousal levels.

Strategies that coaches can give athletes to deal with under or overarousal before or during play

Physical strategies

Underaroused	Overaroused
1. Increase breathing rate (short and deep)	1. Take at least three deep breaths
2. Introduce cheering and yelling	2. Take one or two release breaths, shoulder-shrug breaths that are shallower than deep breaths
3. Play lively or loud music	3. Stretch to relax muscle tension
4. Build from mild to vigorous exercise, such as rapid sit-ups or push-ups	4. Practise technical aspects of technique (slo-mo)
5. Take a cold shower	5. Use progressive muscle relaxation

Mental (cognitive) strategies

Underaroused	Overaroused
1. Give yourself a severe pep talk	1. Focus on your task — 'What do I have to do?'
2. Stress the importance of the competition to yourself and others	2. Use 'thought stoppage' to prevent negative thoughts
3. Consider the strengths of the opposition	3. Use 'switch on, down, and off' concentration skills
4. Set yourself a challenging goal	4. Use visualisation techniques
5. Complete a full pre-competitive workout	5. Use biofeedback to control heart rate by listening to your heart (or taking your pulse) and slowing down your breathing

IMAGERY

Imagery (mental rehearsal or visualisation) is simply creating or recreating an experience in the mind. There are both physiological and psychological reasons for its effectiveness in sport. Athletes can use either internal or external imagery or both, and senses used can include smell, sound, touch, taste and sight. The nature of the task and the ability level of performers can affect the effectiveness of imagery. While both novice and skilled performers benefit from imagery on cognitive tasks that involve decision making and perception judgement, in general skilled performers use imagery more effectively.

Mustafa, the coach and father of teenage golfer Hanna, asked a sport psychologist to help Hanna deal with her inconsistent performances over both one and four-round tournaments. Hanna reported that she had neither developed a solid and consistent pre-shot routine nor made use of imagery on the course. To lock her focus into performance cues for each shot incorporating imagery, a five-stage pre-shot routine was devised.

- A plan was made for each shot that included selecting the target and the type of shot before addressing the ball.
- A picture, sensation and thought of how the shot would look was selected.
- The shot was rehearsed physically and mentally.
- A set-up system of aligning and aiming was developed on the practice range and then used during matches.
- The same thought or image was used as a swing trigger for every shot.

The young golfer immediately noticed how much her task focus improved over 18 holes and subsequently her scores reduced over a month.

(National Sports Information Centre)

A golfer should visualise a shot before playing it.

Principles

Imagery can be used before and after practice and competition, during breaks in the action, and during personal time away from competition. Athletes can also use imagery to enhance both physical and psychological skills, such as concentration, confidence, emotion management, acquiring and practising skills and tactics, and coping with pain and injury.

However, the keys to effective imagery are vividness and controllability. Using all their senses, good imagers make their recalled images as vivid and as detailed as possible. They also manipulate their images so they get what they want. For example, when conjuring up a best-ever previous performance, good imagers see and feel themselves in the actual environment, and performing perfectly — the picture is clear and the result is successful.

At key times during the year, athletes are often very stressed. For this reason, coaches' post-event strategies should include some steps to return the athlete to a normal emotional state. These strategies may vary markedly depending on the personality, maturity and experience of the individual, but they are easy to implement if the techniques are rehearsed regularly after training sessions and before going to bed.

Visualisation, progressive muscle relaxation, slow and deep breathing exercises, yoga, meditation, music, and other relaxation strategies are used by leading Australian athletes to achieve mental and emotional recovery. Using relaxing music during static stretching at the end of train-

ing, and visualisation, are two techniques often introduced to young athletes. Before going to bed the athlete can visualise a calming tranquil scene in order to relax and switch off from the day's events.

Mood-lifting activities can include watching a comedy show on TV or video, reading an escapist or adventure novel or planning a social game of tenpin bowling. For teams or athletes in extended competitions, and competitions away from home, planning such activities as part of training is essential.

Application examples

To make the best use of imagery, Orlick and Botterill (1987) advise athletes to:

- 'Start with skills that you already can do well, then begin to work on skills you are trying to refine.

- Focus on bringing the feeling up when you do your imagery.

- Devote 10–15 minutes daily to your imagery practice.

- On the way to practice run through in your head what you want to accomplish.

- During practice, before you do skills, run through the image of what you want to happen and, when you are given corrections, feel the corrections in your head before you do the skill.

- As you prepare for competition feel yourself in control, doing what you want to do, focusing the way you want in pressure situations, and imagine yourself achieving your ultimate goal.'

(National Sports Information Centre)

Activities such as reading can help athletes to relax.

Visualisation mental skills practice plan for young cricketers at net practice

Learning objective

To introduce visualisation to outswing bowling

Total time: 10–15 minutes

Explanation

Following a period of technical instruction and short practice, say to the cricketers, 'Sit or lie quietly, close your eyes and turn your attention inwards. Take four or five deep breaths and pay attention to the feelings in your body. We're going to learn the skill of visualisation.' Be patient and tolerant as the group settles and calms down.

Key teaching points

Beginning

Continue with 'Now while you are relaxed, imagine you are at the nets bowling, just as you were a few moments ago. See if you can remember what outswing bowling feels like. What is involved? Pretend in your mind that you are bowling again and bowl six deliveries.'

Middle

'It's a bit strange isn't it? Let's try it again and see if you can get it to work a little better this time (repeat above). Feel yourself as well as seeing yourself bowling six outswing deliveries.'

End

Summarise by explaining 'Visualisation is practising or rehearsing in your mind, or picturing yourself in your mind's eye performing. It will help you learn skills more thoroughly. We'll do this again each net practice.'

Equipment and space required

Normal net practice area, cricket ball each

Steps

Once (in their own judgement) players can visualise while relaxed, ask them to repeat the exercise at practice once or twice over, and then before each successive delivery and, finally, transfer it to games.

Comments

Look for non-verbal signs of confusion in players.

Expect

Some negative reactions, but don't dwell on those

Tell them

'Try to be patient, learning will take time.'

CONCLUSION

Coaches can use performance profiling as a self-awareness technique to help athletes work out where their strengths and weaknesses lie and so where work is needed in the future. Readers should now also be equipped with the important principles to apply in teaching mental skills to athletes, particularly the four key mental skills discussed here — goal setting, concentration, arousal management and imagery.

It is critical that coaches understand how important it is to train athletes' minds as well as their bodies. Without the correct mental approach to sport, athletes' performances will always be less than their best. Coaches should feel confident about applying their knowledge of mental skills training by integrating practice plans similar to the samples above within their normal coaching sessions.

COACHING TIPS

- Periodise the mental skills program alongside other components of training.

- Individualise mental skills training to suit different types of athletes. For example:

  use goal setting and management strategies for those who lack confidence and direction

  use relaxation training for those who are nervous before competition, and

  try arousal training techniques for athletes who struggle to do their best in early morning competitions.

- Develop concentration skills within general training sessions through coaching cues, questioning/discussions and practising plans and routines.

FURTHER READING

Butler, R (1996) *Sport Psychology in Action*. Oxford, UK: Butterworth-Heinemann.

Hanin, Y (1999) *Emotions in Sport*. Champaign, IL: Human Kinetics.

Orlick, T (1986) *Psyching for Sport: Mental Training for Athletes*. Champaign, IL: Human Kinetics.

Orlick, T (2000) *In Pursuit of Excellence: How to Win in Sport and Life through Mental Training*. Champaign, IL: Human Kinetics.

Orlick, T, and C Botterill (1987) *Visualisation: What You See Is What You Get* (video). Belconnen: Australian Coaching Council.

CHAPTER 14
ACQUISITION OF SKILL

Bruce Abernethy

(National Sports Information Centre)

INTRODUCTION

Helping athletes improve their movement skills is fundamental to good sports coaching. In this chapter we first examine the processes that underlie the performance of skilled movement and then we look at how these processes change with practice and learning.

PERFORMANCE OF SKILLED MOVEMENT

Stages in the performance of motor skills

The brain and nervous system are responsible for our ability to control and learn movement. They act much like a computer, processing information from a range of sources, both outside and inside the body, in order to produce skilled movement.

To understand how a computer works we cannot simply look at the output it produces; rather we must understand the information processing that has taken place beforehand. The same is true of trying to understand skilled movement. Movement does not simply occur as a consequence of spontaneous, unplanned muscular activity, but is rather the end product of a series of processes within the brain and nervous system. These pro-

cesses are not directly observable, but are nevertheless critical to skilled performance.

There are at least three key processing stages involved in making skilled movement:

- **perceiving** — determining what's happening
- **decision making** — selecting the right movement option, and
- **acting** — planning and controlling the required movement.

Perceiving — determining what's happening

Underlying processes

Perception is concerned equally with determining what is happening in the outside world (for example, where is the opponent located?), what is happening within the athlete's own body (for example, is it in balance?) and the relationship between these external and internal environments (for example, where is the athlete's hand in relation to the approaching ball?). Perception is an active process that goes beyond the simple collection of information from our various senses to detailed analysis and interpretation of the information we receive.

Measuring perception

Perceptual skills are measured in athletes in several different ways. One approach involves measuring general perceptual characteristics, such as visual acuity, depth perception and peripheral vision. A second approach involves using sport-specific stimuli to reproduce accurately the perceptual demands faced by the athlete in competition. While a whole host of different sport-specific perceptual tests are possible, the most common are for pattern recognition and of anticipation.

Sports are full of patterns — **movement patterns** of individual players and movement

In sports such as hockey, the ability to rapidly recognise play patterns is essential to successful performance.

(National Sports Information Centre)

patterns of whole teams. Sport-specific pattern recognition is usually assessed by giving players a very brief (about five seconds) view of either slides or video showing typical scenes from a competition situation (for example, a developing play pattern in hockey). After viewing the pattern, the player is asked to reproduce, as accurately as possible, the positions of each of the players shown in the scene onto a plan of the playing surface. The ability to recognise these patterns rapidly can also be assessed by systematically altering the length of time for which the patterns are displayed.

Anticipation is a specific type of pattern recognition skill for which players must pick up advance information from the early movement patterns of opposing players. By filming videos from a player's perspective and then selectively editing these videos to block vision at different points both before and after the flight of the ball, the coach can work out both when a player first picks up anticipatory information and what part(s) of the opponent's action provides this information.

Decision making — selecting the right movement

Underlying processes

Athletes often have only very limited time in which to decide what movement response, if any, is needed. The process of selecting the best movement option (**decision making**) in-

volves considering both current perceptual information and past experience. The number of decisions to be made, the number of response options from which to select, the total time available for decision making, and the cost in terms of time associated with making incorrect decisions all influence the speed and accuracy of decision making.

Measuring decision making

The speed with which people can make decisions is usually measured by **reaction time**, the time between receiving a stimulus and initiating an appropriate response. When there is only one stimulus and one possible response (such as occurs at the start of a sprint race) it usually takes about one-fifth of a second (or 200 milliseconds) to react. However, as the number of alternatives from which a person must choose increases, so does reaction time. It increases by about an equal amount each time the number of possible responses we have to choose from is doubled.

This has important implications for understanding sports performance. Anything an offensive player can do to increase the number of alternatives facing an opponent will slow the opponent's reaction time and give the offensive player more time. Likewise, anything that the defensive player can do to narrow the range of alternatives available to the offensive player will act to speed up the defensive player's response in the game situation.

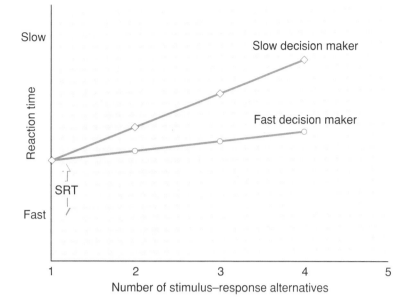

Reaction time as a function of the number of stimulus–response alternatives. Simple reaction time (SRT) refers to the situation where there is only one alternative, and hence no choice to make (after Abernethy et al 1996).

The degree to which reaction time is slowed each time the number of possible responses doubles varies from one person to the next and, importantly, can be reduced with practice. Any advance knowledge an athlete has that either makes some stimuli more probable than others, or that makes event sequences in some way predictable, will help speed up decision making. The more players can learn their opponents' strengths and weaknesses, preferred options and patterns of play, the faster they will be able to respond. Similarly, the more unpredictable players can remain, making all response options and patterns of play equally probable, the more the decision-making speed of their opponents can be slowed to the players' advantage.

Acting — planning and controlling movement

Underlying processes

In order to produce a desired movement, an athlete must organise the movement in advance (by planning the signals to be sent to the muscles), initiate the movement (by sending the necessary signals from the brain to the muscles) and then control the movement (by monitoring feedback about the movement's progress). The speed and accuracy of movement organisation, initiation and control are determined by a number of factors, including the number of muscles and joints involved in the movement, the acceptable error margins for the movement, and the difficulties the movement creates for maintaining balance.

Measuring movement control

Most sports have available skills tests that provide objective measures of a player's ability to execute, with precision or with speed, the specific movements (techniques) required in the sport. However, such skills tests don't provide much insight into the precise movement pattern that is used or the underlying control processes.

With the increasing availability of sophisticated techniques for the biomechanical analysis of movement, the measurement of movement patterns for most sport skills can now be quite precise. Movement patterns can be fully described in terms of the displacement, velocity and acceleration of the athlete's body and limbs (**movement kinematics**), the forces generated during movement production (**movement kinetics**) and the activation of the key muscles controlling the movement (**electromyography**). These biomechanical measures not only let the coach objectively measure movement patterns, but are also a valuable training device for improving movement execution skills.

The amount of attention required to control a movement varies from person to person. Assessing how much attention players need to give to the performance of the basic movement skills may provide the coach with useful information about how well the skills have been learned. For example, basketball players who fail to detect when team-mates are unmarked may do so not because of poor visual perception, but simply because the performance of the basic movement skills takes so much of their attention that there is no 'free' attention left to allocate to other things. Players who display similar basic skills may do so by using different amounts of their limited processing capacity.

The logical way to assess how automatic players have become in the performance of their basic skills (and so how much 'free' attention they have to allocate to other tasks) is to have them perform two tasks at once. This dual-task approach involves the players performing an additional (or secondary) task at the same time as they perform the basic (or primary) movement tasks of their sport. In basketball, for example, the primary task could be any one of the game's basic movement skills, such as dribbling the ball, and the secondary task could be one such as noticing when a team-mate is unmarked or, to make measuring easier, determining when specific lights around the court are switched on. The better the secondary task performance of the player, the more automatic the performance of the basic movement skills will be.

(National Sports Information Centre)

Skilled athletes perform complex movements smoothly.

LEARNING SKILLED MOVEMENT

One way of understanding more about what is learned with practice is to carefully compare the characteristics of highly skilled and less skilled athletes.

Characteristics of skilled athletes

Observable characteristics

A number of differences in performance between the skilled performer and the novice are apparent to even the untrained eye. The expert performs in a smooth, unhurried manner, making appropriate decisions both rapidly and accurately, and acting with maximum efficiency and apparently little attention and effort. The novice, on the other hand, is apparently forced to operate constantly without sufficient time to determine either what to do or how to do it, and the resulting performance is rushed, disorganised and ineffective. The novice is generally unable to cope with the conflicting demands of both speed and accuracy in decision making, and both consistency and adaptability in producing movement.

Skilled perception

Experts are typically little different from everyone else with respect to their general perceptual characteristics. Champion athletes do not appear to possess 'super' vision, when it is measured using standard optometric tests. However, experts are profoundly superior to less skilled athletes in their pattern recognition and anticipatory skills when these are assessed using patterns drawn specifically

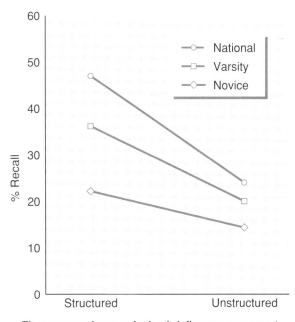

The accuracy in reproducing briefly seen movement patterns of hockey players at different skill levels. Structured stimuli are those containing sport-specific patterns; unstructured stimuli are random configurations (after Starkes 1987).

from their sport. The limiting factor for expert performance appears to lie not with getting the necessary visual information into the brain, but rather with knowing how to interpret and process the information. A good way to improve perceptual skills for sport may be to expose athletes repeatedly to the patterns specific to their sport.

A much-debated issue in coaching circles is whether anticipation and pattern recognition skills (what is often called the ability to 'read the play') are innate or whether they can be learned and improved through practice. A recent study examined whether it might be possible to use video training to improve the speed with which tennis players could anticipate, and return, an opponent's serve.

Some novice tennis players were given training that consisted of watching videotapes of tennis serves, filmed from the receiver's perspective, with vision of many of the serves systematically blocked out early in the server's action. This video training was supplemented by verbal instruction from the coach about specific cues for reading the tennis serve. Over a four-week training period the decision-making speed and the anticipatory ability of the players trained this way improved significantly more than similar novice players who were given either different training or no training. This certainly indicates that these skills can be trained and that relatively simple techniques using video may be sufficient to enhance anticipatory skill (Farrow et al 1998).

Skilled decision making

There are two main ways in which the decision-making processes of expert athletes may differ from those of novices. First, experts appear to have better knowledge of the probabilities, sequences and patterns of play involved in their sport. They have better intuition about their sport in general, and can better analyse the actions of specific opponents, courses and so on. This superior knowledge of event probabilities allows experts to markedly reduce their decision-making time.

Second, in many sport situations the experts can directly influence the decision-making demands placed on their opponents. Experts are typically able to successfully execute a wide range of options within any particular setting, maximising the uncertainty, and so the reaction time, of their opponents. Experts are less likely to respond to false cues than novice players while, through their own actions, they can make it more likely that their opponents will respond to such false cues and 'fakes'.

The differences between experts and novices in decision making suggest a number of approaches that coaches might take to enhance the decision-making skills of their players. One obvious approach is to study in detail the preferred play strategies and options of the opposing player or team. The use of computerised match statistics on the relative use and success rates of different plays may be a useful objective addition to traditional videotape for learning the strengths, weaknesses and probable patterns in an opponent's play. Decision-making training should also focus on developing and systematically practising deception skills. This might include trying out ways of presenting false cues, as well as disguising the critical cues or presenting them as late as possible.

Skilled movement control

It's very obvious that the movement execution skills of the expert athlete are very different from those of the less skilled novice. In sports where speed is important, experts are usually found to move faster than average, and in sports in which coincidence-timing is particularly important for success, experts usually have not shorter, but more consistent, movement times. In sports where the performance environment is highly stable and predictable (for example, 'closed' skill sports such as gymnastics and archery), experts show greater consistency, both in the way they move and in the way they time their movements.

With practice, skilled performers in these sports develop regimented movement routines that allow them to translate consistent movement execution directly into consistent performance. The movement patterns experts use frequently also become more efficient, making them more resistant to fatigue. Experts cocontract (contract opposing muscles together) muscles less than do novices, and use fewer muscles not directly involved in the movement task.

In 'closed' skill sports such as pistol shooting and archery it is important to be able to produce as consistent a movement pattern as possible from one shot to the next. Studies in these sports show that elite shooters consistently begin their movements at the same point in their breathing cycle and in the beating cycle of their hearts. Heart rate is systematically slowed down by some five to ten beats per minute in the last few seconds before the trigger is pulled, and at the same time there are some consistent changes in the brain wave activity. Providing learners with feedback from these different physiological systems may help coaches improve skill learning in these activities.

Consistent movement patterns are essential for pistol shooters.

(National Sports Information Centre)

As performers become more skilful, the control of their basic movement patterns also becomes progressively more automatic, requiring less and less direct attention. This allows experts to pay greater attention to other higher order skills such as 'reading' the game and identifying the position of team-mates and opponents. In dual tasks, experts consistently outperform less skilled players on secondary tasks, even when their performance of the basic (primary task) skills may not be obviously better.

To facilitate skill learning, coaches may find it useful to give athletes feedback on the main features of their movement, such as its time, consistency or pattern. Further, it may be possible to stimulate continued learning of movement execution skills, even by highly experienced players, if coaches progressively overload their players with concurrent tasks, in much the same way as the second task is used in assessing how automatic are athletes' movements.

Stages of learning

Most learners pass through at least three identifiable stages in acquiring any movement skill.

The cognitive stage

The learner in the initial (cognitive) stage is focused on determining what needs to be done in order to perform the skill correctly and successfully. Issues such as 'how do I score points in this game?', 'what is the best way to hold the bat or racquet?' and 'where should I be positioned relative to my team-mates and to the sideline?' dominate. Consequently, enhancing performance at this stage largely involves thinking and planning (cognition) rather than actual motor practice.

Old movement patterns (developed by other skills) are pieced together in a new way. Improvements in performance tend to be quite rapid, but performance levels fluctuate substantially as new strategies are tried and often abandoned. Movement execution is very inconsistent and the perceptual and decision-making aspects of performance are both slow and error-ridden.

During the cognitive phase, good instruction and demonstration may improve performances faster than even task practice. The

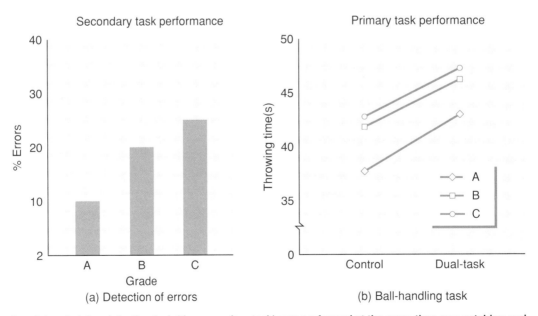

(a) Detection of errors (b) Ball-handling task

A peripheral vision detection task (the secondary task) was performed at the same time as a catching and passing task (the primary task) by netballers of different skill levels. The more skilled (A and B-grade) players performed better on the detection task, even though their primary task performance was largely indistinguishable from that of lower grade players (after Parker 1981).

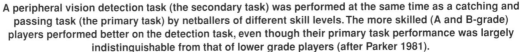

transfer of learning from other motor skills is most likely to be positive at this stage, and the coach may be able to help athletes acquire skills by drawing parallels between the requirements of the new task and those of sports the athletes already know. For example, a volleyball coach may be able to help athletes acquire skills by pointing out the similarities between the spiking action and the overhead service action in tennis. The simpler the lessons, the faster athletes will learn.

The associative stage

The second phase of learning begins when the player has decided on the best way of doing the task and focuses attention rather upon 'fine-tuning' the movement skills. Players at this intermediate stage of learning progressively become both more consistent and accurate in producing particular movement patterns, and more capable of generating new movement responses when required.

Improvement in the associative phase is typically gradual, but performance is markedly more consistent than in the cognitive phase. At this stage of learning, the coach should progressively make the practice situation more complex (for example, by introducing opposing players or new play options), to help players become more familiar with the perceptual and decision-making demands of competition.

The autonomous stage

After extensive practice some, but not all, athletes enter the autonomous phase of learning, where the control of the required motor skills becomes largely automatic. At this stage, control of movement becomes so precise and performance so consistent and accurate that athletes no longer need to keep checking feedback on how well they are executing their movements. This allows them to move their attention to other tasks, such as monitoring the movement of other players.

Even when athletes apparently reach the autonomous phase of learning, they can still continue to improve their skills, providing they undertake appropriate and intensive practice. Indeed, there is no evidence that motor skill learning ever ceases, even after decades of practice and millions of practice trials. Coaches should consider using practice drills with attention demands and difficulties greater than those provided by the sport itself to help the expert performer learn to perform even more automatically. However, they should take care with practice at all stages of

learning to ensure that correct movement technique is developed and maintained. Errors in technique may be extremely difficult, if not impossible, to correct at the autonomous stage of learning.

Factors affecting learning

Instruction and models for learning

The main ways that coaches can teach athletes about the movement patterns necessary for success in their sport are either verbal instruction, visual modelling, or a combination of the two.

Verbal instructions should be restricted to providing only a few key cues or phases at a time. As learners are bombarded with large amounts of information when they first perform a new task, it is essential that the coach not add to this complexity, but rather provide a maximum of two or three key elements on which the learner can focus. These elements should help make learning easier.

The challenge for the coach is to determine what the key elements are at each stage of learning. For example, providing cues about the placement of the arms in downhill skiing might be an appropriate cue for the intermediate skier, but a completely inappropriate one for a novice, who has more basic concerns about balance and weight transfer. Teaching athletes about the mechanical principles underlying the skills being learned can often be helpful, but they can also often perform well without this knowledge.

As long as some simple criteria are met, visual demonstrations are generally more effective than verbal instructions. Models are most effective if they are:

- technically sound

- presented from a perspective that allows athletes to picture themselves as models rather than merely observers

- accompanied by good verbal instruction highlighting the key elements, and

- continuously available during practice as a reference point.

Feedback availability

There are two critical types of feedback information that learners need in order to improve — feedback information about the outcome of their movements (for example, was the arrow on target?) and feedback information about the pattern of movement produced (for example, how much knee flexion was

The relationship between knowledge of performance and knowledge of results provides a guide for directing future attempts at a skill

Type of evaluation	Was the goal accomplished (from knowledge of results)?	Was the movement executed as planned (from knowledge of performance)?	
		Yes	No
	Yes	Getting the idea of the movement; try to repeat	Surprise at a chance success; would not try to repeat movement pattern
	No	Need to adjust movement plan	Everything's wrong; need to attempt to produce the planned pattern

(Adapted from Gentile 1972)

there at landing?). The first type of feedback is often referred to as **knowledge of results** and the second, **knowledge of performance**, and the relationship between these two types of feedback information helps guide the learner.

Achieving positive knowledge of results and positive knowledge of performance motivates learners to try to reproduce and reinforce the movements produced in practice, whereas any other combination helps them to improve what they're doing. The important role for the coach in this whole process is ensuring that the learner has continuous and ready access to clear, concise feedback information, both about movement patterns and outcome.

Knowledge of results is essential for learning. Without information about the outcome of their movements, athletes can't improve their skills, even when they practise a lot. It appears to be best if coaches give feedback about results to players frequently in the early stages of learning, but less frequently as the players' skills develop. This helps athletes develop the important capability of monitoring their own performances, and makes them less reliant on external forms of feedback.

When knowledge of results is given to learners, generally it should be presented as precisely as is useful to them. In sports where precise knowledge of results is not directly available to athletes, it is very important that the coach provides it, and as soon as possible, as any delay may diminish its effectiveness. If athletes perform other skills afterwards, before they receive feedback, and between receiving feedback and practising the skill again, they may not learn as well.

Knowledge of performance is more difficult for the coach to provide and for the athletes themselves to acquire than knowledge of results. To obtain feedback about athletes' movement patterns, athletes or coaches generally need access to either videotape or more sophisticated biomechanical analysis systems.

Amount and type of practice

Provided adequate feedback information is available, the more practice people do, the more they will learn. To reach elite levels in many competitive sports, athletes have to practise basic skills extensively over many years, and so perform literally millions of learning trials. Research on different kinds of experts suggests that a minimum of some ten years (or 10 000 hours) of deliberate, effortful practice is necessary to reach an elite level (Ericsson 1996).

One way to learn which types of practice best help to develop expertise is to look for similarities in the early practice backgrounds of elite athletes. In a recent study for the Australian Sports Commission, researchers examined the practice histories of 15 world-class decision-makers from hockey, netball and basketball. Common among this group of experts were:

- early exposure to a wide range of different sports
- relatively early exposure to competition against adults (and the opportunity to learn to predict adult movement patterns)
- the opportunity, in first learning the skills of their specialist sport, to experiment without heavy emphasis on outcome, and

■ the opportunity to model and learn by watching others, again from an early age.

Playing experience in other sports appears to be a valuable part of the development of expert decision-makers in team sports. The greater the number of other sports these athletes played before specialising in their chosen sport, the fewer total hours of deliberate practice they needed before first being selected for a national team. Variable practice experiences, especially during the formative years, appear to be particularly valuable for developing aspects of expert performance (Abernethy et al 1999).

The type of practice done by athletes appears to powerfully influence learning. Practising under a range of different task conditions better prepares athletes for coping with new task conditions than does practice under unchanging conditions. Providing a range of different practice conditions seems to be particularly important in the training of players in sports where adaptability is essential for successful performance. Expert decision-makers in team sports all share this as part of their practice histories. Surprisingly, variable practice conditions also seem to be beneficial for performance of 'closed' skills. Apparently, the wider their practice experiences, the more adept athletes become at coping with the subtle changes in task that they may encounter in competition.

As a general rule, the more specific the practice drills are to the sport, the more effective they will be in improving competitive sport performance. If athletes are to transfer as much of what they've learned as possible from the practice session to competition, the practice session must mimic as closely as possible the sport itself. This applies not only to the movement execution skills, but also to perceptual and decision-making skills. Practising and learning all the skills of a sport while playing the sport itself (as occurs in the popular 'games for understanding' approach to teaching skills) seems to be a better way to learn than the traditional approach of learning skills in isolation.

CONCLUSION

To design appropriate practice sessions for specific sports and athletes, coaches need to use three fundamental steps. In the first step, they need to assess the specific task demands of their particular sport. They should try to calculate how important skill acquisition is to the athletes' performances, compared to other factors. For the key skills, coaches should also work out how important are the underlying perceptual, decision-making and movement execution processes.

In the second step, coaches need to assess the current capabilities of the athletes, preferably by measuring their ability to perceive, decide and act in the ways outlined in this chapter. In the third step, coaches need to develop sport-specific practice conditions designed to correct any deficiencies in athletes' sport-specific skills. This systematic approach gives coaches great opportunities to help athletes learn skills.

COACHING TIPS

■ Give immediate, accurate and constructive feedback whenever possible.

■ Use videos or demonstrations in combination with key words to teach skills and improve performance.

■ Schedule the learning of new skills early in the practice session, when athletes are fresh and attentive.

■ Include activities that train anticipation and decision-making skills in practice sessions.

■ Provide opportunities for athletes to practise under a range of different task conditions.

FURTHER READING

Abernethy, B, V Kippers, L Mackinnon, R Neal and S Hanrahan (1996) *Biophysical Foundations of Human Movement.* South Melbourne: Macmillan, chapters 16–19.

Abernethy, B, J Côté , and J Baker (1999) Expert decision-making in sport. Report to the Australian Sports Commission.

Abernethy, B, JP Wann, and S Parks (1999) Training perceptual–motor skills for sport. In: B Elliott, *Training in Sport: Applying Sport Science.* Chichester, UK: John Wiley, 1–68.

Christina, RW, and DM Corcos (1988) *Coaches Guide to Teaching Sport Skills.* Champaign, IL: Human Kinetics.

Ericsson, KA (ed) (1996) *The Road to Excellence: The Acquisition of Expert Performance in the Arts and Sciences, Sports and Games.* Mahwah, NJ: Erlbaum.

Farrow, D, P Chivers, C Hardingham and S Sachse (1998) The effect of video-based perceptual training on the tennis return of serve. *International Journal of Sport Psychology* 29: 231–42.

Fitts, PM, and MI Posner (1967) *Human Performance*. Belmont, CA: Brooks/Cole.

Gentile, AM (1972) A working model of skill acquisition with application to teaching. *Quest* 17: 3–23.

Magill, RA (1998) *Motor Learning: Concepts and Applications*. Boston, MA: Wm C Brown/McGraw-Hill.

Newell, KM (1991) Motor skill acquisition. *Annual Review of Psychology* 42: 213–37.

Parker H (1981) Visual detection and perception in netball. In: IM Cockerill and WW MacGillivary (eds), *Vision and Sport*. Cheltenham, UK: Stanley Thornes.

Schmidt, RA, and CA Wrisberg (1999) *Motor Learning and Performance*. Champaign, IL: Human Kinetics.

Schmidt, RA, and TD Lee (1999) *Motor Control and Learning: A Behavioral Emphasis*. Champaign, IL: Human Kinetics.

Singer, RN, and CM Janelle (1999) Determining sport expertise: from genes to supremes. *International Journal of Sport Psychology* 30: 117–50.

Smith, R (1994) Analysing on-water rowing performance. *Sports Coach* 17(3): 37–40.

Starkes, JL (1987) Skill in field hockey: the nature of the expert advantage. *Journal of Sport Psychology* 9: 146–60.

Thorpe, R (1990). New directions in games teaching. In: N Armstrong (ed), *New Directions in Physical Education*. Champaign, IL: Human Kinetics, 79–100.

CHAPTER 15
BIOMECHANICS OF SPORT

Bruce C Elliott

(National Sports Information Centre)

INTRODUCTION

An understanding of sport biomechanics (how and why the human body moves) prepares athletes to learn new skills and coaches to detect and correct flaws in performance. Coaches can then:

- adjust each individual athlete's technique so that they achieve the best performance possible
- select the appropriate equipment for each athlete's size so that the best performance can be achieved at all levels of development, and
- reduce the possibilities of injury.

The true value of using biomechanics in coaching is that it permits athletes to be treated as individuals.

How does a coach decide on the appropriate technique for each athlete? If they understand the mechanical and physical requirements of a particular activity, coaches will not have to rely only on their own experience (intuition), on copying the styles of current champions, or on leaving performers to their own devices. They should integrate these resources with biomechanical knowledge and information, to help them systematically identify and correct performance flaws, producing better performances in future.

ANALYSING MOVEMENT

In order to improve athletes' performances, coaches must first evaluate their technique and then modify it. It is important to ensure that athletes have reached the stage of producing consistent performances before they are biomechanically tested, or the tests may not produce useful results.

Coaches must focus on the critical features of the action if they are to successfully analyse a movement. Inexperienced observers can't generally identify as many key factors in a particular movement as can experienced coaches, mainly because they can't distinguish relevant from irrelevant factors.

The coach must consider the following factors before beginning any analysis:

- what level of performer is being evaluated, and
- what are the aspirations and the ages of the individuals being examined? For example, there is a great difference between the expectations of an under-12 soccer team training three hours a week, and an under-12 elite gymnastics squad, which may train 30 hours a week in preparation for international-level performance.

Rather than immediately attempting to correct a flaw in technique, a good coach should also first check to see if that is the real source of the problem. It may be necessary to assess psychological, physical and tactical aspects of the movement before it is safe to assume that the cause of the error is purely technical.

- The coach should determine whether the athlete is psychologically ready to learn the skill. Factors such as anxiety, caused by fear of failure, can affect technique and should be addressed before modifying technique.

■ The coach must also ascertain if physical factors are causing a technique fault. The reason for a particular error may be low levels of flexibility or strength.

■ Errors in technique may also be the result of a poor tactical situation, rather than the technique itself. A player may choose an inappropriate response to a tactical situation, making the performance of a learned response almost impossible.

Subjective analysis methods

The successful analysis of movement involves planning a routine set of procedures that become easier to structure with practice. In order to analyse a skill, the coach should understand the biomechanical principles involved in it and must be completely familiar with its performance.

Coaches who are subjectively analysing a skill would take the following steps.

Preparing for the analysis

Determine the performance goal: coaches must decide what they are trying to achieve for the performer — a lower time, greater distance, or perhaps a tactical advantage?

Determine the mechanical variables: before coaches can modify technique, it is essential that they have a mechanical model of the performance in mind. This model will help to identify the way different factors work together to influence performance. Experienced coaches will know the mechanical variables that are critical to the performance, and may therefore simply make a list of these factors.

Mechanical variables in a racquet sport

To assess the speed of the racquet, coaches could look at the:

■ number and sequence of body segments in the movement, and list the sequence of movement

■ trunk rotation

■ upper arm horizontal movement

■ upper arm internal rotation, and

■ hand flexion.

To assess the position of the racquet and shoulders, coaches could look at:

■ the angles of selected joints at the completion of the backswing and when the ball is hit

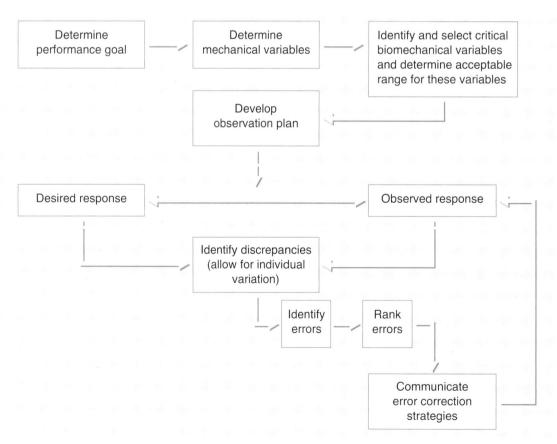

Pre-Observation

Analysing a skill subjectively (after McPherson 1996)

- the angle of the racquet at the backswing position and when the ball is hit, and consider how much variation they would accept, and

- the amount of wrist hyperextension at impact, which will change depending on the type of stroke to be played.

To assess the swing path, coaches might observe:

- the path of the racquet both before and after impact.

Identify and select critical biomechanical variables: some mechanical variables are more important than others and those that are critical to the performance must be identified (for example, the run-up velocity in the high jump or the angle of the racquet in squash).

Determine an acceptable range: an acceptable range must be established for each of these critical biomechanical variables. The acceptable run-up speed in the high jump may be between 6 and 8 m/s, while the angle of the racquet face to the court in squash may be plus or minus 5° of vertical. Coaches usually get these figures from objective data reported in applied sport science research studies or their own experience.

Develop an observation plan: coaches must decide such factors as the directions from which the skill should be viewed (side, front and/or overhead), whether the individual phases of the movement should be viewed separately (backswing, forward swing and/ or impact and follow-through), whether to emphasise particular segments in the movement (head, leg and/or trunk) and so on.

During the observation

Desired response compared with observed response: at this stage coaches compare what they observed about the athlete being assessed with the list of critical variables. They may use video to assist in this process.

A diver or skater with a technique flaw must have this error corrected, because it is directly related to the way in which the routine is judged. However, a netball player with a variation in technique that does not detract from performance may be left alone. The coach must always consider flair in assessing performance.

Diagnosing the problems

Identify discrepancies and errors, and rank errors: any biomechanical errors in technique iden-

tified must be ranked according to their importance, and the time that will be needed to correct them must also be assessed. For example, if a major fault is detected, it may be best to wait until the off-season before correcting it, to avoid upsetting the athlete's performance. On the other hand, a minor fault may be corrected in the weeks leading up to a major event. Coaches must always remember to work on the cause of the problem, rather than the effect.

Some coaches have trouble seeing the wood for the trees, and spend too much time trying to correct the symptom rather than the cause of the fault. A good example of this can be found in gymnastics, when the gymnast takes a step backwards on landing after a back somersault. A coach may then comment, 'Next time make your landing stick', whereas the poor landing may well have been the result of not tucking tightly enough during flight, or opening out too soon.

Correcting the problems

Communicate error correction strategies: the ability to communicate with athletes in a manner that they can easily understand is one of the most important characteristics of successful coaches. All the instructions that are given to the performer during error correction must be as simple as possible. First coaches should describe the error, show it on a video or demonstrate it, then describe and demonstrate the correct technique so that the athlete can 'picture' the correct movement.

Coaches may also ask questions to see whether the athletes fully understand the changes that are being attempted, and the steps needed to correct the fault. At the end of the practice, they should then observe how athletes perform to see if the required changes have occurred. They can then, at least in part, gauge how successful the change in technique has been.

If there has been little improvement after a reasonable period of practice, coaches may have to re-examine the modification process by asking the following questions:

- Was the error in technique correctly identified and was it clearly a cause and not the result or effect of another factor?

- Was the correction sequence appropriate?

- Did the athlete understand the modification needed and the reason for the change?

Objective analysis methods

Video techniques are commonly used by coaches to analyse performance. At the subjective level, coaches can make videotapes that allow them to make general comments on athletes' body and joint positions and movements. For example, after watching a video of a player hitting a baseball, the coach may comment on the flexion of the knee joint or the position of the bat compared to the front foot when the ball is hit. However, any *objective* analysis of movement must be supported by detailed measurements. A biomechanist may help the coach by measuring knee joint angles and the actual distance of the bat from the front foot when the ball is hit.

Scott Goodman coaches Damian Burroughs, a world record discus thrower who has cerebral palsy. When Scott started coaching Damian, he videotaped him in action to assess his ability and throwing technique, and identified a number of areas where improvements could be made. Working with Damian, Scott adapted the standard throwing style of most able-bodied throwers to Damian's needs, with great success.

Other methods of objective analysis that require the assistance of a biomechanist include measuring landing or take-off forces with a force platform, or recording the level of activity in a particular muscle or muscle group using electromyography (EMG).

MECHANICS IN SPORT

To analyse movement effectively a coach has to understand mechanics. To help coaches do that, this section provides a vocabulary of sport mechanics. This will allow coaches to read and understand the literature, and better assess the critical features of performance.

Balance

Balance plays an important role in almost all activities. Some activities demand static balance, where a set position has to be maintained for a long time, as in archery and shooting. Others require dynamic balance that can be altered easily, as in a rapidly changing game such as netball or basketball.

Balance in a sporting activity depends largely on the area of the base that supports the body (for example, how far apart the feet are) and the position of the centre of gravity of the body, or 'weight centre' of the body. Balance is related to:

- the position of the centre of gravity. In wrestling or archery, which require static balance, the centre of gravity is well centred over the base of support. This makes it difficult for the wind or an opponent to move the body from its position. When sudden movement is required, athletes lower their centre of gravity (knees slightly flexed), and position it close to the perimeter of the support area (leaning or tilting the body). For instance, in the 'set' position, 100 m sprinter Patrick Johnson positions his body forward over his hands in preparation for a quick start.

- the weight of the performer. In contact sports, heavier players are more difficult to move because of their weight. The stability of a rugby scrum depends on the weight of the scrum and the techniques used by the players. Similarly, in Australian rules, Tony Lockett was always difficult to move when setting for a mark because of his size.

- the area of the base of support. A wide (but comfortable) positioning of the legs, as in archery or pistol shooting, aids static balance. To achieve good balance, the feet should be placed shoulder width apart and in line with the anticipated direction of movement, as in fencing. However, the feet are often parallel in sports such as tennis or volleyball where movement in any direction is required. The weight should be evenly distributed on the balls of the feet, the knees should be flexed to provide the quick 'spring' needed, and the eyes should be fixed on the ball or opponent.

However, balance is a relative term and should be viewed in terms of a trade-off in body positions. If it is important in a particular sport to unbalance the opponent, as it is in judo, wrestling and rugby, the principles of stability can be used to the player's advantage. To make an opponent unstable, an athlete must move the opponent's centre of gravity beyond any margin of the base of support. An opponent's balance can also be disrupted by pushing or pulling above their centre of gravity to topple them over (judo, wrestling) or below their centre of gravity to take away their base of support (rugby tackle).

Motion

Linear and angular motion

Motion is a combination of both **linear** (movement along a straight line) and **angular** (rotation) motion. Body segments (forearm or lower leg) rotate about an axis of rotation (elbow joint and knee joint, respectively) in order to cause angular motion of the segment and linear motion of the end of the segment (wrist or ankle).

Displacement (or distance) in linear motion is simply how far an object or person moves. **Velocity** (or speed) measures how quickly that object or person moves over a given distance (distance divided by time). Velocity is measured as either the mean (average speed) over a given distance or the highest value (top speed).

Brett Lee bowls at a velocity of approximately 150 km/hr (about 40 m/s) and Mark Philippoussis serves at 200 km/hr (about 55 m/s). These are the highest speeds of the ball in flight. However, Samantha Riley set a 100 m breaststroke record (race time around 68 seconds) by averaging 1.5 m/s over the race.

Acceleration is how quickly a player can change velocity.

At the start of a time trial in cycling, Shane Kelly accelerates from zero to 16 km/hr in 1 second. Shane, who has a mass of around 85 kg, needs muscle power to produce this acceleration, hence his size. However, road racers who need to maintain speed over a longer period are only around 65 kg (less muscle bulk so less weight to carry). The body dimensions of 100 m sprinter Matt Shirvington are different to those of marathon runner Steve Moneghetti for similar reasons.

Angular displacement measures the change of position of a body segment (leg) or an implement (hockey stick). If the stick is pointing to the sky at the completion of the backswing, it is at 90° to the ground. The angular displacement near impact is about 40° forward of the vertical, so the angular displacement is 130°. The **rate of rotation** is determined by dividing the 130° displacement by the time of the downswing (about .1 second).

The hockey player who wishes to hit the ball at a higher speed may rotate the stick at a higher rate (greater angle of swing in the same time or swing through the same arc in less time). In throwing activities, it is important to understand the relationship between the rate of rotation of the body and throwing arm and the linear velocity (speed) of the hand at release. Similarly, a racquet user is concerned with both the angular speed of the racquet and the linear velocity (speed) of the point where the ball hits the strings.

(National Sports Information Centre)

A hockey player's backswing (top) and the same player just after hitting the ball

The length of the rotating body segment or stick and the speed of the rotating segment are important in generating speed in hitting (volleyball), kicking (soccer) or using an implement (golf stick). In golf, the shaft of a number five iron is shorter than that of a wood, which means that the club head doesn't move as fast, even for the same swing velocity. The speed of a hand or a projectile (for instance, while bowling a ball in cricket) can be calculated by adding the run-up speed of the bowler to the length of arm at release of the ball, and multiplying this by the rotational speed of the arm.

The same principle can be applied to a kick in Australian rules football, rugby or soccer, the hammer throw, lawn bowls and probably to a movement in every other sport.

(National Sports Information Centre)

A fast bowler achieves maximum speed with the ball by using a fast run-up and a fully extended arm, which gives greater rotational speed.

Projectile motion

In sport, the most common example of **projectile motion** is the path of an object such as a ball or the centre of gravity of the human body in flight. The path of the centre of gravity of an object (or the body) is predetermined at the moment of release or take-off, mainly by two factors:

- the velocity (speed), and
- the angle of take-off.

When shooting over a longer distance (two-point to three-point shot), basketballer Michelle Timms releases the ball at about the same angle (around 50°) but increases its release speed from about 7 to 8 m/s.

Force

A simple definition of force is a push or a pull. The unit of force is the newton (N). An athlete with a mass of 70 kg applies a force of 686 N (70 kg multiplied by gravity of 9.8 m/s/s) on the ground. Chapter 5, Functional Anatomy, dealt with the muscles that exert a force on the skeletal system to produce movement. Sports performances are also modified by the effect of external forces. In his three laws of motion, Isaac Newton described the relationships between force and motion.

Newton's laws of motion

1. Force is needed to produce motion or change speed during movement.

The ball in soccer is at rest until a force is applied during a penalty shot. Gravity and air resistance (and spin) change the path of the ball during flight.

2. The total force on a body is the mass of the body multiplied by its acceleration (force equals mass multiplied by acceleration).

The force that can be generated with lightweight metal racquets in tennis and squash is higher than was possible with the heavier wooden racquets because the lighter metal racquets can be moved at a much higher speed. Similarly in rowing, carbon fibre/kevlar shells have replaced the wooden ones, which means greater acceleration (and speed) can be achieved by applying the same force. Considerable force must be generated in order to accelerate away from an opponent during a game of hockey. This is why injuries often occur during the acceleration phase of a movement.

Newton's second law also says that force multiplied by time gives the change in **momentum** (mass multiplied by speed) of an object, and can help with injury prevention (see below for more on momentum).

When a cricket ball is caught, the hand absorbs the force with less risk of injury the further it 'gives' (and so the longer the ball has to slow down). This is also why athletes jump into foam pits or sand in preference to landing on concrete, which would reduce the momentum to zero very rapidly. Coaches of sports that produce these large forces at take-off (long jump or high jump) or landing (gymnastics or netball) should be wary of the likelihood of injury produced by repeated maximal performances in training sessions and in a match or competition.

3. For every force there is an equal and opposite force.

The force exerted by the swimmer against the block, which produces no effective movement because the block is attached to the ground, has an equal and opposite reaction force that drives the swimmer into the pool.

Long jumpers land in sand to reduce their momentum gradually. .

A swimmer exerts a force on the block and the reaction force drives him into the pool.

Sport also offers many examples of the angular equivalent of this third law. When a long jumper swings her legs ready for landing, a rotational force equal and opposite to that exerted is applied to the remainder of the body. As the jumper swings her legs forward and up, the trunk and upper limbs move forward and down. In rotational sports such as golf, tennis or field events in athletics, the rotation of the upper body is accompanied by an equal and opposite effect. However, because the feet are in contact with the ground, this rotation is transmitted to the ground and the body doesn't move as a result.

Force and body levers

Body segment rotation is caused by a muscle force or a weight/resistance acting at a distance from a joint. In a biceps curl, the elbow flexes as a result of the muscle acting on the forearm. The distance from the muscle attachment to the joint is termed the **force arm**. Similarly, the elbow may straighten when a large weight is placed in the hand. The distance between this weight and the joint is termed the **resistance arm**.

The force arm is relatively constant for different body segments, as muscles are attached to bone and so always stay in the same position. However, positioning the weight to be lifted, thrown or moved can modify the resistance arm. The shorter the resistance arm, the greater the force that can be applied and the less the velocity/speed that can be developed. Weight-lifters keep the bar close to their bodies to improve their lifting capacity. The longer the resistance arm, the less the lifting capacity, but the greater the speed of movement. The tennis player serves with an almost straight arm and racquet to develop speed.

Ground reaction forces of selected sporting skills

Movement	Footware	Maximum force in approx body weights
Walking heel-toe (at 1.3 m/s)	Casual shoes	1
Running heel-toe (at 4.5 m/s)	Running shoes	3
Running jump take-off	Spikes	8
Fast bowling (cricket) front foot contact	Cricket boots	5
Vault take-off	Barefoot	4–6
Double backward somersault landing	Barefoot	12

Consider the implications of repeated performances of fast bowling where the body must absorb forces of five times the bowler's body weight at front foot impact, or landing in gymnastics where forces of 12 times the body weight are not uncommon.

Summation of velocity (or force)

Generally, the body coordinates a number of forces to produce movement. The principle of **summation of velocity** states that:

- if athletes need to achieve maximum speed, they move each body segment at the instant the previous segment slows down — rhythmic movement. This sequence generally means that the large segments (the trunk) move before the smaller ones (the arm). In this way, momentum (mass by speed) built up in the trunk is transferred to the upper limb.

- if athletes need to achieve accuracy and not velocity (for example, a netball goal shot) they move all the relevant body segments together.

If coaches wish to increase velocity (of the hand, foot or an implement), then they have three alternatives:

- use more body segments (properly coordinated)

- increase the distance over which segments move (allowing greater velocity to be developed), or

- use elastic energy to enhance the movement (if muscles/tissue and tendons are stretched then, like an elastic band that is stretched, they will rebound, providing additional force). Approximately 20% additional velocity is produced if the shoulder muscles joining the chest and upper arm are stretched during the backswing of a throwing action.

Lindsay Davenport, the 2000 Australian Open tennis champion consistently serves at 170 km/hr (around 47 m/s). This is achieved because she is tall (long levers), uses her legs, trunk and arm to generate velocity, and stretches the shoulder muscles during the backswing and early forward swing phases of the serve.

Forces that oppose motion

If a force is applied against a moving object during a sporting activity then the object will be decelerated (slowed down). The three most common forces that oppose movement are gravity, fluid resistance or drag (air or water) and friction. Lift and spin are forces that also affect the movement and acceleration of objects.

Gravity is a force that opposes upwards movement. Runners who raise and lower their body excessively with each stride waste energy by continually trying to overcome the force of gravity.

When a body moves through either air or water, the resistance to the movement is related to the body's velocity. Resistance increases dramatically with increases in velocity. This resistance to the movement of a cyclist, runner or swimmer is called a **drag** force. The composition and shape of the body, and movement of body segments, all contribute to the total resistive force. On a windless day, sprinters use approximately 13% of their energy to overcome mainly air resistance. Cyclists who sit behind an opponent conserve approximately 30% of their energy because they ride where the air resistance is lower.

Another force that opposes motion is **friction**, which is created by contact between two

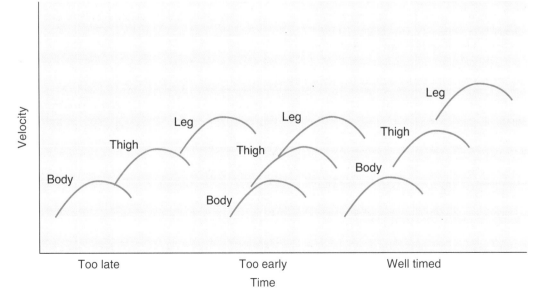

In a well-timed football kick, the leg begins to extend at the knee joint just as the thigh reaches maximum velocity. If this leg action begins either before or after this point, then the final velocity of the foot (and so the ball) is reduced.

surfaces. There are many situations in sport where the performer increases the friction (or grip) between two surfaces to prevent slipping: the baseball pitcher uses resin, the basketballer wears rubber shoes and the table tennis player uses a bat with a special surface. The performer attempts to increase the 'grip' between two bodies by altering the nature of one or both of the surfaces in contact. Remember that an ice-skater reduces the friction between the skate and the ice to reduce the influence of friction.

In throwing events **lift** also plays an important part in the distance a projectile can be thrown. Lift is an upward force that works against gravity, and so holds a projectile in the air longer. In swimming, the limb movements apply both propulsive lift and drag forces to the water, which are maximised in different strokes (see Hay 1993 for sections on fluid mechanics and swimming). For example, drag propulsion is greatest in sprint freestyle, when the swimmer pushes backward yet moves forward (Newton's action/reaction law). Lift forces are applied at right angles to the direction of pull and can be seen in the breaststroke arm action, where lateral sculling results in a forward movement.

If an object is spinning while it moves through the air, its flight path will be altered by forces that are often referred to as the Magnus effect, the result of **spin**. This phenomenon, where increased velocity is associated with decreased pressure, is a part of many sports. In tennis, a ball hit with topspin drops quickly because the decreased velocity of flow on top of the ball is associated with an increased pressure. A golfer imparts backspin to the ball, which causes it to lift, while sidespin can be a constant source of frustration because it often causes the ball to hook or slice into the rough.

Momentum

Linear momentum

Every body in motion has mass and velocity, which when multiplied together represent the **linear momentum** of the body. Tenpin bowlers have a greater chance of success when they use a heavier ball because it has more momentum at impact, although it is harder to control. In body contact sports, lighter players may develop more momentum than heavier opponents because they can run faster. This is why, when players are hit by lighter, faster opponents, they are often more seriously affected than when they are hit by larger, slower ones.

Angular momentum

Angular momentum is the momentum of a rotating body and it equals the body's moment of inertia multiplied by its angular velocity (rotation speed). What then is the moment of inertia of a body and what are its implications in sport?

Moment of inertia

Moment of inertia is a body's resistance to change in its angular motion (rotation). In angular motion, the resistance of an object to turn depends not only on its mass, but on how far this mass is distributed from the axis of

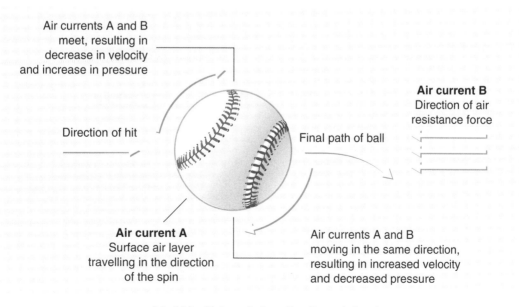

Air currents A and B meet, resulting in decrease in velocity and increase in pressure

Direction of hit

Air current B
Direction of air resistance force

Final path of ball

Air current A
Surface air layer travelling in the direction of the spin

Air currents A and B moving in the same direction, resulting in increased velocity and decreased pressure

A ball hit with topspin travelling through the air

179

rotation. Moment of inertia is less if the mass to be rotated, such as a racquet or the leg in running, is kept close to the axis of rotation. In tennis, small children often grip the racquet midway up the handle, thus reducing the moment of inertia and making the implement easier to swing. The distribution of weight with respect to the axis of rotation (grip) is therefore critical when teaching juniors, who must use shorter racquets.

In sprinting, where stride rate is so important, the leg should be bent at the knee while it is swinging through unsupported. This reduces the leg's moment of inertia and allows for faster recovery during this section of the running cycle.

However, off-centre impacts happen in many sports (for example, tennis, cricket and golf). Equipment has been designed to counteract the rotation produced by such impacts. The oversized tennis racquet has its weight distributed away from its central axis, thus increasing the moment of inertia about this axis and reducing the influence of off-centre impacts. The scooped cricket bat, with a greater proportion of its weight distributed to its sides, maintains the total mass of the bat but increases the moment of inertia about the axis that runs down the length of the bat. Off-centre impacts therefore don't destabilise the bat with rotary effects. Similarly, metal 'woods' in golf are peripherally weighted to make it easier to hit the ball straight and with a higher velocity from a variety of impact locations.

Conservation of angular momentum

This concept plays an extremely important role in many sporting activities. We have seen above that angular momentum is a body's moment of inertia (or resistance to change in rotation) multiplied by its angular velocity (rotation speed). The principle is that a body rotating in the air will continue to turn about its axis of rotation constantly, unless a force is applied to it. If a body rotates constantly in the air (given no other forces are applied to it), its angular momentum stays the same so, if its moment of inertia is reduced, the body must rotate faster. Likewise, if its moment of inertia is increased, rotation will slow.

After leaving the diving board, divers tuck and grasp their legs to decrease the radius of rotation (and so their moment of inertia) and thus increase angular velocity (the speed of rotation). Their angular momentum remains stable so, if one if its components changes (moment of inertia), so must the other (speed of rotation). Divers also straighten their body in preparation for entry into the water to increase the moment of inertia and thus decrease the speed of rotation. Skaters, who start with the arms extended horizontally in pirouetting, bring them to the side to increase the rate of rotation. Golfers are able to increase angular momentum during a drive by applying more force. In fact, the body coordinates angular momentum in much the same way as it does the summation of velocity.

CONCLUSION

The coach who understands the mechanics of movement, and can identify critical aspects of performance, can then tackle one of the most challenging tasks in sport today — modifying technique to improve performance. Only then will athletes be able to improve their performances while continuing to compete in an injury-free environment.

COACHING TIPS

- Consider the unique characteristics of each individual athlete when applying biomechanical principles.

- Aim to develop smooth and efficient movements in maximising performance.

- Improve your coaching by feeling how your own body moves when attempting the same actions as athletes.

- Look at athletes' techniques either with the naked eye or by using video from several different positions (front, back and side). This gives a better all-round perspective of the development of skills.

FURTHER READING

Hall, SJ (1999). *Basic Biomechanics*. Boston, MA: WCB McGraw-Hill.

Hay, JG (1993) *The Biomechanics of Sports Techniques*. Englewood Cliffs, NJ: Prentice Hall.

Hay, JG, and JG Reid (1988) *Anatomy, Mechanics, and Human Motion*. Englewood Cliffs, NJ: Prentice Hall.

Luttgens, K, and N Hamilton (1997) *Kinesiology: Scientific Basis of Human Motion*. Madison, WI: Brown and Benchmark.

McPherson, M (1996) Qualitative and quantitative analysis in sports. *American Orthopaedic Society for Sports Medicine* 24, 85–88.

CHAPTER 16
SPORTS NUTRITION

Karen Inge

(National Sports Information Centre)

INTRODUCTION

It is now well accepted that nutrition plays a vital role in sporting performance. Ongoing sports nutrition research is making it clearer that athletes' dietary requirements are different to those of the normally active population. As well as being important to athletic performance, a nutritionally sound diet is essential to both the immediate and future health of the athlete.

THE TRAINING DIET

The training diet aims to:

- provide athletes with enough fuel and fluid to meet the demands of training
- provide them with all the nutrients essential for good health, and in the right balance
- help them achieve long-term health goals through adequate nutrition, and
- trial various eating strategies for competition.

Energy

To meet the demands of training, athletes need more energy than the normally active population. If athletes are unable to meet these demands by consuming the right amounts and types of food and fluid, they will be more easily fatigued and their performances will be impaired.

The main energy source used by the athlete depends on several factors, including the

Athletes have high energy demands.
(Colin Stuckey)

Estimated energy requirements of certain sports in kilojoules (kJ) and kilocalories (kcal)

Type of event	Sex	Weight (kg)	Energy requirements
Endurance events	Male	70–80	25 200 kJ/day (6000 kcal)
	Female	55–65	18 900 kJ/day (4500 kcal)
Sprint events	Male	65–75	19 320 kJ/day (4600 kcal)
	Female	50–60	14 550 kJ/day (3400 kcal)
Weight throwing	Male	100	29 400 kJ/day (7000 kcal)
	Female	90	23 440 kJ/day (5580 kcal)

(From McArdle et al 1991)

workload required to perform the exercise, the athlete's nutritional status before and during the exercise, and his or her training status. Carbohydrate is the most readily available source of energy for the muscles. Fat has limitations as an energy source for high intensity work because it takes a long time to produce energy from the breakdown of fat, and because the process uses a lot of oxygen.

Even a very lean athlete has a large stored energy source in the form of fat (7 kg of body fat equals 250 000 kJ or 60 000 kcal). In contrast, carbohydrate stores in the body are limited (approximately 100 g in the liver and 400–500 g stored in muscle as glycogen), equalling about 8400 kJ (2000 kcal) of stored carbohydrate energy. The body also has a significant stored source of energy in protein, however this does not contribute significantly to exercise (estimates of the proportion of exercise fuel that comes from protein range from 5 to 15%).

Carbohydrate

The main role of carbohydrate in the body is as an energy source. Intense training makes heavy demands of muscle glycogen, and its depletion is thought to be a major cause of fatigue (see chapter 6, Physiology and Sports Performance, for more information on glycogen). Carbohydrate also has a 'protein sparing' effect: if an athlete has an adequate intake of carbohydrate, then the body will use it in preference to protein (or muscle), thus preventing muscle depletion.

Athletes should rely mainly on nutritious carbohydrate foods that provide other essential nutrients as well, such as protein, fibre, vitamins and minerals (for example, grain foods, sweetened low-fat dairy products, fruits, legumes and starchy vegetables). Meeting their carbohydrate needs is crucial for athletes, yet many find it difficult.

To help meet their carbohydrate needs, athletes should:

- eat carbohydrate-rich snacks throughout the day, such as fruit, yoghurt, and fruit and grain-based bars
- eat carbohydrate-rich meals throughout the day based on breads, cereals, rice, pasta and other grains and starchy vegetables
- consume a variety of carbohydrate-rich foods in solid and liquid form
- consume carbohydrate-rich meals, snacks or fluids as soon as possible after exercise

Estimated carbohydrate requirements for athletes

Daily training level	Daily carbohydrate intake
Light training (<60 min per day)	5–6 g/kg body weight
Moderate training level (60–120 min of moderate to high intensity exercise)	6–8 g/kg body weight
Endurance training (>120 min of intense training)	8–10 g/kg body weight
Extreme endurance (5–6 hr of intense training)	10 plus g/kg body weight

(From Burke 1995)

- plan and organise ahead to ensure that suitable carbohydrate-rich foods are available when necessary, and

- educate themselves about the importance of carbohydrates for performance.

Fat

Fat plays many important roles in the body. It is an energy source, it plays a part in hormone production and the structure of body cells, and it provides fat-soluble vitamins A, D, E and K, and essential fatty acids. The body needs a certain amount of fat, particularly unsaturated fat, for good health. However, in most western countries the average person consumes far more fat, especially saturated fat, than is necessary.

For athletes, the main disadvantages of a high total fat intake are an increase in body weight and body fat level, which can be detrimental to performance and can affect the athlete's intake of vital carbohydrate-rich foods. Athletes should consume around 20–30% of their dietary energy intake in the form of fat. They should also aim to follow a low-fat diet and to obtain their essential fatty acids and fat-soluble vitamins mainly from unsaturated sources (fish, whole grains, nuts and seeds).

Protein

Protein is essential in the diet for building and maintaining the body's tissues. It forms the structure of components such as muscles, hair, skin, blood and antibodies. Protein is made up of basic units called amino acids. There are 20 different amino acids, of which eight are essential in the diet because they cannot be made by the body. Athletes require a greater amount of protein than normally active individuals.

Excessively high protein intakes do not necessarily improve muscle strength or size.

Although the use of specific amino acids to stimulate muscle growth, enhance strength and delay fatigue has been popularised by many commercial companies, studies do not substantiate these claims and more research is warranted.

Protein comes from two main dietary sources:

- animal foods (meat, eggs, dairy produce, fish, shellfish and poultry), which are known as complete protein foods, because they contain all of the essential amino acids, and

- plant foods (nuts, legumes, dried beans and lentils and cereal products), which are usually incomplete protein foods, lacking one or more of the essential amino acids. Vegetarian athletes should consume a variety of plant foods to obtain enough of all of the essential amino acids.

Vitamins and minerals

Vitamins and minerals are required for health and are essential for optimal physical performance. While deficiencies of certain vitamins can impair athletes' performances, there is no strong evidence to suggest that their performances will be improved if they take additional vitamins, provided their diet is adequate. Athletes at risk of developing vitamin deficiencies include those who are pregnant, those taking certain medications, for example, the oral contraceptive pill, and those on low-energy diets. Rather than relying on supplements, 'at risk' athletes should improve the vitamin balance in their diet.

Poor mineral status is also known to affect athletic performance. Most minerals occur in a wide variety of foods and are essential for nerve transmission, muscle contraction, fluid and electrolyte balance, energy production pathways, and bone, muscle, skin and blood structure.

Estimated protein requirements for athletes

Type of athlete	Protein intake
Non-athletes	0.75 g/kg body weight
Strength athletes	1.2–1.7 g/kg body weight, to assist in increasing muscle mass
Endurance athletes	1.2–1.6 g/kg body weight, as an energy source and to assist in repair of exercise-induced muscle damage

The functions of minerals, the effects of deficiencies and how to avoid them

Mineral	Function	Athletes at risk	Effects of deficiency	Food sources
Iron	Haemoglobin production (oxygen carrier), energy production, learning and memory, immunity	Endurance athletes, post-pubertal women, vegetarian athletes, those on restricted energy diets and those following fad diets	Lethargy, tiredness, decrease in performance	Liver, kidney and red meats — easily absorbed from these sources Green leafy vegetables, fortified breads and breakfast cereals, and legumes — not easily absorbed from these sources, but vitamin C-rich food, eaten in conjunction with these foods, will enhance iron absorption.
Calcium	Bone formation and maintenance, nerve and muscle function	Young females restricting their energy intake, amenorrhoeic athletes (females who have stopped menstruating), and those with increased needs, for example, breast feeding	Reduced bone density, and increased risk of osteoporosis later in life	Dairy products — milk, cheese and yogurt Fortified soy drinks Fish with edible bones* Nuts and seeds* Green leafy vegetables* *Not as easily absorbed from these sources
Zinc	Immune function, wound healing, bone health, energy production	Similar to those at risk of iron deficiency, as many foods that are good sources of iron are also good sources of zinc	Fatigue, reduced immunity, lack of taste sensation, slow healing of wounds, failure to grow, hair loss, dry skin	Oysters Red meat, liver Seafood Legumes Wholegrain products and fortified breads and cereals Nuts and seeds Note, zinc from plant sources is better absorbed when eaten with animal protein (such as dairy products).

Hydration

Meeting the body's need for water is essential for both health and physical performance. Athletes typically only replace 30–70% of sweat and other fluid losses incurred during exercise, so they can expect to finish training or competition sessions with a mild to severe degree of dehydration. They can lose very large amounts of sweat (up to 3.7 L/hr), and the greater the degree of dehydration, the greater the negative effect on performance.

A loss of fluid up to 2% of body weight has a continually increasing negative effect on performance, until it becomes substantial at 2% of body weight. Heat stroke and heat exhaustion can become life threatening when fluid loss exceeds 6–10% of body weight.

Hydration recommendations

Coaches should:

- ensure that athletes are well hydrated before training or competition
- ensure that athletes drink two to three cups of fluid at the pre-training or pre-competition meal or snack, and
- ensure that athletes drink one to two cups of fluid just before starting the exercise session.

During exercise, coaches should:

- encourage athletes not to rely on thirst to prompt them to drink
- encourage athletes to aim to consume one cup of fluid every 15 to 20 minutes

- provide cool (not cold) fluids where possible, as these are emptied faster from the stomach and are more palatable
- try giving athletes flavoured drinks, such as sports drinks or dilute cordial, if they are struggling to consume enough fluid, as these may be better tolerated by some athletes, and
- create opportunities for athletes to drink.

After exercise, coaches should:

- compare the athletes' pre and post-exercise body weight, to help determine the amount of fluid required
- encourage athletes to drink a greater amount than the fluid lost through exercise, as fluid continues to be lost after exercise
- encourage athletes to drink to a plan
- ensure enough fluids are available
- consider using flavoured drinks to promote greater fluid intake
- encourage athletes to avoid caffeine and alcohol as they can increase fluid losses
- encourage athletes to consume carbohydrate-containing drinks, such as sports drinks, because, as well as contributing to fluid replenishment, they enhance glycogen resynthesis
- remember that fluids that contain sodium and potassium can help retain fluid, and
- encourage athletes to avoid spas and saunas, as these will lead to further dehydration from additional sweat losses.

(National Sports Information Centre)

Adequate hydration is essential for athletes.

Lisa's tennis coach, Marion, was concerned that Lisa seemed to be suffering from a lot of headaches, and her mother noticed that she was sleeping much more than she used to. Her performance had also not improved and her ranking was falling. Marion decided to investigate this a bit further with the assistance of a sports dietitian.

An assessment of Lisa's diet showed that dehydration was the most likely cause of her problems. Lisa was asked to complete a fluid balance chart to record her weight changes and fluid intake during training sessions. She was also taught about the importance of maintaining an adequate fluid intake.

Lisa now knows she needs to drink approximately one litre of fluid per hour of training and games, in addition to two litres during the day. Headaches are now a thing of the past, her energy levels have improved and she is winning matches again.

COMPETITION DIET

The rate at which muscle glycogen stores are depleted during exercise depends on the intensity of the exercise. Low muscle glycogen levels can affect performance by inducing fatigue.

Carbohydrate loading

Carbohydrate loading can result in muscle and liver glycogen stores twice as large as normal in the trained athlete. The currently accepted technique of carbohydrate loading starts three days before competition, and involves the following:

- tapered training
- a high-carbohydrate intake equal to 10 g/kg of body weight per day
- plenty of fluid (because every gram of carbohydrate is stored with three grams of fluid in the muscles), and
- decreased fibre intake during the day prior to the event (athletes should expect to gain about 2 kg over the carbohydrate loading period).

Because of the weight gain associated with carbohydrate loading, it is *not* recommended for athletes in weight category sports and/or where muscle glycogen is not a limiting factor in performance.

Pre-competition meal

There is no one magic food that can be eaten before a competition to guarantee a win or a personal best. However, there are some guidelines on eating before competition for coaches and athletes:

- allow two to four hours for a big meal to digest, or one hour for a light snack
- choose carbohydrate-rich foods
- avoid very high protein and fat intakes
- drink plenty of fluid, and
- experiment with foods during training to see which best suit the athlete concerned.

Eating during exercise

During endurance exercise, athletes will require approximately 30 to 60 g of carbohydrate per hour. Carbohydrate intake during long-duration exercise helps to delay fatigue, but it may also assist in shorter duration, high-intensity events with several bouts. Drinking carbohydrate-rich fluids during exercise will help to meet both fluid and carbohydrate requirements simultaneously. However, solid forms of carbohydrate can also be used to provide additional energy in such events and, in endurance events lasting longer than five hours, these will also assist in delaying hunger.

Eating between events

In sports in which an athlete competes several times a day, the priority is to replace fluids and top-up blood sugar levels between the events. If athletes have a period of two to three hours between events, they can eat solid foods (for example, sandwiches and fruit), and drink fluids. If the time between events is too short to allow them to eat solid food, fluid should be the first priority. If the time between events is less than one hour, water or fluid containing carbohydrates (such as sports drink) is appropriate. If the time between events is one to two hours, athletes can consume small carbohydrate-rich snacks (such as jelly beans) or liquid meal supplements. If they don't know how long it is until the next event, they should sip sports drinks (500 mL to 1 L per hour).

Recovery

In the early stages of recovery, the ideal carbohydrate intake is around 1–1.5 g/kg of body weight as soon as possible after exercise, leading to a total carbohydrate intake of 7–10 g/kg of body weight over 24 hours. Emphasis should be placed on consuming

quick-acting carbohydrate-rich foods that are quickly digested and absorbed to enhance the rate of glycogen resynthesis. It is important that athletes choose an eating schedule that is practical and comfortable, to ensure that their carbohydrate requirements are met.

Glycogen storage doesn't seem to be affected by whether the carbohydrate is consumed in the solid or liquid form during recovery. There has been little research on the co-ingestion of other nutrients, such as protein, with carbohydrate during recovery. It's possible that protein can help repair muscle damage caused by strenuous exercise and aid the immune response. It is also important to remember that many foods consumed as high-carbohydrate snacks following exercise also contain some protein (such as bread and cereals, yoghurt and milk drinks).

Since Tim has been playing soccer at a higher level, he has noticed his energy levels are low, particularly during the second half of the game. He normally goes out on Friday night (although not late), then gets up at 8–8.30 am on Saturday morning and rushes to soccer for a 10 am start, without breakfast. This kind of fatigue can be caused by inadequate carbohydrate in the diet. When he told his coach, Gerd, how he was feeling, Gerd designed the following plan to help:

1. Two days before the game he should ensure an adequate carbohydrate intake by eating regular meals and snacks, focusing on carbohydrate-rich foods such as cereals, bread, fruit, rice and pasta, and drinking plenty of fluids.

2. On the morning of the game he should get up a bit earlier and have a high-carbohydrate breakfast two to four hours before the game, consisting of one or more of the following:
   - breakfast cereal with low-fat milk
   - toast, muffins or crumpets with a spread
   - spaghetti on toast, and
   - a low-fat milk smoothie or commercial liquid meal supplement, and two to three cups of water, cordial or fruit juice.

3. Just before game time he should have one to two cups of water or sports drink.

4. During the game he should continue to drink water or sports drink (if still needing to top-up energy levels).

Since implementing Gerd's plan, Tim has noticed a significant improvement in his energy levels. Not only can he keep running through until the final siren, but he has also noticed that he is concentrating and focusing better.

WEIGHT CONTROL

Approximately 50% of Australian men, 37% of Australian women and 20–25% of Australian children are overweight. For athletes, excess body fat can adversely affect sporting performance. Athletes are under constant pressure, from coaches, parents and themselves, to achieve 'ideal' body weight. 'Making weight' is also an issue for many athletes in weight-categorised competitions. It is hardly surprising that so many athletes use unsafe practices to achieve rapid weight loss.

Successful loss of body fat is not achieved overnight, and it is important that athletes realise the risks of restrictive diets. While they may appear to work in the short term, most of these diets do not have a good long-term success rate and can be hazardous to health. Continuous restrictive diets can make athletes obsessive about their diets and may lead to dangerous dieting practices.

General guidelines for body fat loss

The safest and most effective way of reducing body fat is the combination of a controlled kilojoule diet, which contains adequate amounts of carbohydrate and is low in fat, with an appropriate aerobic exercise program. Many athletes will lose weight by reducing their intake of fats and alcohol, increasing carbohydrate and fibre, and choosing low-fat

(National Sports Information Centre)

Athletes should eat a variety of foods to ensure a balanced diet.

protein foods. They may need individual counselling and monitoring by a sports dietitian to ensure a safe steady weight loss. Athletes trying to lose weight should continue to eat a variety of foods to make certain that they receive all the nutrients they need and to stop performance deteriorating.

General guidelines for bulking up

Certain groups of athletes need a relatively high proportion of muscle for their sport. However, many are misinformed as to the best way to 'bulk up' for a long-term gain in muscle bulk. While there is evidence to suggest that athletes attempting to increase muscle bulk do need more protein, these levels can be reached by diet alone, without the need for supplements.

The safest way to increase muscle mass is through the combination of a high-energy diet, to allow protein to be used primarily in the growth of muscle rather than for energy, with an appropriate training program. A high-energy diet can be achieved if athletes eat five to six meals a day, and energy-dense foods such as smoothies and other energy-rich drinks, fruit and grain-based bars, dried fruits and some foods rich in good oils, like avocado and nuts. It is important to monitor the athletes' body composition regularly to ensure that weight gain is from increased muscle mass rather than body fat. It's also important for the coach and the athlete to understand the athlete's genetic potential to 'bulk up', so that realistic goals can be set and achieved.

EATING DISORDERS

Coaches and other professionals dealing with athletes should be aware of how eating disorders can affect athletes. Athletes often show personality traits that increase their risk of developing an eating disorder, such as being perfectionists, being very dedicated, being overachievers, and having a narrow focus. Athletes are exposed to even greater pressure than the general public to achieve low body fat levels and attain the ideal body, especially in weight category events, and where low body weight directly affects performance.

The term 'female athlete triad' describes three kinds of clinical disorders that may co-exist in some female athletes. These are eating disorders, menstrual disturbances, and reduced bone density, and they can all affect performance, and short and long-term health, significantly. The 'female athlete triad' is a complex issue and athletes may suffer from one or more of these disorders for a variety of reasons (males can also experience two of the three conditions).

The two main eating disorders are anorexia nervosa and bulimia nervosa. Signs that an athlete may have **anorexia nervosa** include:

- dramatic loss of weight
- preoccupation with food and weight, fat and calories
- relentless excessive exercise
- mood swings
- avoiding food-related activities
- trying to cover up weight loss (such as wearing baggy clothes), and
- bizarre eating habits (for example, strange food combinations).

Signs that an athlete may have **bulimia nervosa** include:

- noticeable weight loss or gain
- excessive concern about weight
- bathroom visits after meals
- depressive moods, and
- excessive behaviour regarding diet and weight, followed by binge eating.

Coaches should be aware of the warning signs that an athlete may have an eating disorder, so that they can arrange an intervention program at an early stage.

The treatment of eating disorders in athletes is a complex issue and requires the expertise of a team of specialists including a psychologist or psychiatrist, a sports physician, a dietitian and the coach. The teamwork of this group of experts will enable them to work effectively with an athlete with an eating disorder.

Rumours were circulating that Maria, an athlete in Bill's netball squad, had an eating disorder. Bill had not noticed weight changes in Maria, but according to others she was very preoccupied, possibly even obsessed, about her weight, although her body fat levels were low. Other athletes noticed that she visited the toilet a lot, especially after a meal.

What should Bill do? The following tips may help:

- Look for signs of bulimia — bathroom visits after meals, mood changes, sores around Maria's mouth or on her fingers, or cuts and wounds that won't heal.

- Organise a sports dietitian to talk to the entire team about healthy eating for performance.

- Approach the athlete with concerns about her health and performance, rather than accusing her of having an eating disorder.

Bill found these strategies worked very well with Maria, who followed up the talk and his suggestions by visiting the dietitian for an individual consultation. She still sees the dietitian regularly for advice and support.

ERGOGENIC AIDS

Athletes striving to be the best are forever looking for that extra edge. Often they are tempted to take substances that they believe would enhance their performance, that is, ergogenic aids. Owing to this continual search for the winning edge, the dietary supplement business is a multibillion dollar industry worldwide. Because of the amount of money involved and the advertising resources available in such an industry, there is an imbalance in the information being given to the general public about supplements. This often means that the scientific facts about whether a particular ergogenic aid helps performance or not may not be heard by the athletic population.

Researchers suggest that coaches and athletes who are considering using ergogenic aids should ask the following questions:

- Is the substance banned by the International Olympic Committee?

- Are there any short and long-term health risks associated with taking this substance, and, if so, what are they?

- What does this substance claim to do? Does it sound too good to be true? If so, it probably is. Does it claim to take the place of training and adequate nutrition? If so, it probably will not work. If it does what the makers say it will, will it improve performance?

■ Is the substance backed by anecdotal evidence or scientific fact? If it is backed by scientific fact, who performed the research and has other research reached the same conclusion (Hawley and Burke 1998)?

Coaches and athletes should also ask a variety of qualified health professionals (sports physicians, sports dietitians or exercise physiologists) if they know anything about this substance. Naturally, if they are in doubt, the athlete should not take the substance.

CONCLUSION

A combination of natural talent, hard training, superior coaching and a positive mental approach is necessary to create potential winners. More recently, nutrition has been added to this list as a critical factor in determining peak athletic performance.

It is important that coaches recognise the contribution that nutrition can make to sporting performance. They are in an excellent position to improve nutrition awareness among athletes, and also among parents and families of athletes. This can be done by providing them with literature on sports nutrition, organising a sports dietitian to give a talk or conduct a workshop, and by being a good role model.

The coach can also play an important role in identifying the athletes most at risk of incurring nutrition-related problems, such as eating disorders and iron deficiency anaemia (see chapter 17, Medical Considerations in Sport, for more information on iron deficiency anaemia). As significant people in the lives of the athletes they work with, coaches are important role models and can help athletes maintain well-balanced diets by being seen to do so themselves.

Coaches must also recognise their limitations with regard to treating dietary problems, and refer athletes to a sports dietitian or doctor when required. To locate a sports dietitian near you, contact Sports Dietitians Australia (see the Further Reading section).

COACHING TIPS

■ Remember that parents usually shop and cook, and are the keys to sound nutritional habits in young athletes.

■ Discourage parents from rewarding young athletes with junk food for good performances.

■ Teach athletes sensible nutrition and good eating habits for life.

■ Encourage rehydration during and after training and competition. Test for adequate hydration by weighing athletes before and after training sessions.

FURTHER READING

Internet

Sports Dietitians Australia, tel (03) 9682 2442, website <http://www.ausport.gov.au/sda/>, email SDA@ausport.gov.au.

Publications

Fluid and energy replacement for physical activity. (1996) *Australian Journal of Nutrition and Dietetics* supplement 53(4) December.

Australian Sports Commission (2000) *A Winning Diet for Sport* (video). Canberra: Australian Sports Commission.

Brand-Miller, J, K Foster-Powell and S Colaguri (1996) *The GI Factor*. Sydney: Hodder and Stoughton.

Burke, LM (1995) *The Complete Guide to Food for Sports Performance: Peak Nutrition for Your Sport*. St Leonards: Allen and Unwin.

Burke, LM, and V Deakin (eds) (in press) *Clinical Sports Nutrition*. Sydney: McGraw-Hill Book Company.

Hawley, JA, and L Burke (1998) *Peak Performance: Training and Nutritional Strategies for Sport*. St Leonards: Allen and Unwin.

McArdle, WD, FI Katch and VL Katch (1991) *Exercise Physiology: Energy, Nutrition, and Human Performance*. Philadelphia, PA: Lea and Febiger.

O'Connor, H, and D Hay (1998) *Competition Sports Nutrition*. Rushcutters Bay: JB Fairfax Press.

O'Connor, H, and D Hay (1998) *Sports Nutrition Basics*. Rushcutters Bay: JB Fairfax Press.

Phillips, J, C Martin and K Baker (1997) *In the Dark about Eating Disorders?: Answers for the Coach*. Adelaide: South Australian Sports Institute and Australian Coaching Council.

Stanton, R (1999) *'Vitamins': What They Do and What They Don't Do*. St Leonards: Allen and Unwin.

CHAPTER 17
MEDICAL CONSIDERATIONS IN SPORT

Arjun Rao and staff of the Australian Sports Drug Agency

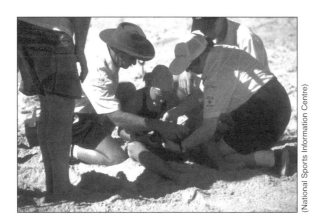

(National Sports Information Centre)

INTRODUCTION

The medical problems of both recreational and elite athletes require a multidisciplinary team approach. Coaches are vital members of such a team. Very often they can be the first to identify an illness or injury and obtain medical assessment. Coaches also play a key role in preventing injury, administering initial treatment and rehabilitating the injured athlete.

Conditions such as overuse and overtraining injuries often result from inappropriate training programs. It is therefore vital that coaches have a sound knowledge of the physiological principles of training and are able to adjust programs to suit each athlete. Coaches should have good support networks, including qualified medical professionals, whose members can offer advice or help where necessary.

Coaches should know if any of the athletes under their supervision need special care or have any medical problems, such as diabetes. It is important for coaches to be able to administer first aid to these athletes if and when required and, more importantly, to know where to get appropriate medical attention. Coaches are not qualified to treat seri-

ous injuries and must always seek medical assistance when these occur.

MANAGING INJURIES

Types of injuries

There are acute or chronic, overuse and traumatic injuries. **Acute** injuries include a dislocated shoulder and a hamstring tear. **Overuse** injuries are usually a result of repetitive activity, and include stress fractures and tendon degeneration. Often overuse injuries are the result of an underlying biomechanical problem, for example, incorrect training techniques or muscle inflexibility. Unless these factors are identified and treated, the problem will usually remain.

Traumatic injuries can result from either direct trauma (for example, a blow from an opponent) or indirect trauma (such as falling on an outstretched hand). The anterior cruciate ligament (ACL) in the knee is often damaged traumatically by a twisting fall.

Signs and symptoms of injury include pain, swelling, discolouration and restricted range of movement at the site. Pain that occurs during warm-up, recedes during play and then returns afterwards, indicates inflammatory pain (for example, an inflamed tendon). Pain that occurs only with activity represents mechanical pain and indicates probable internal damage to a joint (for example, torn cartilage in the knee).

Preventing injury

Several factors help prevent injury, including:

■ adequate warm-up, including psychological preparation, and cool-down (15–30 minutes is recommended for both)

Warming up can prevent injury.

(National Sports Information Centre)

- static stretching (not ballistic stretching, which will cause injury unless the muscles are warmed first. Anecdotal evidence suggests that there are fewer injuries between the muscle and the tendon if athletes stretch, but this is not proven.)
- appropriate graduated training loads (coaches should avoid rapid increases in training intensity or volume)
- appropriate periods of recovery during training
- protective equipment, where necessary, for example, a shin pad in soccer
- taping and bracing (preventative strapping, for example, to prevent an ankle sprain, and therapeutic strapping, for example, to protect an injured shoulder)
- adequate footwear and clothing (for example, loose-fitting cotton clothing in the heat), and
- avoiding exercise if the athlete is already ill and has a temperature higher than 38°C or 'below the neck' symptoms (see Infections in sport on page 197).

Treating and rehabilitating injuries

The first 48–72 hours after an injury are extremely important, as this is usually the 'inflammatory period'. Inflammation is a necessary evil, a part of the body's healing process and usually produces pain, swelling, morning stiffness, discolouration and restricted movement.

Injury management should initially include first aid measures to reduce the amount of swelling and help soft tissue healing. The old acronym PRICE — protection, rest, ice, compression and elevation — is familiar to everyone, but it should be CPRIE, as compression is the most important measure, particularly for stopping bleeding, tissue fluid leakage and inflammation. Compression should be applied as soon as possible after an injury has occurred. An elastic bandage does this best: crepe bandages stretch and are ineffective after the first use. All coaches should take basic first aid courses, so they can learn how to apply bandages to different parts of the body.

Applying ice

Applying ice to an injury decreases swelling mainly by constricting the blood vessels to the affected area. Crushed ice in a wet towel is a good method.

Duration Superficial injuries (for example, to the Achilles tendon) need only ten minutes' cooling, while deeper injuries (such as a corked thigh) require at least 20 minutes, because it takes time for the cooling affect to reach that depth. Compression should be maintained during and after the ice is applied. Try to keep the injured part of the body at around 0°C.

Frequency Ice an injury every two to four hours, because body tissue regains normal body temperature reasonably quickly.

The role of the coach

Appropriate initial management of an injury can significantly reduce the overall recovery

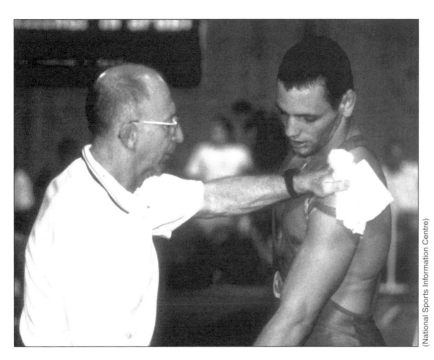

Applying ice reduces injury swelling.

(National Sports Information Centre)

time. Coaches should be well prepared for any eventuality and, in the absence of appropriate medical facilities, carry their own first aid kits. This should include the following:

- elastic bandages
- ice/cold packs
- gauze pads
- rigid strapping tape
- scissors
- disposable gloves
- steri-strips
- alcohol swabs, and
- skin disinfectant.

The coach should instruct the athlete to avoid the following during the inflammatory period:

- heat
- alcohol
- rubbing, and
- massage.

These factors can aggravate the inflammatory process. Heat and alcohol cause increased blood flow to the site of injury, which increases the inflammation. The inappropriate rubbing and massage of an injured muscle can result in the formation of calcium in the muscles and substantially restricted movement.

When the initial symptoms of the injury have settled, the inflammatory response has been reduced, and a full range of movement has been restored, the athlete can then begin recovery. During recovery, cross-training that doesn't use the injured part can improve endurance without stressing the injury inappropriately.

The coach can help by introducing the following activities into the injured athlete's rehabilitation program at this stage:

- swimming — an excellent non-weight-bearing exercise
- cycling — often single-legged to protect the injured part of the leg
- using rowing or step machines, and
- circuit training.

Once the athlete's strength, flexibility, balance and endurance have been restored, functional exercises can begin. These include exercises to develop explosive strength (for instance, bounding and hopping), sprints, figure-of-eight exercises and agility drills (for instance, cutting and side-to-side movements). Exercises and drills should be as sport specific as possible and should be based on the periodisation principle of conditioning.

Coaches have an important role to play in helping injured athletes regain optimum fitness. They can supervise athletes, ensure goals are achieved and liaise with the medical team should a problem arise. Because they have an in-depth knowledge of the sport involved, coaches can often help sports physicians or physiotherapists prescribe sports-specific exercise programs that gradually increase the functional load on the injured body part. Specific areas of weakness and technique errors can also be addressed at this stage. At the end of the day, teamwork is essential.

Andrew, an 18-year-old soccer player, sustained a twisting injury to his right knee at training. The knee was extremely painful and started to swell immediately. John, the coach, helped him off the field and applied an elastic compression bandage and crushed ice in a wet towel. The local sports physician diagnosed an anterior cruciate ligament rupture. Blood was drained from the knee and non-steroidal anti-inflammatory drugs and electrotherapy (including therapeutic ultrasound) were administered.

Andrew started rehabilitation with range-of-motion exercises, balance work, stretching and strengthening. After six weeks he could run in a straight line and do exercises such as leg presses and side step-ups. Cross-training — swimming and cycling — began, supervised by John. At six months, Andrew began some sport-specific exercises, including dribbling, passing and kicking. These exercises were prescribed by the sports physician in collaboration with John and the physiotherapist, taking into account Andrew's age, skeletal maturity and skill levels. Andrew was gradually returned to full activity at nine months.

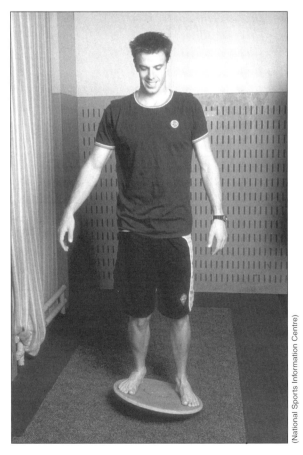

(National Sports Information Centre)

Rehabilitation is essential before returning to sport.

MEDICAL CONDITIONS AND SPORT

Diabetes

Coaching diabetics

Athletes with diabetes can perform most types of exercise, including elite-level competition. Diabetes can be a life-threatening condition, so those who coach diabetics should be prepared to monitor the affected athletes closely and learn to deal with potential emergencies. The coach should work with both the athlete and doctor to develop an action plan to cope with any emergency that might arise.

Emergency treatment for diabetics

The major potentially life-threatening risks of exercise in diabetics are **hypoglycaemia** (low blood sugar), and **diabetic ketacidosis** (high blood sugar with formation of ketones in the blood and urine). Coaches and athletes should make themselves aware of the symptoms of each condition and be ready to recognise them when they occur.

Symptoms of hypoglycaemia often mimic those of strenuous exercise, such as sweating, increased heart rate, tremulousness and fatigue, and it is therefore imperative that both athlete and coach are alert and carefully consider such symptoms. Dehydration, drowsiness, loss of appetite, nausea and vomiting, as well as abdominal pain and increased urine production, are symptoms of diabetic ketacidosis.

Epilepsy

Even in the twenty-first century, sports organisations are reluctant to permit people with epilepsy to participate in sport because they think that exercise could provoke seizures, and athletes could be injured. However, studies indicate that epileptics don't have seizures often during exercise, and that exercising may in fact help prevent them, and so should be encouraged.

Coaches with epileptic athletes should think about factors such as how well the athletes can control seizures, whether there is any previous history of exercise-induced seizures, and whether the athlete could be injured during a seizure, as in sports such as diving, rock climbing or parachuting. Then they should decide if the risk of injury to those athletes, and others, is too great to allow them to compete in that particular sport.

First aid for seizures

If seizures occur on the sporting field, the coach should remain calm and protect the athlete from injury. The athlete should be turned on to one side, in the head-down position, to prevent choking on vomit or saliva. Never force anything into the athlete's mouth during a seizure (especially one's fingers as these can be lost!). It is important to keep the airway clear after the seizure too. Most seizures last less than five minutes; if it is longer or this is the athlete's first convulsion, the coach should call an ambulance or a doctor.

Asthma

Exercise-induced asthma (EIA) is caused by **bronchospasm** (a narrowing of the airways) resulting from breathing cold dry air (below 21°C and a relative humidity of 50%). This kind of asthma usually happens five to ten minutes after strenuous exercise, but it may occur during exercise, particularly in unconditioned athletes.

Athletes recover from these attacks spontaneously, usually within 20 to 30 minutes, and under most circumstances they are not in danger. Athletes may experience a **refractory period** of up to one hour after an attack, in which they won't have another one despite exercising again.

Managing EIA

Coaches should encourage athletes to use the following to control their condition:

- environmental controls, such as face masks, when exercising in cold dry air, or humidifiers when practising indoors
- training modifications, such as slower, longer warm-ups, to induce a refractory period, and
- medication, but coaches should remember to check that any substances to be taken are permitted by the International Olympic Committee.

Lisa, a 16-year-old long-distance runner, started to complain of fatigue and tightness in her chest, particularly when she trained on a cold dry winter morning. Nicole, her coach, had seen these symptoms before and suspected that Lisa might have EIA. Nicole suggested that Lisa see Jenny, a sports physician. Jenny performed some simple lung function tests and confirmed that Nicole was correct. Lisa was prescribed a Ventolin aerosol inhaler and instructed on how to use it. When she took two puffs 15–30 minutes before her training session, she had no further problems.

The tired athlete

There are many potential causes of fatigue in athletes. These include:

- overtraining syndrome
- infectious diseases such as upper respiratory illness, glandular fever or viral hepatitis (viral infection of the liver)
- poor nutrition, especially iron deficiency
- pregnancy
- chronic disease states, such as diabetes, hypothyroidism (underactive thyroid gland) or cancer
- medications, and
- sleep disorders.

Overtraining

Coaches and athletes often resist the idea of decreasing training loads, despite evidence that it would be beneficial to do so. They only see a substandard performance as an indication that the athlete should work harder. In addition, training loads are often not tailored to the individual athlete. For example, athletes and coaches sometimes follow the training program of a highly successful athlete such as the 400 m runner Cathy Freeman, even though the athlete can't tolerate the training loads. Females may be at higher risk of overtraining because of anatomical and physiological differences, and because they often push themselves much harder during training than men.

Symptoms of overtraining can include:

- fatigue
- apathy
- sleep disturbances
- weight loss
- increased resting heart rate
- frequent injuries, and
- poor performances.

See chapter 9, Principles of Training, for more information on the symptoms of overtraining.

Preventing overtraining Early recognition of abnormal or excessive fatigue is the first step towards preventing overtraining. This is vital, as recovery time may take weeks or months. Coaches should consider asking athletes to keep a daily training diary that records their levels of exertion and their attitude to training, and then periodically reviewing these diaries as a way of detecting overtraining as soon as possible.

It is important to vary the training load by cycling sessions of heavy training with sessions of recovery (see chapter 9, Principles of Training, and chapter 18, An Integrated Approach to Planning, for more information on overtraining and planning training programs). Coaches should also remember to ensure that athletes eat and drink properly and have at least seven hours of sleep each night (see chapter 16, Sports Nutrition, for more information on sports diets).

Treating overtraining Rest and regeneration strategies are central to recovery from overtraining, as is regular low-level aerobic exercise. Strategies include:

- massage

- hydrotherapy (water exercises), and

- using medications, such as non-sedating antidepressants, when athletes are depressed or not sleeping well.

Iron deficiency anaemia

Iron deficiency is the most common cause of anaemia (shortage of red blood cells) and often results in fatigue. It is mainly caused by not eating enough iron, but blood loss from either menstruation or the gastrointestinal tract, and pregnancy, are other potential causes. The recommended dietary allowance of iron for women is at least 15 mg/day, but many competitive female athletes, such as gymnasts or ballet dancers, eat only 12 mg/day. Many female athletes are also either vegetarian or adopt vegetarian-like diets that avoid red or dark meat, a good source of iron.

Athletes with iron deficiency anaemia should take iron supplements, preferably in the form of ferrous sulphate.

Preventing iron deficiency anaemia

Athletes should:

- eat lean red meat or dark poultry three to four times each week

- avoid drinking tea or coffee with iron-rich foods, as they absorb iron and carry it out of the body, whereas vitamin C helps the body absorb iron

- cook scrambled eggs and acidic foods such as vegetable soup in cast-iron pots to leach iron into the food, and

- eat white poultry or seafood with pulses (beans and lentils), because the animal protein helps the body absorb iron from the pulses.

There is controversial but anecdotal evidence that suggests that athletes with low iron stores frequently complain of fatigue and an inability to recover after heavy training. Many of these athletes respond to iron supplementation and it may well be that treatment prevents their condition from getting worse.

Special concerns of the female athlete

The 'female athletic triad' — disordered eating patterns (see chapter 16, Sports Nutrition, for more information on eating disorders), **amenorrhoea** (absence of menstruation) and **osteoporosis** (brittle bones) — in the compulsive exerciser is a growing concern in sports medicine. These problems are seen particularly in athletes participating in:

- aesthetic sports, such as ballet, gymnastics and ice-skating

- weight category sports, such as judo, boxing and rowing, and

- endurance sports, such as marathon running and triathlon.

Athletes who suffer from these problems are often self-critical perfectionists, with very low levels of self-esteem, but they are highly motivated and are willing to work very hard.

Amenorrhoea

If a female athlete does not start menstruating by 16 years of age she is said to have **primary amenorrhoea**. **Secondary amenorrhoea** is the cessation of menstrual periods for three to six consecutive months, or less than three menstrual cycles per year. Menstrual dysfunction is a major concern because, if the condition lasts for more than two years, it can result in major bone loss that can lead to stress fractures and premature osteoporosis. Infertility may also result, but this is usually reversible.

Managing these problems

Eating more calories, having a well-balanced diet, and decreasing training by 10–20% will usually help to bring on menstruation. However, many top level athletes ignore this advice and so require hormone replacement therapy, either in the form of the oral contraceptive pill or an oestrogen and progesterone preparation.

Chapter 16, Sports Nutrition, contains information on treating eating disorders and managing diet and nutrition. Coaches have an important part to play in counselling athletes and helping to protect them from self-image problems.

Cindy, a 26-year-old female long-distance runner with amenorrhoea, developed exercise-induced lower leg pain. She was referred to a sports physician who diagnosed a tibial stress fracture and advised six to eight weeks of active rest. Andrew, Cindy's coach, had noticed that Cindy had some obsessive–compulsive tendencies, particularly about food, and had lost weight over the past few months. The sports physician confirmed Andrew's suspicions and instituted a multidisciplinary management plan, including psychological counselling.

Cindy's caloric intake was found to be low and was increased to over 2000 kcal/day including 1500 mg calcium and 400 to 800 international units of vitamin D. She was not prepared to reduce her training activities and so was prescribed the oral contraceptive pill. Twelve months later, her weight loss has improved, albeit slowly, and she has sustained no further injuries.

INFECTIONS IN SPORT

Upper respiratory tract infections

Most upper respiratory tract infections (URTIs) are caused by viruses. The average recreational athlete will experience three or four viral infections each year. The symptoms include fever, sore throat, nasal congestion and myalgia (muscle ache).

While regular moderate exercise probably enhances immunity and protection against URTIs, training at higher levels of intensity or volume may make athletes more vulnerable to these illnesses.

Exercising and URTIs

Exercise in the early parts of a viral illness can potentially increase the severity and effects of the infection. The Coxsackie B virus can affect the heart, and exercise during the early phases of its infection of the body can increase the level of virus in the heart and result in myocarditis (inflamed heart muscle) and sudden death.

Coaches should apply the 'neck check' to athletes with URTIs. If the symptoms are located above the neck, for example, a runny nose or a sore throat, then the athlete should be allowed to proceed cautiously through a scheduled training session for 20 minutes, three times a week, as this may aid recovery. This can be followed by a graduated return to normal training activities.

Athletes with 'below the neck' symptoms, such as fever (temperature higher than 38°C), aching muscles, productive cough, vomiting or diarrhoea, should not train. Exercise will aggravate the illness and prolong recovery. Once the fever has subsided and resting heart rate has returned to within two to three beats of normal the athlete can resume strenuous activity. This can take up to 14 days, but occasionally a few weeks.

Treating URTIs

Coaches should help athletes with URTIs by ensuring that they have plenty of fluids and rest. They should take particular care to ensure that athletes are not prescribed banned substances, such as pseudoephedrine, which is found in many cold and flu preparations. There is now some evidence that zinc and vitamin C can shorten viral illnesses.

Preventing URTIs

Regular hand washing may prevent transmission of these diseases among athletes. Athletes should avoid team-mates when infected and cover their mouths when coughing or sneezing in order to prevent droplet spread.

Glandular fever

Athletes with glandular fever (kissing disease) usually have the following symptoms in the early stage of the disease:

- myalgia (muscle ache)
- headache
- loss of appetite
- malaise (feeling generally unwell), and
- fatigue.

Fever, sore throat (often with enlarged tonsils), and tender swollen glands follow. The virus is carried in saliva so, to prevent it being transmitted, athletes and coaches should avoid sharing utensils and other contact that transfers saliva.

Athletes with this illness will not feel like exercising strenuously. However, there is no need for prolonged bed rest, which can cause deconditioning and possibly slow recovery. However, a medical practitioner must clear athletes with glandular fever before they begin to exercise again. When returning to exercise, recovering athletes should start non-contact training at roughly 50% of maximum. If they manage this for a week or so, they can gradually return to full activity.

Blood-borne diseases and sport

The potential risk of the transmission of blood-borne infections such as hepatitis B virus (HBV) and HIV (human immunodeficiency virus) in sport is extremely low. Of the two, however, HBV is more of a concern as it is present in higher concentrations in the blood and it lasts longer outside the body.

Preventing exposure to blood

Athletes with skin wounds that bleed significantly should be treated promptly. Blood on the skin of the injured athlete should be wiped away with soap and water or a clean towel. Many contact sports have a blood bin for this purpose. The athlete can return to play when the wound is covered securely with an appropriate bandage or dressing.

If an athlete bleeds profusely, it is critical that anyone who treats the athlete, or who handles bloody kit and gear, uses disposable gloves to prevent blood exposure. Blood-soaked kit or equipment should be changed, but small amounts of dried blood on the surface of jerseys or padding can remain. Blood-soiled kit and other gear should be washed with detergent in the usual way. Blood on surfaces, such as bench tops or floors, should be cleaned with soap and water, diluted bleach (one part bleach and nine parts water) or an appropriate antiseptic, such as hypochlorite solution.

Those who could have contact with injured athletes who may bleed, such as coaches of contact sports, should be vaccinated against hepatitis B, which covers them for five to ten years.

Preventing the spread of infection in sport

Infectious disease can be spread at sports events in three main ways:

- person-to-person contact
- common-source exposures, and
- airborne or droplet spread.

Coaches should take these key measures to limit the spread of infection:

- encourage athletes to avoid exposure to saliva and avoid drinking from the same water bottle, sharing towels or other equipment, and issuing ointments and powders by hand from common containers
- encourage athletes to wash with soap and water and have their kit laundered often
- encourage athletes involved in contact or collision sports to have regular checks for abrasions, lacerations and skin lesions that could be infectious
- ensure that athletes are vaccinated for hepatitis A and B, diphtheria and tetanus, particularly those who often compete overseas where these infections are more prevalent
- use first aid and infection control methods to prevent exposure to blood (see earlier section), and
- organise or encourage relevant education and professional development for officials, coaches, trainers and athletes.

Traveller's diarrhoea

Athletes who travel overseas to compete are always at risk of developing traveller's diarrhoea, which is usually a mild, self-limiting condition lasting three to five days. The problem should be managed aggressively in order to minimise the effects on mental preparation and physical performance. Treatment should ensure adequate replacement of fluid and electrolytes, ideally with a glucose–electrolyte solution made up with bottled water.

Symptoms can also be treated with antibiotics, which can limit the length of the attack. Coaches should use the same criteria as for an URTI (see page 197) when deciding whether an athlete can begin to exercise again.

Preventing diarrhoea

Prevention is better than cure, however, and athletes should be educated about appropriate food and fluid intake. Ideally, food should be freshly prepared and served hot. Salads, peeled fruit, tap water and ice cubes should be avoided in high risk areas. Coaches should consult with a sports physician about including antibiotics in their first aid kit, and when to use them, when important sporting events take place in high-risk countries.

ENVIRONMENTAL CONCERNS

Heat illness

Heat illness occurs when the body can no longer manage to regulate its own temperature, and its symptoms can range from fainting and cramps to heatstroke. A combination of high temperature and high humidity can stop the body radiating heat or sweating, the two main ways it lowers its temperature. Children, menstruating females, older athletes and those who cannot control their own body temperature are particularly at risk.

Exertional heatstroke

Athletes with this problem rapidly develop severe central nervous system disturbances, including loss of consciousness. They may or may not sweat. Coaches should call for medical assistance immediately if they suspect an athlete is suffering serious heatstroke, as multiple-organ failure can result if the condition is not treated quickly and appropriately. The coach can assist by initiating resuscitation and rapid cooling by:

- removing the athlete's clothing
- using a warm spray and fan to promote evaporative cooling, and
- placing ice bags or cold compresses over the athlete's neck, armpits and groin (where the large blood vessels come close to the surface) to speed cooling.

Preventing heat problems

In hot environments, athletes' clothing should be lightweight and loose fitting to maximise convective and evaporative heat loss. Natural fibres are better than synthetic ones. Coaches should ensure that athletes are well hydrated before, during and after exercise. They should also remember that, when athletes complain of thirst, they have already lost 2% of their total body water.

Ideally, an athlete should be weighed before and after exercise. Every .5 kg lost should be replaced with 500 mL of fluid. Tea, coffee and carbonated drinks should be avoided, as they promote further fluid loss. Water and glucose–electrolyte drinks are preferable. If athletes' urine is clear and they urinate frequently, they are well hydrated.

Coaches should also ensure that athletes are properly conditioned and undergo acclimatisation if necessary. Exercise should be avoided in extreme heat and humidity. Endurance events, such as a marathon, may have to be cancelled if the wet bulb/globe temperature index is higher than 28°C: this is an indicator of heat stress and combines the effects of solar and ground radiation, ambient temperature, relative humidity and wind velocity. Some athletes require special care to cope with their everyday environment.

Gary is a very good and experienced quadriplegic table tennis player. The state men's coach, with whom Gary has been training, has recently retired and a new coach, Claire, has been appointed.

At her first training session, Claire was a little concerned about how she should deal with Gary's condition, as she was worried about her lack of medical knowledge about quadriplegia. She read through Gary's medical information, and saw that he had quadriplegia as a result of a spinal cord injury. Claire asked Gary to tell her anything about his condition that she should be aware of as his coach. He said that, as a result of damage to his spinal cord and hence his central nervous system, he did not sweat below his neck. This meant that he had to use external means to cool himself when he got hot. He told Claire that he used a bottle to spray water on himself to regulate his temperature and that when he was really hot he used a special jacket full of ice.

Travelling — issues for the coach

Travelling sporting teams are sometimes not accompanied by a medical practitioner so coaches and trainers must be aware of problems that may be encountered. It is essential that they plan ahead and gather information about the travel destination, in particular the likely climatic conditions that will be encountered. Athletes may need to acclimatise, and to do this properly they should usually arrive at the destination a couple of weeks before their event. In addition, coaches may have to plan time for recovery from jet lag.

Certain overseas destinations may have specific health risks, such as contaminated water supplies or malaria, and coaches may have to add appropriate preventative medications to their first aid kits. They should consult with a medical practitioner who can provide advice about these and other problems that may be encountered (including vaccination requirements), and help to establish medical contacts at the site of the event. Any athlete with an existing illness or injury should have this attended to appropriately before they depart. If they are not fit, they should not travel!

Tips for the coach

Air travel   Coaches should ensure that athletes adjust to destination time on embarking from the plane and should always ensure non-smoking seats for the athletes where possible. Preventing dehydration is important because the cabin atmosphere will be dry, and large amounts of fluids should be consumed. Athletes should avoid tea, coffee and carbonated drinks. They should also avoid sitting in the plane for prolonged periods of time, and should be encouraged to get up and walk every so often, and perform some gentle stretches. On arrival, coaches should arrange a light training session and should also ensure that athletes don't sleep during daylight, but sleep and eat in accordance with local time.

Food and water   'If you can't boil it, cook it or peel it, then forget it' is a useful motto to remember when trying to prevent the spread of water-borne disease (see Traveller's diarrhoea on page 198). Reheated foods should be avoided and never assume that water in hotel refrigerators is safe.

Preventing malaria   In areas where malaria is a risk, coaches should ensure that athletes wear long-sleeved shirts and trousers and otherwise minimise exposure between dusk and dawn when mosquitoes are at their most active. Insect repellents and mosquito coils are useful. Malaria medication often has to be started before departure and taken for several weeks after returning.

INJURIES AND EMERGENCIES ON THE FIELD

It is imperative that a coach has an emergency management plan in place for potentially serious or life-threatening injuries. Things for the coach to consider include:

- the ease of access for emergency services on to the field of play
- the location of first aid/medical facilities if available, and the nearest hospital, and
- the availability of emergency equipment, including stretcher, cervical collar and arm and leg splints.

Head injury

Head injuries in sport range from mild concussion through to bleeding within the brain itself.

Concussion

Concussion results in an immediate and temporary impairment of brain function, such as alteration of consciousness or vision, as a result of head trauma. It can be mild, moderate or severe. The majority (90%) of cases are mild with no loss of consciousness and a brief period (less than 15 minutes) of **post-traumatic amnesia** (loss of memory) or confusion. Symp-

toms usually settle within 15 minutes or so and the athlete can return to the field of play.

Coaches should be alert and vigilant to the possibility of concussion, particularly in contact sports. If they suspect that an athlete is concussed, they can ask some simple questions to check:

- Orientation — Where are we? What time of the day is it? Whom are we playing against? What quarter or half is it? Who scored the last goal?
- Immediate memory — give the athlete five words to remember and ask him or her to recall them three times in succession (scored out of 15).
- Retrograde amnesia — ask about events that occurred before the traumatic incident.
- Delayed recall — ask the athlete to repeat the five words mentioned earlier (scored out of 5).

When coaches are wondering whether injured athletes should return to play, they should assess the athletes' mental impairment and coordination by asking them to walk in a straight line, bounce a ball and complete 20 m shuttle runs.

If athletes have symptoms that last longer than 15 minutes, or a brief period of unconsciousness, they should not return to the field of play. In the majority of cases, athletes won't have to be hospitalised, provided they can be monitored by a responsible adult over the next 24 hours. They should sit quietly and avoid reading or watching television. Alcohol consumption should be prohibited.

Criteria for referral to hospital

Athletes should be taken to hospital immediately in the following cases:

- they have loss of consciousness for more than three minutes
- they have convulsions
- their mental status deteriorates, with increased drowsiness or dizziness
- they are very restless or irritable
- they have severe headache, nausea and vomiting
- they have more than one concussive episode during the game, or
- they cannot be properly supervised.

Return to play

Athletes should not recommence training until they are completely free of symptoms.

Their training can be increased progressively and immediately stopped if symptoms re-emerge. They should not participate fully until they have had one week totally free of symptoms.

Mental function tests such as the **digital symbol substitution test** are also helpful in assessing the extent of recovery. This test involves matching symbols to numbers in 90 seconds and the total number of successful matches indicates the score. It should be performed by all athletes before the season begins so that the coach has a normal baseline to use as a comparison.

If athletes train with symptoms then they are at an increased risk of developing **post-concussion syndrome**, continuing concussive symptoms. Sometimes these symptoms can persist over months or years.

Medical evaluation

Any athlete with repetitive mild, moderate or severe concussion requires neurological evaluation, preferably by a specialist sports physician. The specialist can make recommendations about further participation in sport, particularly contact sport. At the end of the day the major concern is the prevention of permanent brain damage, the so-called 'punch-drunk syndrome', as developed by Muhammed Ali.

The unconscious athlete

All coaches involved in contact sport should have first aid certificates so that they know how to implement life-saving measures in an emergency situation. It is vital to have a resuscitation procedure in place in case an athlete becomes unconscious. The DR ABC procedure is recommended:

Danger — athlete and coach must be removed from a dangerous environment.

Response — Can you hear me? What is your name? An unconscious athlete will not respond.

Airway — to clear the airway insert a gloved finger into the mouth to clear away debris such as vomit or a mouthguard. To open the airway use the jaw thrust technique, that is, move the jaw forward.

Breathing — check colour, listen for breathing, look for chest movement. If the athlete is not breathing, begin resuscitation.

Circulation — check carotid pulse (in the neck) and, if it's absent, begin cardiopulmonary resuscitation.

If the athlete is in a prone (tummy down) position, he or she must be 'log rolled' into the face-up position. This requires four people with one person taking charge and manually controlling the head and neck. Those treating an unconscious athlete should always watch for the signs of head, neck or spinal injuries and should not attempt to treat them. They should call an ambulance or a doctor immediately if they suspect an athlete has such injuries.

The rest of the body should be checked for injury, including the scalp, face, nose, ears, neck, abdomen, pelvis and limbs. The athlete should be immediately transported to hospital if:

- resuscitation is required
- other major injuries are present, such as a neck injury
- the athlete develops convulsions, or
- the athlete is unconscious for more than three minutes.

Spinal injury

Any athlete who complains of neck pain should be suspected of having a potential neck injury. Other symptoms can include numbness and weakness affecting either the upper and/or lower limbs, particularly on both sides. When a serious injury is suspected, the injured athlete should not be moved and an ambulance or doctor should be called immediately.

The key to managing these injuries on the field is preventing further injury, including potential paralysis and death, until the ambulance or doctor arrives. Coaches should assess the injury using the DR ABC procedure above. If the injury is spinal or related to the head and neck then the athlete must be immobilised, maintaining the longitudinal alignment of the spine. If an injured athlete vomits, then he or she should be turned to the side (coma position), with the neck held in a neutral position.

If the game has to stop to ensure the safety of the injured athlete and those caring for him or her, then that should happen. If an athlete is wearing a helmet, leave it there. It is better if it's removed in the emergency department at the hospital after appropriate X-rays of the neck have confirmed that no fracture is present. Athletes with suspected lower spinal injuries should also be immobilised until a complete medical evaluation has been performed.

Abdominal and pelvic injuries

The most commonly injured organs are the spleen and liver, and such injuries can rapidly lead to shock as a result of internal blood loss.

Symptoms to look out for include:

- abdominal pain
- nausea, and
- vomiting.

The athlete with this sort of injury will often look pale and have a poor pulse (threadlike) and low blood pressure. Athletes with these symptoms should not be allowed to drink. Coaches should call a doctor or an ambulance immediately if they suspect an athlete has such internal injuries.

Leg injuries

Simple first aid measures for leg injuries include:

- splinting of the injury, for example, a fractured tibia can be splinted to the opposite leg
- covering any wound with a moist sterile dressing

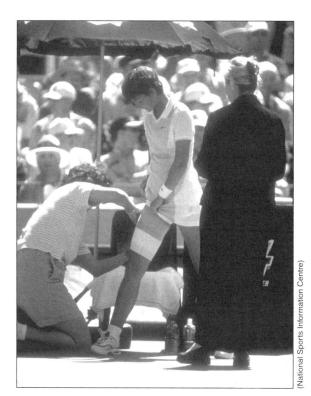

(National Sports Information Centre)

Simple first aid procedures can reduce the impact of leg injuries.

- applying CPRIE (compression, protection, rest, ice and elevation) and particularly pressure to stop bleeding, and
- transporting the injured athlete to hospital, depending on the severity of injury. If nerve or blood vessel damage is suspected, this should be done immediately.

Coaches and other staff should not attempt to relocate a joint such as a shoulder, elbow or finger joint, unless they are suitably qualified, as this can result in nerve, blood vessel or further joint damage.

DRUGS IN SPORT

Drugs in sport are now a significant issue at all levels of sport. It is important that all coaches are prepared to deal with this issue, and have developed their own philosophy and strategies to address it.

The range of issues that coaches may face in relation to the drugs in sport issue include:

- the use of banned performance-enhancing drugs
- the use of medications for injuries and illness that may contain banned drugs
- the use of social drugs
- the use of nutritional and herbal supplements that may contain banned drugs
- athletes being subject to drug testing
- innuendo and allegations about athletes using banned drugs, and
- the use of drugs for body image reasons.

Coaches can influence the attitudes of athletes, and should support and care for them as individuals. This means that they can play a significant role with regard to drugs in sport. Coaches can:

- encourage athletes to abide by the anti-doping rules of their sport
- prevent drug misuse by athletes, and
- help athletes to deal with other issues related to drugs in sport, such as drug testing.

There are a number of reasons why drugs have been banned in sport. These include:

- health reasons — many drugs, especially if they are not used properly, can seriously affect athletes' health

- ethical reasons — some drugs may give an unfair advantage to an athlete, and using them is considered to be cheating, and

- legal reasons — some drugs are banned because they are illegal in the general community.

The coach's role

The coach is one of the most important influences on the athlete, and can play a key role in preventing drug misuse by athletes. Some of the steps that coaches can take include:

- providing athletes with factual information about banned drugs

- being good role models (using social drugs responsibly)

- communicating their beliefs about health and fair play to athletes and reinforcing the idea that using banned drugs is cheating

- discouraging misuse of banned drugs, medications and social drugs

- providing alternatives to drug use to enhance performance, for instance, designing training programs that develop the whole athlete, and keeping up to date with the latest developments in sports science, equipment, techniques and tactics

- counselling athletes they suspect or know are taking banned drugs

- alleviating pressures on athletes where possible, and

- helping athletes to develop skills such as decision making and assertiveness.

As well as preventing deliberate drug misuse, coaches can play an important educative role with athletes regarding other drugs in sport issues, such as drug testing and the use of medications. Coaches who work with athletes who are subject to drug testing should ensure that they know which substances are banned or restricted in sport, and that they advise athletes to avoid using medications that contain banned drugs.

Pressures faced by athletes

There are a number of factors that may contribute to an athlete misusing drugs. Following are some factors that may influence athletes' decisions about using drugs, and some ways in which coaches can help them deal with the issues.

Financial rewards involved in being an elite athlete

Coaches might discuss the possible consequences of drug use with athletes, instilling the attitude that 'there is no honour or pride in winning by cheating'. They should encourage athletes to develop work and personal skills for life after sport.

Athletes' intense will to win

Coaches should encourage athletes to achieve personal goals, rather than those achieved by others, and instil the importance of fair play. They might also reinforce the idea that doing well as a result of hard work, talent and skill is something of which athletes should be proud, but using drugs to win is not.

Other athletes are using banned drugs

Coaches should reinforce the importance of achieving personal goals. They should also discuss with athletes any relevant national and international developments, such as state legislation for testing and the creation of the World Anti-Doping Agency to conduct testing at the international level.

Prohibited substances and methods

Most national sporting organisations prohibit the use of substances and methods outlined in the *Olympic Movement Anti-doping Code* (appendix A, Prohibited Classes of Substances and Prohibited Methods) (International Olympic Committee 2000). The list is reviewed annually and it is important that coaches check with their relevant national sporting organisations for any amendments.

The following substances are subject to certain restrictions and coaches should consult the relevant policies to find out what restrictions apply under their sport's rules:

- cannabis

- alcohol

- local anaesthetics

- beta-blockers, and

- glucocorticosteroids.

The classes of prohibited substances under the *Olympic Movement Anti-doping Code*

Type of substance	Examples	Results	Possible side-effects
Anabolic agents	Anabolic androgenics, such as nandrolone and stanozolol Non-steroidal agents, such as beta 2 agonists	Increased muscle strength and power	Liver damage Violent/aggressive behaviour Irreversible damage to both sexes' reproductive organs
Diuretics	Frusemide Spironolactone	Short-term weight loss (through fluid loss)	Dizziness and fainting Headaches Nausea Loss of coordination and balance Kidney and heart failure
Narcotics	Morphine Heroin Pethidine	Strong pain relief	Loss of balance Decreased concentration Sleepiness Slower breathing Nausea and vomiting Ongoing aggravation of injury if an athlete continues to compete
Peptide hormones, mimetics and analogues	Human growth hormone (hGH)	Muscle growth	Cardiac disease Grotesque overgrowth of hands, feet and face
	Erythropoietin	More red blood cells, improving the body's ability to transport and use oxygen	Blood clots leading to heart attacks and strokes
Stimulants	Pseudoephedrine Amphetamines Caffeine (if above the reportable level of 12 micrograms per millilitre)	Increase in mental alertness Decreased sense of fatigue Increased sense of aggression	Lack of coordination Dehydration Weight loss Rise in body temperature

In addition the following techniques for improving performance or avoiding the detection of banned substances are also banned:

- pharmacological, chemical and physical manipulation of test samples
- blood doping (the administration of blood with higher concentrations of red blood cells), and
- the administration of artificial oxygen carriers or plasma expanders.

Inadvertent doping (including supplements)

Inadvertent doping can occur when an athlete accidentally takes a medication or supplement that contains a banned medication. Athletes are ultimately responsible for the medications they take and coaches should encourage them to use the appropriate sources of information, such as the Australian Sports Drug Agency (ASDA) Drugs in Sport hotline and the *Drugs in Sport Handbook* (ASDA 1999),

The affects of some social drugs on athletes

Social drug	Likely effects on training athletes
Alcohol	• can delay the healing of soft tissue injuries
	• combined with lack of sleep from staying out late, may suppress immune function
	• is high in kilojoules, and so affects athletes who are trying to reduce or maintain body weight and skinfold levels
	• is a potent diuretic, and can reduce athletes' ability to fully replace fluid losses, and
	• can prevent a recovery plan being implemented effectively.
Cannabis and other 'party' drugs	• can impair balance, coordination and concentration and can have adverse psychological effects, such as anxiety, paranoia and lack of motivation
	• can increase blood pressure, pulse rate and body temperature, which can result in overheating and dehydration (as does the combination of ecstasy, alcohol and speed or amphetamines), and
	• can produce after-effects that include loss of energy, irritability, depression and anxiety.

to ensure that what they are taking is permitted under their sport's doping policy (see Further Reading).

The use of supplements is becoming increasingly popular among athletes. Herbal preparations, vitamins and food supplements are not subject to the same stringent testing as pharmaceutical products, so such a product could contain a banned ingredient that is not listed on the label. Supplements that are bought via the internet or mail order from overseas do not receive any testing or assessment by Australian authorities. There are also some locally produced supplements, such as those produced by naturopaths or homeopaths, that are not assessed at all.

To reduce the risk of inadvertently testing positive to a banned substance in a supplement, athletes may choose to use sports foods or supplements that are produced in Australia by companies with a known record of good manufacturing, who can guarantee that their products contain no banned substances.

Therapeutic use of banned medications

When athletes have illnesses that medical practitioners can only treat with banned medications, the athletes must check the legitimate therapeutic use of the banned substance with their national sporting organisations. Athletes

using asthma medications must refer to the rules outlined in their sport's doping policies to find out the status of the medication, and whether and how they should notify their sport.

Handling athlete drug misuse

The following are some basic guidelines for handling an athlete's misuse of drugs. Drug misuse can be a complex issue, and these guidelines are merely a starting point. Coaches may have to refer the athlete for professional assistance if the situation is beyond their expertise.

■ If the athlete's drug misuse appears to be an isolated occurrence, it may be best if the coach does not make a big deal about it, but speaks to the athlete privately about the incident. They should discuss what led to the situation and discuss the harm that occurred (or could have occurred) as a result of the athlete's actions. The athlete should be made aware of his or her responsibilities to the team or club, and what action will be taken if the incident is repeated. The coach should be firm but reasonable, and be open to the fact that the athlete may have made an error of judgement and learnt from it. Coach and athlete should agree on a course of action to prevent the situation happening again.

- If a coach has suspicions that an athlete is using or planning to use banned substances, the coach should raise the issue with the athlete. Determining the reasons behind the drug use is an important step in finding a solution to the problem. The coach may be able to suggest alternatives to drug use, or refer the athlete to professional assistance.

- If the drug use is serious or an ongoing problem, there are no easy solutions. If the coach has a good relationship with the athlete, they may discuss the situation (as with the earlier examples). The athlete should be made aware of the consequences of continuing to take drugs. The coach should try to determine whether the athlete is prepared to change his or her behaviour voluntarily and, if so, could provide support and assistance during this process. If the athlete is not prepared to change, then the coach may wish to consider whether he or she should continue to coach the athlete.

Coaches also need strategies for dealing with the abuse of social drugs by athletes, which is often linked to post-game celebrations (see chapter 1, Roles and Responsibilities of the Coach, for further information on dealing with social drug use).

Kareem had coached Justin for many years, and found him a dedicated and hard-working athlete. However, recently Kareem began to notice a change in Justin's behaviour — he arrived late at training sessions and moved to a new gym. Kareem was concerned because he had heard that the new gym had a culture that encouraged drug taking. Justin had also started to question some of Kareem's training methods, insinuating that there were easier ways to make it to the top.

Kareem was concerned about these changes, and suspected that they resulted from drug use.

- Kareem reviewed Justin's current performance against the planned performance for that period, and found that it was much better than expected.

- Kareem also looked at other factors influencing Justin's life that may have affected his attitude and performance levels.

- After reviewing these factors, Kareem felt that drugs were involved and so he approached Justin to discuss the issue.

- Justin confirmed his suspicions and told Kareem that he was taking anabolic steroids.

- Kareem encouraged Justin to stop taking the anabolic steroids, reminding him that it was against the concept of fair play, that it could have adverse effects on his health, and that he was a talented athlete who could achieve the desired results with hard work.

- Kareem also encouraged Justin to seek counselling.

- When it became apparent that there was no change in Justin's attitude and his performance continued to improve, Kareem had to decide whether to continue to coach him.

- After much anguish and discussion with Justin, Kareem decided that he was unable to continue coaching him.

- Kareem spoke to Justin's family regarding his decision and thought about whether he should communicate the information any further within his sport.

Drug testing

Athletes competing at national level can be subject to drug testing by a range of national testing authorities, such as ASDA, the World Anti-Doping Agency and their international sports federation. Testing is increasingly conducted with no notice, so it can happen at any time and any place. It is important for coaches of athletes travelling or training overseas to be abreast of international testing arrangements. They should contact ASDA or their national sporting organisation for up-to-date information on international testing.

The way samples are collected may vary according to the drug testing authority concerned, for athletes with disabilities and for those athletes who are tested overseas. If athletes are concerned with any part of the sample collection process, they should note their concerns on the drug testing form and notify their national sporting organisation in writing as soon as possible.

During a drug testing session, athletes have a number of rights and responsibilities, one of which is that they may have a representative with them. Coaches may be asked by athletes to play this part.

Athletes who are to be tested will be permitted to participate in normal post-game cool-down activities, but the chaperone must always have the athlete in full view. During the drug testing process, athletes are responsible for maintaining control of their sample. The only exception to this is athletes with a disability, who may have the help of their representative. Athletes must also ensure that their sealed sample collection kit is secure and that all appropriate documentation is accurate, complete and signed.

Positive test results and sanctions

Results management and appeals procedures for athletes may vary depending on whether the test is international or domestic. For more information, refer to your sport's doping policy and/or ASDA.

It is important that coaches encourage athletes to know their rights and the penalties involved in returning a positive drug test result under the doping rules of their sport. It is also important for coaches to encourage those athletes who refuse to participate in drug tests to do the test. A refusal constitutes a doping offence under sports policies, and athletes who refuse may face disciplinary procedures, including a sanction.

CONCLUSION

Coaches are an integral part of the team involved in ensuring the medical care of athletes. They must be familiar with:

- injuries and illnesses that can occur in sport
- the principles of rehabilitation
- drug abuse issues that can occur in sport
- the simple strategies that prevent injuries and illnesses, and
- the emergency protocols for assessing and managing accidents that can occur in the sporting arena.

Establishing a good relationship between the coach, the team doctor or local sports physician and the physiotherapist is central to the wellbeing and ongoing good health of the athlete. Open lines of communication and a collaborative spirit are essential ingredients in modern sporting life.

The sports organisation provides an important setting for the education of young athletes about healthy behaviours. Through coaches' influence and the environment created by the sports organisation, athletes can develop healthy behaviours that will allow them to enjoy their sport and enhance the quality of their lives. Coaches should work directly with their national sporting organisation to develop and implement an appropriate strategy that is relevant to the level of the athletes they coach.

COACHING TIPS

- Enlist medical and physiotherapy support to identify potential physical problems before they occur.

- Obtain basic training in first aid and resuscitation, and keep a well-maintained first aid kit always on hand.

- Modify the training load to aid the injury healing process.

- Encourage safe change room practices to minimise the risk of infection and disease transmission.

- Develop a drugs in sport education program to alert athletes to the physical and health risks, as well as the ethical issues, associated with using drugs.

FURTHER READING

ASDA resources

Australian Sports Drug Agency (ASDA) website <www.asda.org.au>, Drugs in Sport hotline tel 1800 020 506.

Australian Sports Drug Agency (1996) *Drugs in Sport Coach Education Manual.* Canberra: Australian Sports Drug Agency.

Australian Sports Drug Agency (1999) *Drugs in Sport Handbook.* Canberra: Australian Sports Drug Agency.

International Olympic Committee (2000) Appendix A: prohibited classes of substances and prohibited methods. In: *Olympic Movement Anti-Doping Code.* <www.asda.org.au/fs_public.html>, 1 April 2000, Australian Sports Drug Agency.

Australian Sports Drug Agency (nd) *Athlete's Guide to Drug Testing* (brochure). Canberra: Australian Sports Drug Agency.

Other resources

Bloomfield, J, P Fricker and K Fitch (eds) (1995) *Science and Medicine in Sports.* Carlton: Blackwell Scientific Publishing.

Brukner, P, and K Khan (2000) *Clinical Sports Medicine.* Sydney: McGraw-Hill.

Fields, K, and P Fricker (1997) *Medical Problems in Athletes.* Oxford, UK; Malden, MA: Blackwell Scientific Publishing.

Ringhofer, K, and K Hardin (1996) *Coaches Guide to Drugs in Sport.* Champaign, IL: Human Kinetics.

Sports Medicine Australia (1994) *Sports First Aid Course Manual.* Belconnen: Sports Medicine Australia.

Williams, JGP (1980) *A Colour Atlas of Injury in Sport.* London, UK: Wolfe Medical.

Wilson, W, and E Derse (2000) *Doping in Elite Sport: The Politics of Drugs in the Olympic Movement.* Champaign, IL: Human Kinetics.

INTEGRATING THE PROGRAM

CHAPTER 18
AN INTEGRATED APPROACH TO PLANNING

Peter Spence and Roger Flynn

(National Sports Information Centre)

INTRODUCTION

Coaching should revolve around a plan that will create a performance-enhancing environment for athletes. Planning in coaching is both a science and an art: the science describes what is to be done and what will be measured; the art determines when and how it will be done. Planning provides the means of organising training and preparation so that the various program components work well together. How well these elements are balanced is crucial to the success and wellbeing of the athlete.

INTEGRATED PLANNING

Coaches can meet the changing needs of athletes by integrating all the factors that affect their performances into a training plan. Fundamentally, they achieve this by dividing the training year into a system of fluid and overlapping training periods that vary in their purpose, volume and intensity, depending upon the stage of development of each athlete and when competitions occur. This is often referred to as **periodisation**.

Integrated planning assists the athlete and coach to:

- recognise strengths, while acknowledging any weaknesses
- set realistic performance goals
- establish steps and action plans to improve performance, in both the short and the long term
- instil and develop confidence in the program, and
- achieve enjoyment and satisfaction.

Creating the environment

Coaching should provide opportunities for the athlete to develop and learn. The objective must be to establish a fertile, challenging, yet supportive environment that will best develop the athlete's unique abilities. The coach is a manager of resources, and successful coaches are those who can tap as many of these as possible (see chapter 3, The Coach as a Resource Manager, for more information on using resources). The primary resource is the talent of the athlete, though this may not be fully appreciated, even by the athlete. In many cases, this talent is grossly underdeveloped because of insufficient planning.

Many other resources and factors influence the environment and the development of talent, including relationships with other athletes, peers, parents and support personnel. Because many of these relationships are beyond the control of the athlete or the coach, the environment is, in many ways, chaotic. The management of relationships is arguably the most critical issue for the coach and the athlete. The ultimate challenge in planning is providing sensitive support within a disciplined system that will enable athletes to draw upon the positive elements of their environment.

The athlete–coach relationship

Each individual has a unique background in terms of personal goals, natural capacities, previous training and life experiences. Coaches aim to help athletes find a path towards achieving their goals. In order to do this, they should aim to empower athletes and encourage their eventual independence. Athletes must be continually encouraged to learn, to work closely with their coaches to drive their programs, and to progress to a more self-sufficient position in the future.

The planning process should evolve as the relationship between the athlete and coach matures and they grow to understand the processes and each other more completely.

When asked about the relationship with his coach (his father), outstanding English middle-distance runner Sebastian Coe remarked that they had a marvellous relationship and could always discuss things. However, he added that the role of the coach changes as athletes grow older and, in some ways, the coach becomes 'another set of eyes'.

With this comment, Coe was reaffirming the contribution that athletes can make to their own coaching, with increasing knowledge, experience and understanding. The coach has to be able to recognise when it is necessary to adopt a different role in terms of the athlete's program and the overall support system that surrounds the athlete (Spence 1998).

While face-to-face contact between coaches and athletes is best, it can be difficult to coordinate, particularly with squads or teams of athletes. Many coaches find that questionnaires help with collecting information from athletes. Such information should be confidential and only shared between the coach and key support personnel. Planning and evaluation questionnaires ask athletes to identify, on a ten-point scale, the current and desired levels of performance factors and life factors. They also ask athletes to list, in priority order, the factors that they wish to develop further.

Planning and evaluation sheets for forthcoming training sessions and for competition can also initiate valuable exchanges of information between coaches and athletes and encourage athletes to participate directly in the planning process. This helps to make the environment more stimulating and meaningful for all concerned.

Establishing goals

To create a long-term planning model, athletes and coaches must establish goals in the long term (perhaps 10–20 years), mid term (3–5 years) and short term (usually within the scope of the annual training plan). This provides a great opportunity for interaction between athletes and coaches.

Performance components

Systematic goal setting helps coaches and athletes identify the components of performance, frequently referred to as 'training factors', that have to be integrated through the program. Integrating these components of performance is the key element that allows athletes to best develop their unique capacities, and achieve their goals.

The integration of these components should be a fluid process, with components constantly overlapping and in a state of flux. The plan should not become mechanical in nature: coaches deal with human beings, not machines, and the wonders of human consciousness offer advantages far beyond those of machines. Coaches must recognise the interdependence of all components, as each one influences the behaviour of others and their contribution to the final outcome.

Squash coach Roger Flynn says, 'To be truly effective the coach has to understand the impact of the specific area of training on other aspects of the athlete's development, otherwise it can become a piecemeal, patchwork, reactionary process that segments the player's training into unrelated and potentially counterproductive processes.

In our program, I have specialists in each of these areas working with the players during the same training sessions, with each participating and sharing in the feedback process to the player, resulting in a dynamic, holistic environment that really optimises the player's development.

Coaches have to adopt an integrated/interdependent approach in their operations, even if specialist support personnel are not available.'

Basic principles of integrated planning

- The training plan must be *individualised* for the unique talents, background and experiences of each athlete. It must be dynamic and should evolve as the athlete develops.

- *Dreaming* should be encouraged, so athletes can imagine what might be. Remem-

Squash player with specialist coach

(National Sports Information Centre)

ber, they are repositories of gifts and talents, many of which haven't been developed. In the right environment, dreams can come true.

- *Documentation* that records the responses of athletes to stimuli is vital to facilitating progressive, individualised planning, and delivering and reviewing the program.

- *Injury prevention* and *medical screening* should be completed at the beginning of the program and then at regular intervals. The coach must be aware of any existing injuries that may affect the developmental process and which could have legal consequences in the event of injury, accident or misadventure. Intensive training should not be introduced until the athlete has been screened.

- Coaches should encourage *concurrent development* of athletes' capacities, to challenge them and to stimulate the relationship between the various factors that contribute to performance. Although specificity of training is important, it should not be viewed too rigidly and coaches should not emphasise one element at the expense of the others.

- *Enjoyment* should be a prime consideration, and *varied activity* and *cross-training* should be encouraged at various stages of the year. This helps the athlete to maintain motivation levels and discover and stimulate underdeveloped abilities.

- Some athletes are exposed to a restricted range of activities in their formative years and their 'movement vocabulary' may be limited. *Body management training* provides variety and can enhance an athlete's range of movement by introducing gymnastics activities. These activities also help athletes avoid injuries, as they learn to absorb force in landing and falling, and can give them more enjoyment, self-satisfaction, motivation and opportunities for creativity.

- Athletes should be encouraged to *develop creative and spontaneous abilities* by using stimulating activities, imagery and creative language to recruit 'right-brain' activity. (The right hemisphere of the brain is generally associated with spontaneous and automatic response, while the left hemisphere is mostly responsible for logical, controlled and deliberate thought and actions.)

- Coaches should *innovate* so that they can meet the changing needs and interests of athletes. They should also think about new approaches to old problems and ask themselves what athletes will best respond to, rather than merely relying on what has been done in the past. They should dare to be different and creative in the way they plan the program!

- They should also adopt a *holistic approach* to promote a balance between sport and life, to ensure that athletes plan for life after sport, and also to introduce life skills and encourage career development during athletes' time in sport. This will help to develop the athletes' time-management skills, allowing them to undertake a variety of activities and preventing them from concentrating too heavily on analysis or on one element of the program.

Athletes in team sports should be as individually focused as those in individual sports, and should develop detailed individual plans for their future in the same way. However, there are special planning considerations for coaches who have to mould individuals into a unified team with goals and characteristics of its own (see annual planning for team sports on page 220).

Long-term planning

Integrated planning should be based upon a whole-of-life approach. Depending on the age of the athlete and the type of sport being played, high-performance planning may cover a period of 20 years or more. Sometimes, such progress will be smooth and sequential; at other times it will be erratic, as talent and a fertile environment combine to produce quantum leaps in development or performances. A model has been developed of the stages through which athletes progress, from beginning in sport to achieving their aspirations.

The model's career stages are:

- *FUNdaMENTAL (pretraining) stage*, when athletes develop a love for participation in activity and an awareness of how sport is played. The focus is on the foundations of enjoyment and coordination rather than future goals (ratio of preparation to competition is 4:1).

- *Training to train stage* (generally two to six years long), when athletes develop the skills and capacities to participate in a sport. At this stage, competition is part of the process, but is incidental to long-term developmental objectives (the ratio of preparation to competition is 3:1).

- *Training to compete stage* (generally two to six years long), when athletes focus on the development of competition skills and strategies, and learn to compete in various environments and against different types of opponents (the ratio of preparation to competition is 1:1).

- *Training to perform/win stage* (the number of years in this stage is sport and athlete-dependent), when the focus is on competition priorities and achieving peak performance (the ratio of preparation to competition is 1:4) (Balyi 1996, Balyi and Hamilton 1995 and 1996, and Balyi and Way 1995).

In some sports, and with talented individuals, these stages may be compressed or overlap significantly. In sports where specialisation occurs early, such as women's gymnastics, the FUNdaMENTAL stage may be very brief or non-existent.

THE ANNUAL TRAINING PLAN

Purpose of the plan

The annual training plan is the pathway to achieving the athlete's short-term goals. It provides the framework for the stimulation, development and recovery of the human body by integrating activities and systematically setting progressive training loads. The plan also becomes the basis of a monitoring system that coaches can use to check progress and to prevent overtraining. Ultimately, the annual training plan must strike a balance between developing athletes and helping them to achieve their best performances at times of peak competition (for more developed athletes).

The plan must be fluid and adaptable, to meet the changing needs and the varying environments of athletes.

(National Sports Information Centre)

Fitness training is included in the annual training plan.

Conventional divisions of the training year

Training phase	Subphase	Purpose
Preparation	General preparation	Foundations established in all components of performance (and the relationships between components)
	Specific preparation	More sport-specific preparation of the components of performance and of the relationships between them
Competition	Pre-competition	Stabilisation of the components of performance and the relationships between them; and basic competition simulation in training/competition (or early season competition)
	Competition	Maintenance and refinement of the components of performance and the relationships between them; specific competition simulations (like a dress rehearsal), that is, preparing athletes for the actual stress of competition; pre-competition unloading; competition; and post-competition recovery
Transition (off-season or recovery period)		Active recovery and/or participation in alternative sport or activities that maintain existing capacities and stimulate underdeveloped capacities

Structure of the plan (training phases, cycles and sessions)

In order to make the coaching process manageable, the annual plan is usually broken into the following divisions.

Training phases are the broad divisions of the training year that differentiate the aims and priorities of the program (particularly with regard to competition priorities, for example, preparation, competition and transition phases).

Training subphases are subdivisions of a training phase that have more specific purposes.

Macrocycles, or training months, are training blocks, usually two to six weeks long, during which there is a common theme to training or competition.

Microcycles, or training weeks, are blocks of training sessions that are often seven days long for simplicity of organisation, but can be of any length from one to ten days. Microcycles are sequences of training sessions coordinated in the most suitable way to achieve the aims and the planned training loads (volume and intensity) of the macrocycle.

Training sessions are units of work and/or recovery designed to fulfil the specific aims of each microcycle. Ideally they are between 30 and 90 minutes long, but sometimes shorter or longer, depending on the aims of the microcycle and the components to be developed.

Developing the plan

Annual plans must be developed in a fluid and adaptable way to ensure that they meet the changing needs of athletes and coaches. These steps will give coaches a starting point for the planning process.

1. Identify commitments

Sport Coaches should list the competition schedule and rate each competition in terms of importance. At this early stage, they should consider identifying the approximate number of peaks that they should be achieving, relative to the career stage of the athlete.

Life Coaches should discuss with athletes the other life commitments that may contribute towards cumulative stress, in terms of time and emotional pressures (such as exams, work or relationships), and list them.

2. Think about the identified commitments

Coaches should then establish the peaking index (PI) for each athlete, in both sport and life, for the entire year. The PI ranges from the most important competitions (rated 1) to less important competitions (that may be rated as low as 5). A PI of 4 or 5 could be reserved for competitions that the athlete will merely 'train through' or for the preparation phases of the plan.

When reviewing the overall distribution of competitive peaks, coaches should focus on the last peak competition in the year and work

Annual Training Plan

Phases	Subphases	Macrocycles (months)	Microcycles (weeks)	Sessions
Preparation	General preparation (GPP)	1	1 2 3 4	
		2	1 2 3 4	
		3	1 2 3 4	
	Specific preparation (SPP)	4	1 2 3 4	
		5	1 2 3 4 5	
Competition	Pre-competition (PCP)	6	1 2 3 4 5	
		7	1 2 3 4 5	
	Competition (CP)	8	1 2 3 4	
		9	1 2 3 4	
		10	1 2 3 4	
		11	1 2 3	
		12	1 2 3	
Transition		13	1 2 3 4 5	

Conventional structure of the training year

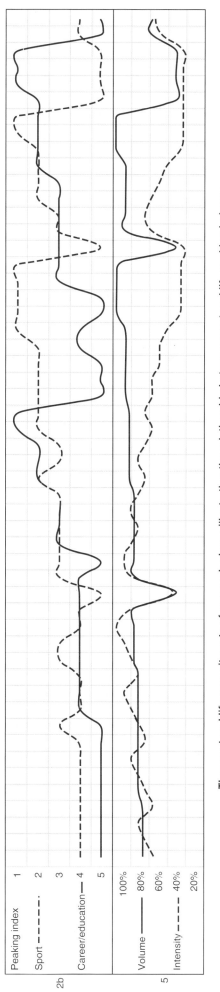

The sport and life commitments of a squash player, illustrating the relationship between sport and life peaking indexes back from there, in order to determine the sequence of priorities. Note that the PI curve should be smooth and not jump up or down dramatically, as it must allow for athletes to develop progressively.

For developing athletes, particularly those in transition from the FUNdaMENTAL to training to train stages, it may be more appropriate to allocate a mid-range PI of 3 for all competitions, so that the developmental goals may be highlighted without distracting the athletes with more intense competition objectives. The life PI uses a similar process to identify peak times in terms of life demands.

When the PI has been established, it should be drawn on a graph. The graph of the life PI may show commitments that clash with the sport PI. In such cases, it is the responsibility of the athlete to convene a meeting with the coach and significant others (such as parents, teachers or employers), to negotiate changes and manage the clash effectively. Some coaches clarify the life PI before attending to the sport PI, as they maintain that life considerations are essential to establishing a balanced and integrated program for athletes.

3. Allocate training phases that generally align with the training PI

The link between the training phases and the PI is usually as it is in this table.

Training phase	PI
Main competition	1–2
Pre-competition	2–3
Specific preparation	3–4
General preparation	4–5
Transition	5

4. Specify and integrate the training components to be developed

Coaches should plan the content and delivery of training so that all aspects peak at the same time. They should recognise that athletes will have different training histories ('training ages') and that this factor may also vary across the training components of each athlete. It is common in many sports for athletes to have a sound training history in certain technical components, yet be relatively undeveloped in physical, mental or strategic development.

On the annual plan sheet, each training component (such as strength, speed or endurance) should be developed (horizontally) and then coordinated or integrated (vertically) with the rest of the plan. The vertical integration minimises interference from other activities and allows coaches and athletes to best coordinate the various training components.

5. Volume/intensity guide

The volume of training is the total number of sessions and the total time allocated to them. The intensity of training can be calculated by comparing athletes' target heart rates to their maximum heart rates; by the rating of perceived exertion, the athletes' rating of the intensity of the activity/session; or by blood lactate levels. Intensity can also be calculated by noting such factors as whether the level of skill being applied has declined and whether cues are being misread.

Coaches should remember to consider psychological stress (and all stressors, as they have a cumulative affect) on athletes when they are trying to determine the intensity of a training session. Volume and intensity should generally be inversely proportional — when volume is high, intensity is low and vice versa.

Sport   In this step coaches should allocate estimated recovery/regeneration periods. They should also graph the approximate volume and intensity of training to provide guidelines for the general management of training load (for example, volume in minutes multiplied by the rating of intensity out of ten) and recovery.

Life   Coaches and athletes should also graph a total load (stress) curve, or the volume and intensity (if appropriate) of other aspects of life.

6. Macrocycles

The next step is to apportion macrocycles based on the planned sequence of training. Some coaches prefer to work in blocks of three to six weeks/microcycles, while others elect to vary the length of the training 'month' according to the training phase and the time available between certain landmarks in the program.

7. Microcycles

The training weeks or microcycles are the next planning element. Because it is important to be flexible and to vary the program according to the way in which the athlete is responding, it is usually not necessary to prepare detailed plans for more than two to six weeks ahead of current training.

Developing and integrating training components in Australian rules football

Training components	Preparation		Competition		Transition
	General	Specific	Pre-competition	Competition	
Flexibility	General	Specific	Specific and ballistic	Maintenance	Active rest, regeneration and review
Endurance	Aerobic	Aerobic and anaerobic	Develop the foundation of specific endurance	Specific endurance	
Strength/power	General strength	Maximum strength	Conversion to power or muscular endurance	Maintenance	
Agility	General mobility	Specific mobility and tumbling	Specific mobility and tumbling	Maintenance	
Skills • individual	General skills and remedial	• Specific skills	• Competition skills	• Competition skills under pressure	
• team		• Skills in small groups	• Group skills for attack and defence	• Competition simulations	
Tactics	Understanding style of play	Basic tactics	On-field team decision making (competition simulations)	Situational problem solving	
Psychology	Self-monitoring skills	Perceptual skills and decision making	Pressure, exertion and coping strategies	Automatic response (right brain control)	
Group dynamics	Group goals	Awareness of individual differences (group discussions/ active involvement in planning and evaluation)	Team-building tasks	Team activities and recreation	

(after Bompa 1990)

8. Session plans

Finally, the training sessions are planned.

Angela is an experienced softball coach, who works mainly with teenage athletes. Angela is Indigenous, and has encouraged many people within her community to take up the sport. Angela found that the traditional style of session planning — skill practice, then a game — didn't work for many of her Indigenous players. She realised that she had to be flexible and develop a program that suited the needs and preferences of the players with whom she was working.

She now uses an approach in which the team plays a game first, then breaks down the skills for development, then builds back up to another game. Angela has found that this approach keeps the interest of her players, and makes the development of skills more relevant to the game itself.

Annual planning for team sports

Planning the most fulfilling program for an individual athlete is a challenge. Developing a similarly fulfilling plan for a team is more complex, as the needs of each athlete must be considered and then coordinated to create the team unit. If the team unit is well developed, then it can produce more than the simple sum of the parts: there is a multiplier effect that is apparent in good teams and noticeably missing in poorly performing teams.

The key training principle of individuality (see chapter 9, Principles of Training, for more information on individuality and other training principles) must be applied with any team. Coaches should remember that each athlete is unique in terms of goals, natural capacities and life experiences and deserves an individualised program. The individual athlete's plan must be closely linked to the team plan and team structures. The real balancing act in team coaching is being able to stimulate each individual athlete, while coordinating the team plan to meet the objectives of the team.

Fundamental to the team training plan is defining a playing style and team culture that will guide preparation and performance and also assist with establishing individual performance goals. The coach can achieve this by encouraging the team to develop a mission and a set of values for the year ahead, so that they feel as though they are strongly connected to the plan and its underlying principles.

The agreed style of play is the basis on which the coach and the team then decide which components of performance (such as speed, psychology or endurance) they will concentrate on, in order to satisfy this style. Performance indicators in training and competition can then be used to show whether the plan is working. These may include performance data such as achievement of targets and numbers of forced and unforced errors, and other details from training or competition.

It is best to plan the training components for both individuals and the team separately, though obviously these should be closely linked. Many of the individual component activities may be included in each athlete's personal training program, while the team components can be addressed at the scheduled team training sessions.

Planning for team sports is more complex than individual planning.

(National Sports Information Centre)

Sample annual training plan for a calendar year

Sample annual training plan for a squash player in the training to compete phase

Soccer coach Ernie Merrick says, 'First of all, you must decide how you want to play the game (determine the style of play that suits your team and the systems to be used in attack and defence) so that you can then prioritise the components that you want the athletes to develop.

Then you need a team plan and an individual plan for each player, particularly for the training that they do in their own time. The structure of the plan provides the system to which the players and the team work. This also integrates the development of the technical/tactical, physical and psychological components, which are all dependent upon each other.

In the past, I have had success in concentrating on individual development in preparation phases and then developing the team focus, as the competition season approaches. However, in recent years, I have found that the early emphasis on the team, through establishing the team mission and team values, helps to set the culture that "glues" things together.

As the competition phase develops, I encourage the athletes to consult with the specialist support personnel in order to tend to their own needs, within the team plan' (Spence 2000).

Cyclical teamwork

One of the limitations in team sport coaching can be the reliance on repetitive training routines that aim to achieve consistency of performance, but can fail to stimulate individual talents and may be boring. Athletes respond well to variety, so coaches should structure the team plan around varied themes that will stimulate individual enthusiasm and develop the special talents of team members.

It may even be profitable to have individual athletes in a team on different training cycles, particularly during preparation and early competition phases. Some athletes may be on loading cycles (with progressively increasing training loads), and some may be on unloading (with reducing training loads) or very individualised cycles, and yet this may enhance the overall performance of the team while still promoting individual development and recovery.

Some team coaches alternate skill and fitness microcycles, in order to stimulate and balance development. Others radically reduce training volume to orchestrate an unloading effect at the end of each macrocycle, to prepare for the next cycle.

Ernie also says, 'I individualise within the team structure by focusing throughout the year on decision making. Much time is spent in modified, small group, match simulations where each player develops his own style of decision making and is encouraged to develop his own particular way of doing things. In defence, it is important for the player to fit tightly into the team structure, whilst in attack, individual flair is valuable to create opportunities. The players find this motivating and enjoyable — and they learn better when they are creating their own way, rather than following a stereotype that may not utilise the player's talents and level of development' (Spence 2000).

(National Sports Information Centre)

A soccer player attacks with individual flair.

Sequence of training

Training divisions for both teams and individuals must be sensitively planned in order to achieve the best outcomes and satisfaction levels.

Macrocycles (training months)

The structure of macrocycles may vary according to the stage of the year and the type of sport. Usually, in preparatory phases, there is a progressive build-up in training load, and training in the last week (microcycle) is usually at a reduced load to speed recovery and prepare for the progressively increased load of the next macrocycle. In competition phases, it is common to progressively reduce load in ensuing weeks, as the athlete tapers in order to prepare for the stress of competition.

A different macrocycle structure is used in endurance and explosive sports. In endurance sports, where athletes' metabolisms must be adapted to the needs of their sport, macrocycles are usually longer, with a progressive cumulative build-up, because endurance sports put less stress on the central nervous system than do other sports. In explosive sports, macrocycles are generally shorter and training load is frequently reduced in ensuing weeks (microcycles) in order to allow for the greater stress on the central nervous system and to help neuromuscular recovery.

Microcycles (training weeks)

The training week should be planned carefully to achieve the best training effect and provide for recovery and regeneration in preparation for the next microcycle, or for forthcoming competition. This may be achieved by simply using a higher training load early in the week and reducing it later in the week. During regular (weekly) competition, it is essential to allow for recovery after competition, before applying a substantial training load again. Particularly in contact and impact sports, coaches should constantly re-evaluate the health and injury status of athletes to ensure that they are fully recovered and ready for ongoing competition preparation.

Training sessions

Training sessions are usually 30–120 minutes long and often follow a conventional format:

- warm-up
- skill development
- competition simulation, and
- cool-down.

However, this format should be adapted to suit the specific aim of the session, which will vary according to the training phase, the readiness of athletes (in terms of background and health and injury status), external conditions (weather or the state of facilities), the proximity of competition, and relationship,

education or career issues. Being prepared to adapt to the needs of athletes is an essential part of good planning.

Training load (volume and intensity)

For each session, training loads should be set to meet team and individual goals and adapted to respond to the progress of the athletes and the team. Each session must be dynamic and varied according to the responses of the athletes. Subsequent sessions may have to be structured to include elements that could not be achieved in previous sessions.

Achieving optimal performance

Unloading or tapering is used before competition to help athletes recover and to elevate performance levels. Peak performance cannot be maintained indefinitely, and achieving it takes careful planning to coordinate unloading phases and concentrated, intense activity. Above all, when aiming to achieve peak form, the athlete must not be feeling the effects of fatigue. Peak performance is likely to occur when the difference between training effect and fatigue is greatest and the athlete is psychologically ready.

Athletes at any level may experience 'flow' or being in 'the zone'. However, high-performance athletes, who have stable preparation and performance routines, report this state more frequently. They experience a calm state of heightened awareness, when things seem to happen effortlessly and automatically (and frequently appear to them to occur in slow motion). This seems to happen more often when athletes are at ease with their talents and preparation, and allow their actions to evolve automatically, rather than trying to force the outcome.

CONCLUSION

There are many different and interconnected factors that affect performance. Because coaching deals with human beings, there are also many different ways of achieving outcomes. It is sensible, therefore, for the coach and the athlete to find ways of operating that suit both — including in the planning process.

Coaches should remember that enhancing one or two training components in isolation will not usually achieve the goals. Rather, it is the relationship between the training components that provides the magic that produces quantum leaps in performance. Integrated planning of all components of training is essential to achieve this.

While there is no proven formula for the best coaching environment, coaches generally have to be caring, sensitive, inquisitive and well organised to establish a stimulating relationship with athletes. Good planning alone may not do the job, but without careful and flexible planning a coach will have little chance of success. Ultimately, the ideal outcome of a training program is that it gives all athletes a desire to continue playing the sport and to follow their dreams in sport and life — then everyone wins.

COACHING TIPS

- Use integrated planning to emphasise certain types of training at particular times of the year. It's a bit like cooking: you must add the right amount at the right time to get the best results.

- Explain the long-term plan to athletes and parents, setting targets along the way that will be indicators of improvement.

- Keep a diary to record training activities and practices, and the outcomes achieved.

- Be prepared to modify training plans and practices if progress is not being made.

FURTHER READING

Balyi, I (1996) Planning for training and performance: the training to compete phase. *BC Coach* winter/spring: 9–14.

Balyi, I, and A Hamilton (1996) Planning for training and performance: the training to win phase. *BC Coach* summer: 9–26.

Balyi, I, and A Hamilton (1995) The concept of long-term athlete development. *Strength and Conditioning Coach* 3(2): 5–6.

Balyi, I, and R Way (1995) Long-term planning of athlete development: the training to train phase. *BC Coach* fall: 2–10.

Bompa, TO (1990) *Theory and Methodology of Training*. Dubuque, IA: Kendall/Hunt Publishing Co.

Gorgenyi, I (1998) Hunting territory: the structure of team life. *Sports Coach* 21(1) and (2).

Rushall, BS, and FS Pyke (1990) *Training for Sports and Fitness*. South Melbourne: Macmillan.

Spence, P (1998) Record of discussion with S Coe.

Spence, P (2000) Interview with E Merrick, June.

CHAPTER 19
WORKING WITH TEAMS

Jill McIntosh

(National Sports Information Centre)

INTRODUCTION

Building a cohesive unit of players who can perform in harmony is one of the most satisfying experiences for a coach. As any coach does, a team coach faces many challenges, but there is immense satisfaction in seeing a perfectly executed passage of play resulting in a score. This chapter will outline the differences between team sport coaching and coaching individuals.

Although team coaches must be able to deal with individuals, it is their ability to build and mould a team unit that sets them apart. Dealing with the many and varied personalities that make up a team is a skill such coaches must possess, along with the ability to balance individual needs with team needs while building a good team. The structure of training sessions becomes a delicate balance of individual needs with team requirements. All of these factors make team coaching an enjoyable challenge.

KEY CONSIDERATIONS IN TEAM SPORT COACHING

Game requirements

General skills

Regardless of the sport it is imperative that the fundamental skills are taught extremely well. The backbone of any good team is its members' solid performance of the basic skills. If these skills can be executed without error consistently, then the flair and creativity that each individual brings to the team can also come into play. If the fundamental skills are not performed adequately, this flair and creativity cannot rise to the surface, as the athletes will be concentrating on performing the basic skills.

Mental skills

Sports psychology is a vital component in any team training plan. Coaches should consider the following aspects of team psychology:

■ If the arousal level required by the team for the best performance is too high or too low it can have a detrimental affect on the team's performance. Individuals' responses can differ, so coaches must know their players and whether they need 'geeing' up or calming down before a match.

■ The team's goals must be realistic and achievable. This will keep players striving to perform at their best to achieve their goals. If a coach sets unrealistic goals, the players will lose heart and the desire to reach these goals.

■ Players must concentrate for different lengths of time in different positions. Because, if they concentrated for every minute spent on the field, they would lose focus quickly, players must be able to turn concentration off, and back on when it's needed. For example, a slips fielder in cricket and a netball goal shooter both require intermittent periods of intense concentration, but players in other positions may need different patterns of concentration.

Refer to the chapter 13, Performance Psychology, for more information on this subject.

Tactical skills

The coach should analyse the team's strengths (for example, speed, height or set plays) and try to capitalise on these when developing tactics and strategies. Key questions coaches should ask themselves include:

■ What does the team do well when under pressure?

■ What are the 'bread and butter' plays (that is, those with a high rate of success)?

■ Will the players need to make major changes to their individual games in order to be successful?

■ What aspects of the team will have to change to ensure success?

When developing team strategies, coaches must beware of information overload — too many different tactics or complicated and intricate moves can just worry players and distract them from their game. Each player will bring special qualities to the team, which should be used wisely to ensure that the team plays as it should. At this stage coaches should address any weaknesses in the team that may be targeted by opponents. It is also a good idea to have a tactical 'plan B' ready: how many times do the best laid plans fail?

Once the team tactics have been finalised, it is time to focus on the opposition and plan training strategies accordingly. Coaches must do their homework and take the time to watch future opponents performing under pressure. They should make notes about what their opponents do well and where they falter, and about the habits of individuals. Every little bit of information helps the coach and players to devise successful strategies.

Individual and positional requirements

Evaluating individual skills and talents

Some coaches try to look at everything and therefore miss details that they should be picking up. Coaches of teams have to be able to focus on the team as a whole, as well as on individual players. There are times when focusing on one player can provide vital information, there are times when viewing an area of the court/field is more beneficial, and other times when seeing the whole picture is essential. Video and statistics are valuable tools that can reinforce or correct coaches' impressions, but they must also learn to trust their own instincts, experience and judgement — the coach's eye. The opinions of other respected coaches can be valuable in evaluating players too.

Matching individuals to positions

Knowing the requirements of each position and what is expected of the individual, both physically and mentally, is paramount when selecting an individual for a position. Some positions have added responsibilities, such as a rugby goal kicker, or a softball pitcher. Individuals need special qualities to perform these tasks. A coach's knowledge of the individuals and the special skill requirements of each position can help them decide which players are best suited to specific roles. The next challenge is blending the players from particular positions/areas so they have a thorough understanding of each other. To help with this, coaches may include activities in training sessions that require players from particular positions to work together.

(National Sports Information Centre)

Some positions have added responsibility.

Training individuals to positions

It is essential that coaches allocate time at training for individuals to practise the unique skills related to their positions. It is easy to become engrossed in the team situations at training, to the detriment of the individual. Starting at the beginning, coaches should break down the individual skills of every position and player and ensure that each skill is adequately addressed in training.

Avoiding stereotypes

One of the pleasures of coaching is working with athletes who can add their own flair and creativity to any new skill or tactic, and adapt that skill to many different on-court or on-field situations. Every individual will bring something unique to the team. Where possible, coaches should encourage natural flair and creativity, but try to mould it into a framework that will also suit the rest of the team. Most teams operate best when they have a basic structure or framework to which they can add their own flair.

Carrie Graf knows about coaching creative individual players, as she has coached women's basketball superstar Lauren Jackson, who shot to fame as a 15-year-old and joined the Australian women's Opals basketball team by 16. But is it a difficult task allowing Jackson's flair and creativity to surface within a team environment?

'I'm sure that all coaches at the top end struggle with that at times', she said. The coach has a team structure, but how much do they need that when they have such a talented a player? 'It is a matter of getting to know the players and having them understand your concepts. You understand their creativity and then try and blend the two together. It's not a perfect science by any means. One of the things that I like is working with different people and learning they do have different talents. But there needs to be a common understanding from both the players and the coach when "showtime" is appropriate and when it is not.'

Graf is an assistant coach with the Australian Opals and has learnt much about developing a team culture from head coach, Tom Maher. She says there are concrete Opals philosophies that every player follows. 'My style is to involve the players in the creation of those themes, so that they have to take ownership of how the team will act and respond. I like to lead and manage but I like the players to have some input.'

Graf embraces the buddy system (see Developing a team culture below), both on a formal and informal level, and has set up a subcommittee of senior players where any grievances that might surface can be aired. She believes that friendly rivalry and competition for places is a common thread among successful teams. However, 'when players are involved in quality competition every day at practice, when it comes to the game, and they pull on the same suit, all that generally flies out the window, because everyone wants to win' (Kirkpatrick 2000).

TRAINING METHODS FOR TEAM SPORTS

Developing fitness requirements

Each sport has different physical requirements, but some are also common to several sports. Coaches need a thorough understanding of all the physical elements of their sport, and if they aren't sure how to assess them they should ask an expert. In analysing the movement patterns that each player performs during game time, coaches might ask how much of this time is actually resting time and how long each player is active before a rest? The energy demands will differ from position to position and player to player.

When determining the make-up of the conditioning program for the team, a coach should think about whether all players need the same program, or whether the program should be specific to positions or to individuals. Different teams will require different approaches. As the Australian netball team's coach, I consulted the team's physiologist and strength and conditioning specialist to identify five areas that needed attention: endurance, speed, agility, strength and power. The team's strength and conditioning program is based around these five areas throughout the year. Naturally, the program is adjusted throughout the year to fit with the training plans of both individuals and the team.

Developing technical requirements

It is vital that athletes learn to successfully perform the various skills of their sport, and practice is important for both the beginner and the elite athlete. Coaches' knowledge of each skill component of the sport must be thorough so they can give players the right information. The annual training plan should include the development of different skill components at different stages of the year.

Match simulation

The best players make good decisions consistently and appear to have more time to make their decisions (see chapter 14, Acquisition of Skill, for more information about developing decision-making skills). However, coaches shouldn't assume that all players have this ability. Like any physical skill, decision making should be practised, over and over again. Players should experience game stresses in training to develop their ability to make good decisions under pressure, a factor essential to the success of any team.

Nothing substitutes for the real thing, but these training sessions should reflect match conditions as closely as possible. If the sessions begin with simple activities, where simple decisions are required, then gradually increase the degree of difficulty until players must cope with a variety of activities and decisions, players will be better prepared for the real thing.

Vision plays a major role in decision making. Coaches should check that players are absorbing all the vital cues before they make their decisions. To do this they must position themselves at training so they can see what the players are seeing, and change position regularly to ensure that they aren't missing something that others are seeing.

Planning and organising

At the beginning of every season, coaches must decide what they wish to achieve in the season. This becomes the basis of the annual training plan (see chapter 18, An Integrated Approach to Planning, for more information on planning).

As a part of the process, coaches should consider the needs of each player in the team. Different players will need training in different areas (for example, fitness, speed or skill development). The plan should also include time for dealing with tactical issues, either with individuals or with small units, for instance, backs, forwards, attackers or defenders. It is very important that the development of the individual is not overlooked as coaches concentrate on team practice.

Training sessions aimed at moulding the team into a unit are also vital, however. Coaches should take into account such things

as tactics and team activities, both on court and off (such as 'bonding' sessions). Training sessions should be well balanced and cover all aspects of team play without emphasising, for instance, the attack to the detriment of the defence.

Athlete involvement in planning

Athletes are one of the coach's best resources. Coaches should listen to what they have to say, especially the more experienced players, who can provide valuable input into planning, and feedback on the overall program.

OBSERVING AND EVALUATING TEAM PERFORMANCE

Training performance

Throughout the year, coaches and athletes should refer to the annual plan to make sure they are on track. They should also take time to reflect on their performance at training, and consider whether their sessions are achieving what they planned and, if not, why not. The level 2 workbook that accompanies this manual contains some useful self-reflection sheets that may help coaches assess their performance at training sessions.

At times, it may be useful to take a step back and ask an assistant coach to take the training session. The coach can then become a spectator for a session and cast a critical eye over the players in action at training. In this way she or he may see something that has escaped notice on previous occasions. Videotaping a training session can also provide another perspective on a training session (see chapter 2, Coaching Methods, for more information on self-reflection and evaluation).

Using information about opponents and dealing with officials

An important part of preparing a team for match day is collecting and using information on the opposition and the respective umpires or referees. It is important for team coaches to know their team's opponents and how they play. Scouting or studying the opposition is an important step in pre-match preparation. This information is vital to the coach and the team when they are devising their game plan.

When watching another team, coaches should look for such things as key players, team strengths, individual habits or weaknesses, commonly used set plays, and team weaknesses on which they can capitalise. Again, video can be a useful scouting tool. The organised coach will analyse this information and then decide what players need to know (they shouldn't be overloaded with irrelevant information). Players should be told about what to expect from their individual opponent, then the coach should run through the opposing team's traits, patterns of play and set plays.

Coaches should prepare players so that they avoid the frustration and time-wasting involved in trying to interpret refereeing or umpiring decisions. Some basic information on the interpretations used by different officials can be valuable to the players. However, coaches should emphasise to players the need to adapt quickly during a game to a variety of different rule interpretations. There are many things coaches can control when preparing a team, but umpiring is not one of them, so they should instruct players to adjust, and not react to umpires' calls.

Video analysis

When using videotaped analyses of play, coaches should decide what they need to see and give specific instructions to the camera operator. The coach may wish to view the game as a whole or only specific areas, or just particular individuals. When they are watching the tape with players, coaches should be prepared to tell players what to look for, because some will have difficulty concentrating on one person during footage of other action.

Statistics

Statistics are a great tool for supporting observations. Before they begin collecting and analysing statistics, coaches should determine what they need and when they need it. Statistics are commonly collected on individual player success and error rates, shooting/scoring percentages, possession turnovers, team offensive and defensive success, error rates and the success of set plays.

Statistics can be used by coaches to make decisions on line-ups for matches, as well as what sort of offensive and defensive patterns are appropriate. They can also help coaches determine the focus for the next training session, and modify the annual plan if need be. It is important that coaches have reliable assistants to collect statistical information for them — it is too difficult for coaches to carry out this task while coaching on game day.

Beyond statistics — knowing the athlete

All team coaches should make sure they schedule time for individual meetings with athletes so that both parties can communicate their perspectives and feelings. It's important for coaches to understand the likes and dislikes of players. Statistics will show that a player did not play well, but they will not be able to say why. Each team contains a variety of personalities, and coaches have to work out the best way to handle each of them. Less experienced coaches can often find it helpful to talk to other coaches if they are having trouble working with a particular player. Sports psychologists may also be able to help with insights into dealing with particular personality types.

The Australian cricket team has been very successful recently, and squad members are under constant pressure to justify their place in the side. Coach John Buchanan believes performance evaluation is a crucial component in maintaining the team's dominance. He says, 'The team performance can always be evaluated by results, but I think there other key measures we can include to improve that system. As far as the individual goes, we work with what we call a skills matrix, and this monitors a range of skills, as well as team orientation, which is aimed at giving players their best chance of performing at the top level.'

Buchanan's major evaluation tool is a complex computer system that provides precise analysis of technique, not only of his own team, but also of the opposition, allowing the Australian team to pinpoint possible areas of weakness. It also allows Buchanan to better target and plan for the individual physical and mental requirements of his players.

'In the physical sense, we have developed individual programs for each player, and that also takes into account what we perceive to be the needs in, say, the test and one-day arenas', he said. 'Mentally, I think there is a strong involvement from the players themselves as to how we approach games, both technically and tactically, because in the end if they have an input into the system they have greater faith in what they are setting out to achieve as a group' (De Kroo 2000).

THE COACH ON MATCH DAYS

Selecting the squad/team balance

On match days coaches should make sure they have dealt with all the potential problems, such as injury, illness, family-related matters, or educational or work commitments. Throughout a season or tournament all of these issues will arise, and coaches have to be prepared to cover the loss of any player in the team. They should ensure that they have a good balance within the team, and players who can cover all positions. Most teams will need to call on their 'bench players' at many stages in the season, often during a crisis.

When selecting the last few players in the team, coaches should ask themselves whether they would be prepared to put that player on in a big game. If the answer is no, then they shouldn't select them. Selecting squads and teams is a very difficult and time-consuming job. Each player should be considered carefully as an individual and what he or she brings to the group, then in combination with other players.

Team selection on match day

The final decision on who plays each match rests with the head coach. Coaches may choose to seek the advice of their match committee or selectors to make sure they are thinking objectively about all players. They may ask the captain and vice captain to help, but the responsibility for the final decision is still theirs.

Coaches should know their opponents and what to expect from them as well as their own players. They may choose to play 'horses for courses', for example, height on height or speed on speed. It is important, though, to ensure that the reasoning behind selection decisions is sound, as coaches must talk to those players not chosen and be open and honest about why they weren't selected. Players should know exactly where they stand and what they need to do to 'get the nod' next time.

Match day procedures

It is vital to the players' confidence and wellbeing that coaches maintain similar procedures on each match day. Players must be familiar with everything that will take place before they have to deal with the pressures of the match, including things such as training on match days; what, where and when to eat; team announcements; pre-game procedures at the venue; warm-up; and access to toilets before and during the match. All these elements must be dealt with before match day. Players don't need the distraction of having to sort out such problems when the coach hasn't attended to them.

Effective use of time-outs, breaks and substitutions

Time-outs can be very effective coaching tools. Coaches should be well prepared when thinking about calling a time-out. Their feedback must be precise to make the best use of the very short time allowed. Used well, time-outs can change the course of a game. They provide the opportunity for coaches to talk to their players, to remind them of the game plan or to alter team tactics, to calm volatile tempers or to change the tempo of the match, or may be used just to give the players a breather. Coaches should remember, though, that their opponents will also have the opportunity to use the time-out, and try to anticipate what the opposition coach may be planning.

Coaches can use quarter and half-time breaks in a similar way, reinforcing good play, delivering constructive feedback to players on their performances and those of their immediate opponents. It is a time to talk team tactics and possible changes, or to introduce short-term tactics to confuse the opposition. Once again, coaches should try to anticipate their opponents' every move and try to upset their rhythm.

Before the break, coaches should prepare what they want to say so they are ready to pass it on to players. Time is short so they must deliver their feedback and move on, otherwise they will not cover everything they have planned. Player seating arrangements can also assist in the succinct delivery of feedback. Coaches should think about whether they need to speak to the entire group as one, smaller groups, or individuals, during the time available.

The wise use of substitutions can also be a very effective coaching tool. Coaches should make players aware of their views on substitutions and how they will deal with this during a game. Sound reasons for making substitutions include replacing a tired player, using a player to achieve an impact, replacing a player who is not performing well, or changing team tactics. Players will accept substitutions more easily if they understand the reasons behind the decision.

Handling players in the heat of the game

During the heat of the game, when tempers are sometimes frayed, it can be difficult for the coach to deal with the angry player who has been taken out of the game. The coach should be thinking about the game at hand

(National Sports Information Centre)

Breaks provide an opportunity for the coach to give feedback.

and not consoling upset players at this crucial time, and so should have to give nothing more than a few calm words and a very brief explanation at the time. Later, and in a more appropriate place, the coach should discuss the situation with the player concerned. In these situations it's important that coaches give constructive feedback.

This also applies to players who have 'blown-up' during a game because of their frustrations either with themselves or with the umpire. The coach's manner should reflect the personality of the player, so they must know their players and how to deal with each of them as individuals. Sometimes a few concise, carefully chosen words spoken with authority is all it takes to remind players of their responsibilities to themselves and their team-mates. The same applies when coaches are addressing a team: they should choose their words carefully and be concise but authoritative. This is not the place to criticise players — all heated debates should be held behind closed doors.

Assessment and follow-up

When coaches are considering the post-game feedback and assessments, they must first decide which is the best time to talk to the players, both as a group and as individuals. Coaches should discuss this with their players and establish a time when the players will listen to what they have to say. Straight after the game is usually not a good time, as players are either on a high or in the depths of despair, and may not absorb the information. Instead coaches should give players just a few words at this time — perhaps something positive, followed by a constructively critical comment for them to think about for the next game — and keep detailed feedback for the later session. At this later meeting, the coach can then present feedback and engage in productive discussion with the players.

Self-evaluation

Most players are their own harshest critics. They are never satisfied with their performances and will always strive to be better. Coaches should work with each of the players to establish what they should be evaluating, and to ensure that they are being honest, yet fair to themselves. Players should know that it is okay to give themselves a pat on the back if they feel they did something well.

There are players, however, who never see that they have done anything wrong, and who always blame someone else. Coaches should go through the same process with these players — finding positive points and then constructively analysing their game. It is not an easy process and if coaches feel they need assistance in this area, they should speak to a sport psychologist, who can advise on the best methods to use.

Coaches should also take time to think about and analyse their own performances on match days. They might consider whether they could have handled events in a different manner, and whether their feedback was constructive. They may also find it useful to monitor their own demeanour on the bench. A coach may ask a reliable person, such as a sport psychologist, to watch him or her on match days and offer feedback on his or her performance.

After bronze medals at the Atlanta and Sydney Olympics, it would appear the Australian women's softball team is heading in the right direction. Under the watchful eye of coach Bob Crudgington, the Australian team has developed into one of the most professional and well drilled in the softball world, which is confirmed by their number two ranking. Crudgington believes his team is narrowing the gap on the leading United States team, and part of this process has involved developing a team culture and structure that will hold fast under the pressure of a major tournament.

'We want to go to the next level and part of that is having good communication amongst the team and having faith in each other's ability. We continue to experiment to find ways to get the best out of everybody and while we don't have a set structure so much, we certainly want to develop a strong team network.' During training, Crudgington's role is very much one of leadership and pointing people in the right direction, but once a major tournament begins his role is management.

'The coach's role does change on game day because, in our sport, you call all the strategy in offence. You decide when to bunt or steal or whatever, so you are very much the playmaker and that is a big difference from other sports. As coach you are still calling the shots during the game', he said. Before that his role deals with the physical and mental requirements of the players, and he and the team have 'worked with a sports psychologist who has profiled all our athletes so we know as a group who we are dealing with. We have some players we call mosquitoes because they tend to become distracted easily, but are very good reactive players and then there are the deeper thinkers who are a lot more concerned with strategy and whatever.

If we all know what we're like and our respective strengths then it is easier to work with and get the best out of each other. Physically we are a little more general, but then also skill specific for players in certain positions.'

Crudgington is also working to forge the right mix between competition and cooperation within the team unit. 'I think it is something we are still working on. For example, we have four pitchers in the team and only one or maybe two are going to pitch in the gold medal game. At the moment we are trying to take the approach that every game we play is an Olympic game and everyone that steps up is doing the job to get us to the medal round. It is a mix we work hard on and a lot of our training and drills are focused on keeping healthy competition within the squad, and I think everyone knows no matter what role they end up playing, it will be important to our overall success.'

Come match day, Crudgington said his team's routines are fairly well set in place, with the focus on the job at hand. 'We usually go through and analyse the opposition, and then settle on our own line-up', he said. 'The game is dominated by the pitchers, so we will work with them, and then it will be a warm-up and into the game.'

With a near faultless preparation, Crudgington hopes that on match day it will be relatively smooth sailing, but said that dealing with players during the heat of games follows a fairly standard procedure. 'It depends greatly on who the player is. Some players you can encourage, others don't want to be distracted, but it is something we monitor through the game', he said. 'If we see someone struggling, we have steps in place to pick that up and we are very open about it, and in many ways it helps the players help themselves' (De Kroo 2000).

Bob Crudgington, softball coach

(National Sports Information Centre)

DEVELOPING A TEAM CULTURE

Leadership, management, head coach and staff

Head coaches provide the philosophies on which the team is built. They are the leaders, the people to whom everyone looks for guidance and inspiration. The person taking on this role is accepting a big responsibility and must be prepared to distance themselves from the players to some extent, because they must be able to think clearly when making decisions, without being influenced by friendships.

All coaches are different, and each must establish a management style from the beginning, thereby setting the tone for the team. One of the main attributes of any leader is the ability to be firm but fair in judgements of team members. Coaches in such positions can expect to be challenged often by well-meaning people who think they know better and question decisions. Above all it is imperative for such leaders to believe in themselves and their ability to make the right decisions. They may use their support staff to help with decision making, but should also ensure that everyone knows that the final word rests with them.

Team values

It is important that all members of the team abide by a set of values or standards that reflect the wishes of the entire group. This set of values is often called a mission statement or a code of conduct and both players and staff should be expected to adhere to it. It is best if all personnel contribute to the development of this code or set of rules — so that they all feel as though it is relevant to them — and all agree to abide by the standards. It can also be useful if the group develops a set of disciplinary measures that can be applied if players or staff break the rules. These are set by the players and enforced by the team management.

Team structure

A positive initiative that has been introduced into the Australian netball team is a senior management group. This consists of a group of five players selected by the head coach to look after any issues and grievances that may arise within the team. This group is also involved in planning and discussion with team management. It reduces the pressure on the captain and vice captain, who are otherwise the ones making decisions on behalf of the group. The captain and vice captain have a very important role to play and are seen as the team leaders both on court and off, but the senior management group helps with the off-court work.

Captains and vice captains can be very influential people in a team. It is important that they respect and follow the coach's philosophies and set a positive example. There will always be a pecking order in any team, with captain and vice captain often at the top. Younger and newer players in the team will look up to and are sometimes intimidated by these players. When coaches are selecting captains and vice captains, they should make sure they consider matters such as:

- whether the players under consideration have the respect of their peers

- whether they can listen
- whether they can take on extra responsibilities
- whether their relationships with team management are healthy
- whether they are honest and objective, and
- whether they are calm in a crisis.

The captain and vice captain must not place themselves above the rest, but must exemplify the values of the team and remember that they are also part of the team.

New or young players in any team can often find it difficult to blend in straight away, and often feel lonely and doubt themselves. One way of overcoming this is to introduce the buddy or mentor system, in which older or more experienced players take on a buddy/mentor role with the younger/newer players and introduce them into the ways of the team. This can help to make the transition into a well-established team much easier for new players.

Team dynamics

The dynamics of any team can be the single most important factor in the team's wellbeing and success. Just one disgruntled player, or a long-serving player at the end of a career, can destroy team harmony and subsequently produce a drop in performance levels. Subgroups or cliques can form and divide a team. It is important for coaches to be aware of the informal structure of their teams, that is, who

(National Sports Information Centre)

Team harmony is vital.

socialises with whom, which players always eat together, whether some players have difficulty talking to others, and whether there are any loners in the team.

Most teams contain a blend of age and youthful inexperience that can sometimes be difficult to manage. Older, longer serving players sometimes place themselves above the younger or newer members in the team hierarchy. Dealing with these sensitive issues is not easy, but ignoring them will be detrimental to the success of the team. Communication is the key when dealing with subgroups or cliques and the best way to resolve conflicts is often face to face.

Players don't have to be best mates, but they should show respect to their team-mates and the team management. Disrespectful players can be the most difficult of all to manage. By showing no respect for their team-mates' or coach's abilities they quickly alienate themselves from the rest of the players, to the detriment of the team's performance. Others in the team may also be influenced by this behaviour if it is allowed to continue, and the problem may then escalate. It can divide the group and place undue pressures on the coach and the rest of the team. Dealing with these players can be difficult, but if coaches use a firm and authoritative manner to reiterate standards and face the culprits when problems arise, such issues should be dealt with promptly.

Player rivalry, competition and cooperation

Competition within a team is healthy, provided the team is not divided by spiteful, bitter or resentful players who were not selected. Coaches should be aware that they can alienate players if they never select them for important games. These players can often feel left out or unwanted and may begin to doubt themselves. Coaches should be prepared to give their inexperienced players adequate time on field, and develop a culture whereby any player on the team can be used in an important game.

They must be honest in their assessments of and feedback to the players. Player attitudes will determine the ultimate success or failure of the team, and how much the coach enjoys the sport. Dealing with the long-serving star whose performances are on the decline is a very delicate issue. These players sometimes find it difficult to acknowledge that their time is limited and that younger players have overtaken them in ability. Sports psychologists can help with this, but coaches should always be fair and honest with players and treat them all on an equal basis.

CONCLUSION

The better teams balance all the ingredients of playing team sports very well. Good team coaches also balance individual and team needs very well. They select the right combination of players for the team. They use their support staff to best service the team and have the physical, mental and tactical preparations right. Good team coaches communicate well with all members of the team: they listen to what their players have to say and how they are feeling. They treat all players equally and do not play favourites, realising that to do so would compromise the team's success. Good team coaches are prepared to make the tough decisions and will remember that the final decision, on all matters pertaining to the team, rests with them.

COACHING TIPS

- Understand that the needs and goals of each athlete in the team may be different.

- Develop and blend individuals within a group, knowing that the whole is greater than the sum of the parts.

- Establish a culture of excellence, in which everyone associated with the team operates in the best interests of its success.

- Help new, young or inexperienced players become integrated into the team through a mentor system.

FURTHER READING

Clifford, C, and R Feezel (1997) *Coaching for Character*. Champaign, IL: Human Kinetics.

De Kroo, K (2000) Interviews with John Buchanan and Bob Crudgington (undertaken for the Australian Sports Commission), May.

Gorgenyi, I (1998) Hunting territory: the structure of team life. *Sports Coach* 21(1) and (2).

Hessert, K (1998) *Coach's Communication Playbook*. Charlotte, NC: Sports Media Challenge.

Kidman, L, and S Hanrahan (1997) *The Coaching Process: A Practical Guide to Improving Your Effectiveness*. Palmerston North, New Zealand: the Dunmore Press.

Kirkpatrick, D (2000) Interview with Carrie Graf (undertaken for the Australian Sports Commission), May.

Launder, A, and W Piltz (1999) Becoming a better bench coach. *Sports Coach* 21(4).

Maher, T (1999) Formulating a successful team culture. *Coaching Australia* 3(1).

CHAPTER 20
ADOPTING A BALANCED APPROACH

Deidre Anderson

(National Sports Information Centre)

INTRODUCTION

Coaching has been described, among other things, as both an art and a science, but it can often be more than that. For many coaches, it is a lifestyle that can quickly exhaust both their physical and mental capacities. This chapter will help coaches work towards a more balanced approach to their work through a greater understanding of their skills, attributes and personal and professional development needs. They should then be able to create a happier, healthier environment in which both they and their athletes can reach their full potential in life and sport.

DEALING WITH CHANGE

Everyone knows that change is an inevitable part of coaching, as it is of life. Sport has developed enormously in recent times and the changes that have occurred have affected all coaches and athletes.

Coaches' ability to deal with change will be determined by their capacity to develop their problem-solving and systematic planning skills and use their experience, knowl-

edge, skills and networks to meet changes head-on. Changes will also the affect athletes with whom they work.

Australian women's water polo coach, Istvan Gorgenyi, maintains that dealing with change by involving players is essential, although he warns that coaches have to think it through carefully, as some players might take advantage of the situation. He was once burnt when he tried to introduce change by involving his senior athletes in the planning process.

'They tried to show it as my weakness that I sought their opinions, so I think that the coach has to be very cautious', he said. 'I have practical sessions where I openly ask the players' opinions; even when all the players are not there I might ask some of the key players their opinions. I might ask them if a certain play will work and then they give me their feedback.'

Whenever Gorgenyi needs to implement change, he likes to talk it over with his players so they are not shocked by the move. 'I'm always working a lot individually with the players — workshops and the like — so it is not difficult to implement change. My philosophy is that I want all the players in my squad knocking on the door' (Kirkpatrick 2000).

Change can often be associated with conflict, as it can result in opposing views. Coaches may have seen this occur within their sporting organisation, during the allocation of resources, or between athletes. Conflict usually manifests itself through fear, dislike, mistrust, resentment or anger. The process of settling the conflict can take many forms, including fighting, surrender, breaking the relationship, making changes to rules or involving a third party to help settle the debate.

Communication

Knowing their own style of communication can help coaches deal with conflict, as it can provide a platform for developing the best approach to solve the problem. To analyse their communication style, coaches should ask themselves what their frame of mind is when they are communicating. Is it competitive or cooperative, or even aggressive, or do they see the other person as the enemy? If so, they are **competitive communicators**. Some people, however, look for mutually acceptable solutions and are assertive rather than aggressive, and coaches who adopt this approach are **cooperative communicators**.

A successful coach should work towards becoming a more cooperative communicator and remember that managing change should not be about winning or losing, but about taking something positive from every situation and building on it. Sport never remains static, so managing change and conflict are part of the coaching role.

For many years, officials, players, coaches and administrators have considered Bill Harrigan to be the National Rugby League's number one referee. The same people considered Bob Fulton to be one of the best coaches, and his appointment as national coach recognised this.

A conflict situation developed between referee Harrigan and coach Fulton after a Brisbane versus Manly game. Fulton made some derogatory comments about Harrigan after he had sent a number of Manly players to the sin bin. All those involved in rugby league considered the incidents a serious problem for the game. How could such a rift between two talented individuals be resolved?

The answer was communication. The conflict was resolved when Harrigan attended a Manly training session with coach Fulton and the Manly players. Issues were openly discussed between players, coaching staff and referees to ensure that each party understood why decisions were made during the game. The players, coaches and referees, through better communication, mended the rift.

Taking the lead in conflict situations usually requires a degree of assertiveness. Being assertive means saying and doing the things that are needed without necessarily offending others or violating their rights. Assertiveness fosters improved communication, openness and understanding. The saying 'If you are patient in one moment of anger, you can escape a hundred days of sorrow' sums up this communication style.

To be assertive, coaches must first decide what is fair, so they know what they want to achieve in negotiations. They should be prepared to take risks, express their feelings openly and give and accept fair criticism. Assertive communicators state their reactions rather than making accusations. To achieve this, successful communicators use 'I' rather than 'you' to describe feelings and situations, and use a calm tone of voice. 'You' statements can be interpreted as aggressive and critical and can be met with hostility.

The following case study may provide some insights into better communication.

A coach and assistant coach have been disagreeing for some time on a particular coaching method. The head coach is concerned that it is starting to affect the athletes. Each time she has told her assistant coach that she wants a task done in a particular way, an argument or defensive behaviour inevitably occurs.

Coaches in similar situations should start by asking themselves the following questions:

- What is the actual point of disagreement?
- What approach can I use to work towards an agreement (for example, what evidence do I have that suggests that my way is the right way)?
- What are the consequences if it is not done my way?
- On which aspects do the two parties agree?
- What degree of compromise am I prepared to accept?
- How can I be sure that both parties have reached a workable level of agreement?
- How can I summarise the discussion and agree on the actions?

Some coaches may use a perceived lack of time as a justification for not coping well with conflict and change. Everyone knows that it can take longer to discuss issues cooperatively, but in the long run it is usually more effective. There may be times when just 'telling' is appropriate, but this approach should not be used because of a perceived lack of time. If coaches maintain a good communications style and develop their time-management skills, they will be able to work with change more effectively.

TIME MANAGEMENT

Most coaches know that, despite their best intentions, they often face time-management challenges (see chapter 1, Roles and Responsibilities of the Coach, for more information on time management). Coaches can find themselves playing many roles — coach, friend, employee, employer, counsellor, parent and family member. Often better coaches find that more demands are made on their time (for instance, speaking engagements and specialist training sessions).

If coaches find they are constantly running out of time, they should ask themselves the following questions:

- By the end of an average day, have I accomplished at least the most important tasks I set for myself?
- What are my priorities during each month, what compromises will I have to make and with whom do you need to discuss these compromises?
- What strategies am I presently using to deal with all the demands on my time?

Causes of poor time management

There are a number of common causes of time wasting and poor time management:

- underestimating the time demands of routine tasks (such as phone calls, paperwork, meetings with athletes and other coaches)
- procrastinating (putting off tasks that should be done now)
- saying yes to new tasks without considering the demands or completing existing tasks
- jumping from task to task because of too many deadlines or a lack of clear priorities, and
- spending too much time socialising or helping others.

Coaches who find themselves in any of these positions need to make some changes to the way they operate. They should particularly try not to be drawn into situations over which they have no power, and should refuse to be caught up in anything other than what contributes to achieving their goals.

Improving time management

These practical points are useful guides to managing time better.

Planning

Coaches should develop an annual plan as a general guide to the tasks that they must complete during the year (perhaps in conjunction with the preparation of athletes' annual training plans), and then schedule a quiet hour each day to review shorter term goals and weekly plans. Using tools such as planning calendars and diaries, they can identify and schedule their daily/weekly/monthly/yearly tasks.

Goal setting

In planning the year's tasks, coaches should set realistic goals for the short, medium and longer term, and integrate their coaching and personal demands. It is important to stick to these goals.

Prioritising

It is essential for coaches to rank tasks from the most important to the least important and ensure that they work to these priorities.

Setting limits

They must only take on additional work if they will have spare time after completing all high-priority tasks.

Systems

It's a good idea to develop systems for completing routine tasks (see Planning). If they know they are easily distracted, coaches should set aside time each day when they are accessible only in emergencies, to make time to get things done.

Reorganising

If they reorganise their work areas, people can often use their space more efficiently, find items more easily, improve concentration and avoid distractions.

Delegating

Successful delegating is one of the responsibilities of coaches, but they should remember to spread tasks around evenly and not to keep all the interesting ones to themselves. Tasks can be delegated to athletes as well. Delegating means developing trust and training those who want the job to do it properly. Even if coaches can pass only 5 or 10% of their tasks to others, this could free up to 50% of their time for planning and innovation.

Managing stress

Those who manage their time efficiently will usually be less stressed. In stressful times, though, coaches should stop, re-establish their goals, check their plans and schedules, and decide on their next action. They should remember to take some time for themselves to maintain health and manage stress.

A mentor coach can provide valuable feedback.

(National Sports Information Centre)

Supporting structures

Many coaches use a mentor coach to (among other things) help with time management (see chapter 2, Coaching Methods, for more information on mentoring). Coaches should also develop a network of other support personnel to whom they can delegate tasks and who can help with other aspects of coaching.

PERSONAL AND PROFESSIONAL DEVELOPMENT

Professional and personal development begins with gaining a greater level of self-awareness. This improved self-awareness should direct coaches to the most appropriate courses, programs and extracurricular activities for achieving their best in their coaching and non-coaching roles. Self-awareness can be improved by learning about its three main components: the physical, social and spiritual selves.

Physical self-awareness is self-image, the way people think of their own bodies. For example, they may think themselves too fat, too skinny, good looking or ugly. **Social self-awareness** means how people think others see them, for example, confident, assertive, aggressive, happy or positive. **Spiritual self-awareness** is concerned with how people interpret their intellectual experiences, such as learning and religion.

The three components, combined with people's values, skills and interests, provide them with a level of self-esteem. The following exercise will help coaches improve their self-awareness.

In the coaching environment, coaches should consider which of these elements they value:

- achievement
- working with people
- independence
- flexibility
- high salary
- high pressure
- high status
- job security
- helping people
- creativity
- leadership
- variety, and
- challenging work.

They should then ask themselves which of these are the most important, why this is and whether, in their current position, these values are rewarded. If they aren't, coaches should think about what they could do to change this. It is important to remember that such values do not alter much over time, and it is therefore wise to check regularly whether they are being acknowledged and rewarded. Lack of value reinforcement can lead to loss of motivation and personal drive, which are two key elements necessary to sustain coaching commitment.

Skills on the other hand, are constantly changing, and therefore should be reviewed from two perspectives. First, coaches should identify and list their present skill bank and, second, the skills they will need in the future (a personal needs analysis). Remember that a skill is something that a person has learnt to do. Skills should be grouped under the following headings: practical, creative, people and communication (both spoken and written). By showing coaches both what they have already learned and what they still need to learn, this exercise can provide direction for future personal development.

The development of coaches' skills and interests should be incorporated into their annual plan. Contact the relevant state coaching director or the state coordinator of the Athlete Career and Education (ACE) program for more information on expanding your skill base. Other coaches or sports organisations can also provide assistance.

Coaches should then list their interests, grouping them under the following headings: helping/advising, practical/mechanical, scientific/technical, business, artistic/creative, nature and motivating/sales. They should then ask themselves how many of these interests they are presently fulfilling, and which are their leisure interests and which their professional interests? In this way coaches can gain an understanding of how well they are satisfying their needs in these areas, and what might still be done to improve the situation.

In their many roles as coach, friend, partner and family member, sports coaches bring together different values, interests and skills. Most of their skills have been gained from personal experiences and the experiences of others. The role of others in learning is paramount. Some of the best coaches in the world have learned from mentors, with whom they have shared challenges and debated issues.

Mentoring

To maintain an edge, coaches should find and practise working with a mentor (see chapter 2, Coaching Methods, for more information on mentoring). To select a mentor, they might start by asking themselves which coach, sports administrator or leader in their field they admire most, why they admire this person, and what qualities does this person have that are admirable. The answers to these questions will direct coaches to suitable mentors, with whom they can work formally and informally.

A formal arrangement might involve the coach meeting with the potential mentor or even going to watch him or her coach. An informal arrangement might happen through reading about, watching or even mimicking certain areas of the mentor's coaching performance. Coaches should be careful, however, not to merely mimic their mentors' skills or attributes, but to use what they learn to further develop their own unique skills and attributes. Adapt don't adopt!

Chris Nunn, head coach of the Australian Institute of Sport Athletes with Disabilities program, has been a mentor coach for many years, guiding the coaching careers of numerous young coaches through the Australian Sports Commission's coaching scholarship program.

'[The] philosophy that I teach to my new coaches is that ideally the coach eventually becomes redundant', says Nunn. 'Every athlete who steps on the track has to ensure that they are not reliant on anyone when it comes to competition day. If the coach has to be there in the stands giving out instructions, then the coach has not done their job. It is important that the coach empowers the athletes to be able to make correct decisions

(National Sports Information Centre)

Chris Nunn working with Paralympian Hamish MacDonald

in pressure situations. And, thus, I empower the coaches that I mentor. I give them full responsibility for one or two athletes, and I just supervise the program as far as their workload and I show them how to implement the program and then how to communicate with the athlete. I like to give them a hands-on approach.'

Nunn also believes that learning occurs both ways in a mentoring relationship. 'I haven't once had a scholarship coach where I haven't learnt something from the coach — I learn from them and they learn from me'. He continued, 'I really do enjoy seeing a new coach coming in, enthusiastic and wanting to learn. You can really focus on teaching the things that are important to coaching, such as rehabilitation, injury prevention, balancing, periodisation and planning. They usually respond so well — all I do is steer them in the right direction.'

Nunn believes that sharing information between all coaches is important. 'There are many, many good coaches, but not all of those good coaches are good mentors. I think some people are actually reluctant to pass on too much information to scholarship coaches. But my attitude to that is that the sport actually misses out in the long run. I think it is a problem within Australian sport that there is often this jealousy and withholding of information. But I believe, if we share more information amongst other coaches, we can only develop our sport more and it will leave a lasting legacy for the other coaches who are out there trying to achieve' (White 1998).

Mentors can help coaches when they are lost for answers or need stimulation. Making time for this will always be valuable. When selecting mentors, coaches should make sure potential mentors will be available to meet with them on an irregular basis. They must be sure to select someone who is an expert in the field and is prepared to share their opinions and ideas. It is also essential to choose someone who is an exceptional leader and a person who can listen and empathise.

Burnout

Good mentors can also help coaches monitor themselves so that they do not burn out. Burnout is prevalent within the coaching community, and generally occurs because many coaches find it difficult to separate their coaching and non-coaching roles, and don't have enough time to rest. Better time management helps to prevent burnout.

To identify burnout, coaches must monitor themselves carefully. The physical and emotional signs are similar to overtraining in athletes, so coaches should keep a check on their own sleep patterns, eating habits and relaxation levels.

Olympic track and field coach, Frank Dick, describes coaching eloquently and in this passage he gives an insight into why many suffer burnout.

'We are coaches of people. We set our own personal standards of quality and performance, and measure ourselves against these standards. We are accountable to ourselves and achieve and fail accordingly. Our greatest moments and our disappointments are our own and will seldom be understood by those who cannot taste our sweat, our tears, our pain, or our moments of ecstasy and quiet satisfaction. We are not only dreamers of dreams, we deliver on them. That's who we are' (Anderson 1990).

When people have such a strong sense of purpose, it is easy for them to forget about the other areas of life. There are also ethical issues to consider when coaches ignore the balance for both themselves and the athletes with whom they are working. If coaches aren't functioning well, they risk not only their own safety and health, but also that of the athletes.

Many athletes place their absolute trust and faith in their coach's ability. If coaches push them too hard and don't set a good example of a balanced life, they can influence the athletes' capacity to reach their potential. Every athlete has a different level of physical and mental maturity, and a different capacity to handle the demands of sport. Each athlete will also have to deal with issues outside sport that may influence performance.

Coaches must monitor how well athletes are handling these matters by setting realistic, achievable and manageable goals that are holistic and integrated with each other, and regularly evaluating athletes against these goals (see chapter 18, An Integrated Approach to Planning, for more information on planning). Coaches are responsible for creating an environment that permits them and the athletes they train to excel in a balanced program.

Working with others

Earlier in the chapter, the Fulton and Harrigan conflict emphasised the importance of communication. Good communication is vital to good coaching practice, particularly

Many athletes place absolute faith in their coach.

(National Sports Information Centre)

if coaches have to work and communicate with a range of people in a consistent and effective manner. Much of coaching is about selling an idea and activating a continuous shift in thinking.

Often when coaches need support for their ideas, it involves convincing more than just the athletes. They might also need to convince committees and funding agencies. Coaches often invest a lot of time in preparing the information required to support the idea, but little time and effort in thinking about how to influence the decision makers.

There is no secret formula to achieving this. However, it will help to get to know a little more about the decision makers. Coaches should prepare for presentations by knowing why people are on the committee, what the personal agendas of each committee member are, and how they will be affected by the idea to be discussed.

It can be useful to find out which committee members like to talk and which don't — coaches should beware of encouraging unproductive chatter in their presentations, as their time will be wasted. They should also be sure to involve all members of the committee in the discussion so that they have the opportunity to find out how everyone feels about the project. This also gives them the opportunity to persuade those who may not agree with the project if it's necessary. Obviously it's vital that the person who's making the presentation has all the facts and figures straight. There are all types of people on committees, so it is important to be as well prepared as possible.

Sometimes having a different approach to coaching can lead to success, as the Australian cricket coach, John Buchanan, found out. Buchanan was appointed to the top job, not because he had been a great player, but because he was seen as a very good coach. Unlike his predecessors, Geoff Marsh and Bob Simpson, Buchanan had not played test cricket, and his only claim to fame was seven first-class games for Queensland.

Buchanan believes that the fact that he hasn't previously been part of the international program has allowed him to bring another perspective to the job. While initially it may have been more difficult to gain the respect of his players, he thinks this perspective is one of the major assets he has brought to the team.

'Possibly I bring a degree of objectivity, because I have not really been involved in test cricket and the whole international scene before', Buchanan says. 'I think my management and communication skills are also reasonable, but I think my main asset is that I'm never satisfied with the job we are doing. It is called the Fred Flintstone principle. Fred Flintstone drove around in a serviceable car, but it could be improved. I don't subscribe to the idea if it isn't broken don't fix it.'

Buchanan believes his dealings with senior players are an important component of his job. 'The beauty of the elite or experienced player is they always want to be an elite player and therefore they are constantly looking for ways to maintain or improve their skills', he said. 'Most are very open to new ideas, provided they are not overly complicated or time consuming and distracting from the technique they have already developed' (De Kroo 2000).

COACH CAREER AND EDUCATION PLANNING

Developing the coaching pathway involves developing an effective career and education plan or a life plan. Whether coaches are volunteers or professionals, they must think about how they want to develop in all areas of life. Identifying their values, skills and interests will help coaches better understand who they are and what motivates them.

A career needs assessment will help all coaches recognise where they may need to focus their attention in future. They might ask themselves, for instance, how they feel about their performance and their work as coaches; whether they are spending enough time on the other things that are important to them and, if not, why not; when they think they will stop coaching and what they would do instead. The assessment should aim to discover how satisfied coaches are with their present situations, what they want for the future, and when that should happen. They should also consider where they could get help or advice about career development and about changing careers, and how they could plan to deal with such matters in the future.

Coaches should review their responses to the above assessment, develop a prioritised list of issues that have to be dealt with as a result, then list the steps that can be taken to deal with these issues. As a final step towards developing a life plan, they should identify their transferable skills (those coaching skills that are applicable to other aspects of life and those life skills that are applicable in coaching). These are usually the personal qualities that others admire in them. These skills will often be their greatest strengths and will help them to adapt to a change in their lives, whether they continue in sport or move away from it altogether.

CONCLUSION

For many coaches and athletes, participation in sport involves a significant amount of time and energy. Although it provides many op-portunities, exclusive commitment to sport may reduce their ability to deal with the many transitions associated with sport and life, and subsequently be detrimental to achievement in both areas. A more balanced approach will help to achieve success in both life and sport.

COACHING TIPS

- Maintain outside interests and friendships as a counterbalance to the stresses and strains of the coaching environment.
- Work to a long-term plan, rather than just responding to crises.
- Become an efficient and effective time manager — plan, prioritise and act promptly on decisions.
- Regularly ask yourself whether what you are doing will assist the athletes.

FURTHER READING

Anderson, D (1990) Personal record of speech by Frank Dick, Coach 98 conference, Scottish Institute of Sport.

Australian Coaching Council (1996) *Video Self-Analysis: A Lens on Coaching* (video and study pack). Canberra: Australian Sports Commission.

De Kroo, K (2000) Interview with John Buchanan (undertaken for the Australian Sports Commission), May.

Dickey, T (1992) *The Basics of Budgeting.* Melbourne: Crisp Publications Australia.

Emery, L (1990) *Stop Procrastinating: Change Your Habits — Change Your Life.* Sydney: Hutchinson.

Kirkpatrick, D (2000) Interview with Istvan Gorgenyi (undertaken for the Australian Sports Commission), May.

McCann, S (2000) Can elite coaches have a balanced life? *The New Zealand Coach* 9(1), spring.

Orlick, T (2000) *In Pursuit of Excellence: How to Win in Sport and Life through Mental Training.* Champaign, IL: Human Kinetics.

Petitpas, A, D Champagne, J Chartrand, S Danish, and P Murphy (1997) *Athlete's Guide to Career Planning.* Champaign, IL: Human Kinetics.

Rovillard, L (1993) *Goals and Goal Setting.* Melbourne: Crisp Publications Australia.

Stevens, P (1994) *Planning for Me: Setting Personal Goals.* Melbourne: the Centre for Worklife Counselling.

White, B (1998) Mentoring: coaches who lead the way. *The Sport Educator* 10(3): 7–10.

APPENDIX
THE COACH'S CODE OF ETHICS

Coaches should . . .

- be treated with respect and openness
- have access to self-improvement opportunities, and
- be matched with a level of coaching appropriate to their level of competence.

The Coach's Code of Ethics

1. Respect the rights, dignity and worth of every human being.	• Within the context of the activity, treat everyone equally, regardless of sex, disability, ethnic origin or religion.
2. Ensure the athlete's time spent with you is a positive experience.	• All athletes are deserving of equal attention and opportunities.
3. Treat each athlete as an individual.	• Respect the talent, developmental stage and goals of each athlete. • Help all athletes reach their full potential.
4. Be fair, considerate and honest with athletes.	
5. Be professional and accept responsibility for your actions.	• Display high standards in your language, manner, punctuality, preparation and presentation. • Display control, respect, dignity and professionalism to all involved with the sport, including opponents, coaches, officials, administrators, the media, parents and spectators. • Encourage all athletes to demonstrate the same qualities.
6. Make a commitment to providing a quality service to all athletes.	• Maintain or improve your current NCAS accreditation. • Seek continual improvement through performance appraisal and ongoing coach education. • Provide a training program that is planned and sequential. • Maintain appropriate records.
7. Operate within the rules and spirit of your sport.	• The guidelines of national and international bodies governing your sports should be followed. Please contact your sport for a copy of its rule book, constitution, by-laws, relevant policies (for example, anti-doping policy), selection procedures and so on. • Coaches should educate all athletes on drugs in sport issues in consultation with the Australian Sports Drug Agency.

(continued)

The Coach's Code of Ethics *(continued)*

8. Any physical contact with athletes should be: • appropriate to the situation, and • necessary for the athletes' skill development.*	
9. Refrain from any form of personal abuse towards athletes.*	• This includes verbal, physical and emotional abuse. • Be alert to any forms of abuse directed toward athletes in your care from other sources.
10. Refrain from any form of harassment of athletes.*	• This includes sexual and racial harassment, racial vilification and harassment on the grounds of disability. • You should not only refrain from initiating a sexual relationship with an athlete, but should also discourage any attempt by an athlete to initiate a sexual relationship with you, explaining the ethical basis of your refusal.
11. Provide a safe environment for training and competition.	• Ensure equipment and facilities meet safety standards. • Ensure equipment, rules, training and the environment are appropriate for the age and ability of the athletes.
12. Show concern and caution toward sick and injured athletes.	• Provide a modified training program where appropriate. • Allow further participation in training and competition only when appropriate. • Encourage athletes to seek medical advice when required. • Maintain the same interest and support toward sick and injured athletes.
13. Be a positive role model for your sport and for athletes.	

* Please refer to the Harassment-free Sport guidelines available from the Australian Sports Commission for more information on harassment issues.

Bold page numbers refer to photographs or drawings. *Italic* page numbers refer to graphs, tables or diagrams.